W9-DDA-390

Case Book in Abnormal Psychology

Case Book in

ALFRED A KNOPF NEW YORK

1962

Abnormal Psychology

BY *Henry Weinberg*

DEPARTMENT OF PSYCHOLOGY

BOSTON UNIVERSITY

AND *A. William Hire*

DEPARTMENTS OF PSYCHOLOGY AND PSYCHIATRY

BOSTON UNIVERSITY AND

MASSACHUSETTS MEMORIAL HOSPITALS

L.C. catalog card number: 56–5396

THIS IS A BORZOI BOOK, PUBLISHED BY ALFRED A. KNOPF, INC.

 Manufactured in the United States of America. Published simultaneously in Canada by McClelland and Stewart Limited.

PUBLISHED MARCH 23, 1956
SECOND PRINTING, FEBRUARY 1962

Acknowledgments

Many institutions and many individual colleagues have been helpful in the selection and preparation of the following cases. To all of them we are indeed grateful. Since a more explicit and detailed statement of our indebtedness would be incompatible with preserving the anonymity of the patients for whose welfare they have labored we trust they will understand our not mentioning them by name.

H. W.

A. W. H.

Contents

Case Book in Abnormal Psychology

Introduction

A CLINICAL CASE STUDY may be considered the organization and interpretation of observations, communications, and test findings within some theoretical framework. The requirements of a useful framework are that it be broad enough to encompass a variety of data yet specific enough to be applicable to the individual case. There are many theoretical frameworks that more or less satisfy these criteria. Which one the investigator chooses to use will be a function of his intellectual affiliations and personal inclination. Whatever his choice he will have to begin his work of organizing and interpreting with a single datum: the presenting complaint or symptom of the patient. This may be the patient's version of what is wrong with him, or the complaint of others regarding some aspect of his behavior. In either case the investigator may consider the symptom an explicit index of dysfunction, and look further to discover the particular nature of the dysfunction and its severity.

The same symptom may indicate entirely different degrees of severity depending upon its relation to the total context of which it is a part. Through making the symptom as explicit and differentiated as possible one begins to see differences in what is thought to be wrong. Two five-year-olds may both be referred to a clinic as "behavior problems," but are quite different in respect to the seriousness of their respective problems: the five-year-old who cannot yet talk and has learned little about caring for his routine needs can be said to have a more serious problem than his age equal who provokes his mother to anger and is rough and aggressive toward a younger sibling.

To take some other examples: A child of ten about whom there are complaints of sex play with other children does not present a problem so severe as when a grown man tries to lure children into sexual activities. A child of eight who sits quietly in school, does not learn or play with other children, and is fearful, is likely to have a more serious problem than one who does poor school work and is defiant or mischievous. An adult who feels tense and must force himself to work probably does not present so severe a problem as the adult who begins to say or do odd things while at his work. And as a final example, the person who feels depressed and has no interest in life after the death of a loved one is probably less "sick" than the person who feels like destroying himself even without any such precipitating loss. Unless the symptom is elaborated and placed into a larger context it cannot be adequately assessed and dealt with.

Over and above all of these aspects there must be considered at least one other: the attitude of the patient toward his symptom. Not only will this give further clues regarding the meaning of the symptom but also the degree of resistance one might anticipate to its removal.

The individual may be conceived of as maturing in terms of reality demands and opportunities, developing in the process assumptions about his world that he can later use in organizing and interpreting new experiences. His growth may be defined in terms of an ever-increasing, ever-widening scope in an outward direction. Beginning with mastery of his bodily movements, the individual moves outward in progressively broader social relationships involving family, school, work, and marriage. In this development one may delineate a number of focal points or transitional stages. Complexes of attitudes are learned at all of these points, and in some cases may be of such a nature as to frustrate the individual's mastering of a particular stage of development. In addition to seeking relationships between a particular symptom and these attitudes learned in the past, one must at the same time be aware that the symptom exists in the present and derives a good part of its meaning from current experiences. Even the question as to why an individual reacts to a current problem with a particular symptom, i.e., the problem of symptom choice, may be answered to some degree through study of the present as well as in study of the past.

If these factors are kept in mind one can then formulate the patient's problem and the way in which it has developed. Information about the focal areas of emotional development and the relevant personal-social contexts helps not only in the evaluation of the symptoms but also in discerning the significant relationships in the development of the individual that have been their source. Some of these contexts and the problems that may arise within them will serve here as examples of the many possibilities that must be evaluated in each case.

First of all there is the family. The current and past family constellation should be considered, including all significant changes within it. One should be aware of the age at which the child began to walk and talk as indicative of his readiness to master achievements, and the degree of support offered by the family. Nightmares, temper tantrums, enuresis, somnambulism, stuttering, and nail biting are only a few of the signs of difficulties in handling the normal stresses of childhood. Another context of development is the school. Not only are there new reality demands made on the child, but he may use the school as a place to act out his feelings against parents who are overcontrolling or favor another sibling. If we consider the family as the most important personal-social context, disposing the individual to react to others in terms of those attitudes and strivings learned at home, we can see that not only teachers but playmates, business associates, and lovers are "seen" differently by different individuals. This does not mean that new learning does not take place; rather we are trying to point up the varying strengths of mental sets developed by the individuals on the basis of an interplay of social experiences and the properties within the organism. One method for pointing up these relationships in the individual case is through the use of a chronology that shows the coincidence in time of the developing behaviors of the person and the various experiences occurring at these periods.

Uses of the Case Study

The purpose for which a case study is used will, to a great extent, determine the questions to be asked of the data. Of these uses we may point up three that seem to be most common: Treatment, Research, and Teaching. The case study may be used as the basis for treatment of symptoms and problems underlying them — diagnosis that must precede or accompany therapeutic intervention. The research use of a case study may or may not affect the particular patient involved, concerning itself primarily with extending knowledge. It is in the use of the case study as a heuristic device that this book is primarily concerned. Case data have been presented with relatively little explicit interpretation or theoretical formulation so that the student, under the guidance of his instructor, may retrace the empirical steps that were taken in achieving understanding. It was inevitable that our own theoretical orientation should contribute to our organization of the material. Nevertheless, the case presentations should adequately fulfill two main purposes: (1) The provision of representative empirical data or "pictures" of various psychological disorders, and (2) presentation of the data in such a manner as to facilitate theoretical interpretation of the development of these disorders. The level of interpretation will vary with the background of the reader. The case studies should lend themselves to sound interpretation by the beginning student as well as to the more profound interpretations by those psychologically more sophisticated.

Dramatis Personae

The following case studies seem to us to be a reasonable sampling of the various categories of psychological disorders. They do not represent all disorders, nor was this our intention. Given the usual limitations and pressures of space and theoretical orientation, this is our selection.

The reader has probably already noted from the table of contents the general trend in the presentation of cases. Beginning with child-behavior problems we have gone on to adolescent then adult disturbances, all of which could without difficulty be encompassed by the term neurotic. The next grouping of cases brings together psychological disturbances or limitations that constitute problems with which society has been forced to deal. The cases that follow become more serious whether it be through the irreversibility of brain damage or severe psychosis.

The first two cases, *Tommy Hawkes* and *Harold Bernhardt,* have in common the problem of ego control, but at opposite extremes. In the former there is a lack of control in a boy with difficulties in socialization who lashes out aggressively when his demands for love are not met. Treatment served to help him in bringing his impulses under control. In the case of the latter the problem is one of overcontrol, of severe inhibition of ego function. Treatment served to make apparent what had been inhibited and to release it so that Harold could be free to continue normal development. Both had been referred to the clinic as "learning problems," one a "bad boy," the other a "good boy." *Gerald Bittinger* had also been referred as a learning problem because of failing in school. As the case study unfolds the reader will see that underlying the complex of symptoms (of which the school crisis was only one) there was a common psychodynamic core based in disturbances of early mother-child relations. The picture is drawn of the development of a passive-resistant individual as a function of unusual experiences in early childhood.

The next two cases stimulate thinking about the emotional components of a somatic symptom. In the case of *Roberta Hackett* we are concerned with the emotional features of epilepsy, an illness not ordinarily thought of as having emotional components. At the other extreme is *Roland Beechberger* whose illness, asthma, is one in which psychological features are more commonly granted to be playing a part.

The case of *Elizabeth Fearchild* portrays the meaning of a phobic symptom and the unraveling of its basis as treatment went on. *Mary D'Amore*'s symptoms consisted of many physical complaints for which no organic basis could be found. In the course of treatment the meaning of her symptoms also was made clear.

The case of *Lionel Guttman* is that of a long-standing obsessive neurosis in a man who in addition to lifelong problems now has gerontological problems as well.

The following group of cases represent problems that are actively of more concern to the community, and point up the role of social forces in psychological disturbances. The cases of *Mollie Stein* and *Patrick Michael Quinn* were selected to give representation to chronic and episodic alcoholism. In Mollie's case one sees the use of alcohol partly as a defense against murderous impulses in a socially deprived woman. Patrick is a passive-aggressive individual who turned to alcohol during a time of stress. *Mary Fearing* represents the complicated intertwining of social, psychological, and neurological instability in a young girl and the role of guilt in seeking punishment.

The problems of differential diagnosis and of rehabilitation in mental deficiency are represented in the next three cases. The long case, *Callie Kakes,* is that of mental deficiency in a girl with severe lifelong personality disturbances. In contrast the short cases of *Fanny Staggles* and *Clarence O'Rourke* are much more clearcut and point up some common problems in rehabilitating men and women of inadequate intellectual endowment.

The next three cases all involve brain damage, with its consequent impairment of higher mental processes and social relationships. *William Glanvin* is a case of endogenous or internal cerebral changes in an individual of superior endowment; *Frank Brown* was the innocent victim of severe exogenous brain injury. Different in source but similar in consequences is the brain deterioration due to alcohol in the case of *Tony Rolando.*

The case of *Carol Bottomley* represents not only a character disorder in an individual with early narcissistic disturbance but also the problems in the administrative and therapeutic management of such patients. In retrospect one is in a more favorable position to be more firm with such cases; at the time of treatment, however, the depressive and suicidal features make one very cautious in the handling of the patient.

The final pair of cases, *Sam Godsky* and *Cluny Standish,* describe in varying degree the development and course of two psychoses. *Sam Godsky* is the description of the ultimate development of paranoid schizophrenia in a youth and the effects on him of radical therapy. *Cluny Standish* is typical of the psychotic mood disorders. In her case one can clearly see the relation between periods of stress and the onset of her mood disturbance, at first briefly depressed, then actively manic for a relatively long period, followed by ever-decreasing mood swings until she is back to normal.

With these introductory considerations we trust we have provided an overview for the presentations that follow and a broadly structured basis for thinking about them.

Tommy Hawkes

CHILD BEHAVIOR PROBLEM

THE HAWKES FAMILY felt that Tommy had always been the most difficult of their children to manage. Since he had started school there had been continuous complaints from his teachers about his behavior and poor school work. Finally, when he was between eight and a half and nine years old, he had a marked recurrence of an old problem of bed wetting. Mrs. Hawkes took him to a children's hospital, hoping that she could get help with this as well as other troublesome aspects of his behavior. After the physician examined Tommy, he recommended that Mrs. Hawkes take him to a child-guidance clinic.

As she recounted her difficulties with Tommy to the social worker at the guidance clinic, she presented him as getting along poorly at home and at school over a long period of time and as having always been overactive and daredevilish. She said it seemed to her that he never sat down from the time he was seven months old until he was five years old. When he was two and a half years old he had climbed a ladder to the roof of the house and would not come down at her entreating. Mrs. Hawkes was pregnant at the time, but climbed to the roof anyway, only to have Tommy refuse to come down unless he came alone. Particular precautions around the house have always been necessary, such as special locks on the windows and an enclosure around the porch, to guard against his climbing out the windows or on to the roof from the porch.

He has been irresponsive to all restrictions or direction given by the parents. His mother cannot cope with him at all and he obeys his father when he is present only because he is afraid of him. His mother says that when Tommy is around it is "like having a tiger by the tail" and that he has so much energy he is like "chained lightning."

In school he has never conformed. He fools away his time and gets his class in an uproar. The teachers try to ignore him. On two occasions he has been temporarily demoted in the hope that it would improve his behavior. He rarely does what is expected of him by way of assignments in class, but he can accomplish his work easily if forced to do so at home. When he was in the first grade the teacher reported to his mother that he got the lowest rating on a psychological test ever obtained in the school. This was because he would not take it seriously but tried to be funny, as, for instance, putting four tails on an animal. When first seen at the clinic he was in the fourth grade and had received eight D's on his most recent report. He told his mother that he has never had a teacher he liked. When given individual attention, however, he did his work quickly and easily, but the family could not afford a special teacher.

From the time Tommy was two until he was seven he had what his mother described as "a mania for matches." She and his father were unable to check his fire setting. On one occasion they burned him with a match hoping that it would make him afraid of fire. When he left the house, they had to frisk him to make sure he did not have matches with him. The fire setting appears to have stopped with an incident when he was seven. He was alone one day in the rumpus room playing with matches and set fire to the curtains and shades. This apparently frightened him, but he extinguished the blaze without anyone knowing about the incident at the time it happened. Then Mrs. Hawkes discovered the burned curtains and shades and, after first denying any knowledge of the matter, Tommy admitted what had happened.

He has wanted privileges of an older child, but always abused them, according to his mother, going too far and doing things that are not safe. For instance, once he ignored prohibitions about the boats at the beach, loosened one from the mooring, and drifted out into deep water. The parents had to swim out to bring the boat ashore, while he acted unperturbed. In recent years he has not played with children his age but has gone around with a gang of boys several years older.

Tommy's enuresis is occasional. He goes for months without wetting his bed and then may do so for a series of nights. After toilet training was accomplished at two and a half years he had no further trouble until four, at which time he began bed wetting again. After his father spanked him, he stopped wetting except for an occasional lapse.

In presenting these complaints about Tommy, Mrs. Hawkes said that she could understand his behavior if he had come from a broken home with alcoholic parents, but he comes from one which is well run. She added that she came from a home broken by alcoholism. She also said that his teacher tried to discourage her from coming to the clinic by telling her of other mothers who came and disliked it because the clinic found things wrong with them. She courageously said that she and his father must not be handling the situation correctly and they want to find out where they are wrong.

As Mrs. Hawkes came to the clinic each week, to bring Tommy and herself to visit the social worker, she unfolded accounts of Tommy's developmental history, the family, and further problems she had encountered in Tommy's behavior. Tommy's birth was by normal delivery while her other children had been instrument births. She described Tommy as a very lovable, "cuddly" child in contrast to his older sister who was never responsive. He was breast-fed for only eight or ten days, as she had insufficient milk. Even this initial feeding had to be supplemented with a formula. He was weaned to the cup at eight months and has never presented any problem in feeding. Except for the lapses in bed wetting there was no difficulty in bowel training and bladder training, which was accomplished at two and a half years. Tommy was an active child who liked to spend hours rocking in his crib.

He was described by both parents as having a very pleasing personality. However, in response to the criticism which his misbehavior has provoked at home and school, they feel he has developed a "chip on the shoulder" attitude. During the year prior to bringing him to the clinic they were considering sending him away to a school to see if he could be trained to accept some regulation of his behavior. Once, when the family were driving along the highway and Tommy was being boisterous and would not sit down in the car, his father stopped the car, put him out, and pretended that the family were going to abandon him. This frightened Tommy very much. He cried for a long time but has since sat very still in the car. Some of the neighbors seem to think his misbehavior is very cute and have shown their amusement at it. Mrs. Hawkes said laughingly, however, that he was such a horrible example that he scared all her sisters out of wanting boy children. Once, when he was being difficult at the family's summer place, she let his aunt drive him some distance in the car as a threat that he was being sent away. He seemed stunned at this drastic action. On another occasion at the summer place he walked out into deep water with his clothes on while friends and neighbors stood by and laughed because his father had to go in after him.

In discussing the family, Mrs. Hawkes expressed the feeling that Mr. Hawkes is overstrict with all the children, but particularly with Tommy. She feels that he and Tommy are much alike, and that Mr. Hawkes realizes it. Tommy cried when Mr. Hawkes entered the Army, especially in resentment of youngsters whose fathers did not go. Mrs. Hawkes was also resentful of his going because of the hardship it placed on her when he could have been exempted had he so chosen.

Mr. Hawkes did not have a notably easy time as a child himself. He was the second of eight children. His older brother was a quiet withdrawn boy, but his father was always aggressive, domineering, and given to vicious outbursts of temper. Mr. Hawkes was his mother's favorite, and she still relies very much upon him. When he was twelve his mother was hospitalized with a combination of physical and emotional difficulties. She was ill for a long time following a miscarriage, then became depressed. Just before she was to return home he ran away, was picked up in a distant city and returned. He became a behavior problem in school and subsequently quit going. All in all he was a source of considerable difficulty and worry to his family.

After Tommy had been in treatment a few months, Mr. Hawkes visited the clinic to talk with the social worker. He was described as a slight, good-looking man with a free, spontaneous manner. The social worker noted a blinking in one eye which Mr. Hawkes said had started after he had been in the Army about five months. He talked freely, giving the impression of wanting to be co-operative in the treatment of his son. He expressed guilt over the fact that he is sometimes harsh with the children. He said that he and his wife recently had been looking back, trying to understand Tommy's situation. He recalled being teased by a boy when he himself was eleven. He threw a brick at him which had paralyzed him temporarily. He said that his fright and anxiety at this had made him try to control his temper. He added that Tommy's temper is really not the ungovernable kind he himself had had.

Mrs. Hawkes was described as quiet and self-contained. She felt that she was more lenient with the children than her husband because of the freedom and flexibility that existed in her own home where she was the youngest of six children. The situation in her home prevailed because her mother was obliged to work and leave much of the running of the house to the children. Her father was an alcoholic; her mother separated from him when Mrs. Hawkes was five years old. When drinking, he was quite aggressive, sometimes making it necessary for her mother to sneak out of the house and hide. He is still a heavy drinker even though he is well in his eighties. Mrs. Hawkes described her mother as easygoing with a delightful sense of humor. She would never believe her sons did any wrong until it was clearly proven to her. Though they were truant from school and ran away from home at an early age, all eventually became respectable and responsible adults. Tommy's behavior reminds Mrs. Hawkes of one of her brothers in particular. This brother is now married and has a son of his own, but is so much aware of Tommy's propensity that when Tommy visits in the home he locks up his guns and hides the key. Her mother confided in Mrs. Hawkes, who was, as she describes herself, a "steam valve" for the whole family. In contrast, her husband "keeps things to himself" and does not tell her. He is worse in this respect since he was in the Army. Before they were married he had ulcers and was a light sleeper. Now, he is not bothered with ulcers and sleeps well; so Mrs. Hawkes felt marriage had been fundamentally good for him.

In addition to Tommy they have two daughters and a younger son. The older daughter, three years Tommy's senior, was getting all A's in school and was well liked by her associates and teachers. The teachers sent Tommy's homework to his parents by her in an envelope. When she was young, she responded quickly to prohibition. Mrs. Hawkes felt that Tommy was resentful and jealous of her because, being older, she could have privileges which he could not.

A sister three years younger was Tommy's favorite. He was protective of her and had taught her such things as telling time. He got along best with her. Mrs. Hawkes laughed and said: "Maybe he is nearer her age mentally." His young brother, only one year old, he ignored in so far as he could.

When Tommy was seen at the clinic for a physical examination he was described as an active, non-apprehensive, dark-haired boy, four feet three inches tall, weighing sixty pounds. Neurological examination was negative; vision was normal. Except for being very thin he was found to be a physically normal boy.

Psychological examinations showed him to have intelligence at the upper range of average. On school achievement tests he scored one year below his grade placement.

Treatment

Tommy was seen for psychotherapy once a week for a year and a half. As we follow the course and content of the major aspects of his treatment we can see what his behavior is knowingly and unknowingly proclaiming to the adults in his life and what anxieties chafe and, at times, harass him.

When Tommy was seen for his first treatment session, preceding both the physical and psychological examinations by several months, the nature and function of the clinic and the treatment process were explained to him in simple terms. In effect, he was told that the clinic was a place where children come who have problems for which they need help; and that sometimes parents talk it over with them and sometimes they just bring them without explaining very much about it. It was also indicated that the therapist tried to understand the child's feelings and see matters through his eyes and talk to him about things on his mind. The various materials around the room were pointed out as things for children to use or play with while getting acquainted and talking with the therapist.

This introduction to the clinic brought forth none of the usual immediate questions and discussion from Tommy. Instead he was tight-lipped and acted like a little culprit in a school principal's office. He merely answered upon inquiry that his mother brought him and that he did not ask why, because he "wanted it to be a surprise." At this point the therapist pressed no more, changing to general inquiry about home and school and what Tommy liked to do. With this he began to warm up to the situation. He said that at school he liked baseball and that he especially liked to be the batter. When asked what else he did at school he said that he made book reports and learned about Eskimos. When asked what he learned about Eskimos he became more spontaneous and communicative. He said: "Eskimos go to bed when they want to and get up when they want to. They can stay up all night; they eat blubber and raw fish." Tommy added that he eats raw fish also. When asked about this he explained that he went fishing when at their summer place and sometimes ate the fish raw, but at other times made a little fire to cook them. Immediately following this he told about walking into the water once with his clothes on and his father's having to come in after him.

He was wearing a cowboy outfit with boots and a highly decorated belt, with a chain swinging from the belt with a number of trinkets on it, including a skull, change holder, and a small pistol. The therapist considered each of these trinkets with him as Tommy came around the desk to stand by the therapist's chair. Tommy told of how he got them by saving coupons, producing a ring from his pocket from which he could remove the large setting, and explaining that it was for carrying secret messages.

He then turned his interest to the play materials that had been pointed out to him earlier in the session. Selecting from these modeling clay, he occupied himself with it for the remainder of the hour. He constructed a "jail" with a watchtower and a wall enclosing it. He put a pencil through a flattened piece of clay and called it a plane. Then, with appropriate imitative noises, he dive-bombed and machine-gunned the wall by jabbing holes through it with the pencil as the "plane" swooped down time and time again. He commented that the destruction of the wall would allow the prisoners to escape. When the wall was demolished, he rebuilt it and repeated the procedure several times.

Thus in his first meeting with the therapist Tommy engaged in only minimal verbalization, but managed to convey rather clearly some of the intensity of pressures he felt in the situation in which his parents and teachers were so exasperated with him.

At the beginning of the second visit Tommy returned immediately to the clay which he had used before, this time making an "igloo." In further talk about Eskimos Tommy said: "The father Eskimos kill whales and the mother Eskimos fix the meat and the mother goes out and flaps skins to help the men find deer." He then added: "And the son can go hunting alone when he has killed a polar bear, and he can go hunt whales, too." The therapist made comments to the effect that all boys were eager to grow up so they could do the things older people do and feel they were their own boss.

Tommy later rolled the clay into a ball, took a coin from his pocket which he then rolled into the clay, and began a game in which the therapist was not to look, and then see how quickly he could find the coin. This game he continued for quite some time, soon changing it to the therapist hiding the coin and Tommy searching for it in the clay. This was modified to a game in which Tommy not only hid the coin but hid the clay also. He wanted to introduce more complexity by leaving the room and hiding the clay somewhere in the clinic building. At this point the therapist resisted and made comments concerning the interesting nature of the game and suggested it was all right to play, but that he hoped it did not mean Tommy just wanted to play a game of "hide" with him instead of feeling free to talk.

On his next visit Tommy did not return to his play with the clay. Instead, in exploring the room for something new he found a set of form boards that were graduated in difficulty for use as a psychological test. He surmised the nature of the task immediately without asking questions or receiving instructions. He appeared to be so adept at the procedure that the therapist decided to stimulate him a little by timing him with a stop watch. This became a fascinating game for Tommy, and one at which he really excelled. When the novelty of this waned, he became interested in the stopwatch and then in the therapist's wrist watch which he studied by lying across the desk and holding the therapist's hand.

Later he became interested in a printing set, designing what he called a game where he was the "postmaster" or "boss." The therapist was to write messages on cards which Tommy would stamp with his initials from the printing set. He would pressure the therapist to write fast, but would not read what was written on the card, merely stamping it in an official manner and placing it quickly aside. The therapist complied to the point of stepping the game up to a lively tempo with Tommy becoming quite arrogant in his comments and demands to hurry. Finally, as the end of the hour was approaching, the therapist commented on the feelings Tommy must have about being bossed and on the fact that his visits with the therapist were not to prove anything about who was boss.

In the next session Tommy returned to playing with the clay. He constructed what he called a "native place," saying that he had studied about "natives" in school and that they kill people. When a "native" kills someone he can go to the place of refuge and will not be killed himself. Over the native place he hung what he called a bees' nest, saying that they could "sting, sting, sting." The bees were to guard and protect the place against intruders.

In the following session, which was the fifth, he chose to color outline figures with crayons. He selected all the Indian and Eskimo figures from a varied assortment and colored them all brown, not using bright colors even for trimming. As he colored, sitting across the desk from the therapist, he asked how long he would have to come to the clinic. The therapist went back to previous statements about the nature of the clinic and the fact that someone always feels a boy should have help with some problem before he is seen at the clinic. The therapist asked Tommy what his mother had told him about bringing him, and he still insisted she had not discussed it with him and that he could not see any reason for coming. The therapist suggested he talk with his mother and father about it and then the therapist would discuss it with him when Tommy would speak more freely about what help he needed. Or if he felt he did not need help, the reason his mother and father gave for his coming could be discussed.

The social worker learned that Mrs. Hawkes did not talk with Tommy before bringing him to the clinic. In response to the social worker's request, she and Mr. Hawkes did talk with him after the first session about why he was coming, but he had merely listened without comment or protest. For the first two months he showed no reluctance at home toward coming and then complained one day when reminded of his appointment. Mrs. Hawkes noted, however, that when they approached the clinic he became eager and bounded on ahead of her. After his first appointment at the clinic Tommy got lost from his mother when he went on ahead of her and took a different course. She returned to the clinic but did not find him there. Worried, she called home, and finally notified the police, who said he was in the station. Reporting to a policeman that his mother was lost, he was taken to the police station, where he was waiting calmly with an air of amusement when she arrived. Tommy says nothing at home about what goes on during his visits to the clinic.

On the sixth visit he brought with him a water gun. As he entered the office, he squirted water at pictures on the wall, the modeling-clay figures made by other patients, the ceiling light, a staff member who was passing by in the hallway, and then shot a stream past the therapist with a skillful, close aim. Next he extinguished the light on the therapist's cigarette burning in an ash tray. He took the gun apart to demonstrate its structure to the therapist, discussing how he had devised an alteration so that it would shoot more times on one filling, but "not as far." He commented that he was going to shoot his father's "old pipe" and put it out because when his father smoked and Tommy was on the floor around his feet he dropped ashes on him. He was extremely active, wanting to destroy the creative products of other patients' efforts, and frequently kept running from the office to explore and look around the building. Finally he placed the gun on the desk before him and sat down in a chair across from the therapist. He sat down apparently with the attitude that he had completed his activity and it was now time for the therapist to take over.

The therapist commented on the gun, saying that it was on the desk as in Western movies when they don't trust the person across from them. To this Tommy made no comment but uttered a faint laugh. The therapist then remarked that people used guns this way to protect themselves when they were scared and to shoot with when they were mad. His shooting around the office and clinic was interpreted to him as indicating he was angry and that it perhaps meant he didn't like to come to the clinic. The therapist then suggested that if they could talk about why he was coming maybe they could come to an understanding.

The social worker had had an account from Tommy's mother during this visit of his having wet his bed several times during the week. He had also repeated his complaint of not wanting to come to the clinic when she reminded him of his appointment. He had received his report card from school and had three D's in the area of conduct but an improved grade for "effort." Also, he had been feuding with his older sister and in one of their tiffs had spattered her new clothes with mud.

On Tommy's next visit to the clinic his father came with him for his session with the social worker. Tommy entered the office in a very subdued and quiet manner, then sat in the chair like a little culprit, very much as he had done on his initial visit. The therapist initiated conversation by inquiring into Tommy's activities since the last visit. He had been having a spring recess from school, Tommy said, and told an elaborate story about going into the woods with older boys where they had cut young trees, against regulations, taking them home to make bows and arrows. They had taken along some old paint to smear on the wood. On the way home the policemen would look at them and say: "Well, it looks like you boys just took some old rotten wood," implying that the police were aware of the real facts but were being generous and understanding of their petty violation. He a few weeks, but, in the meantime, the therapist continued to see him during the two months until camp.

During these two months Tommy alternated between some extremely active behavior, the telling of fantastic aggressive tales in which he was involved in conflict and danger, and regressive, infantile behavior in which he spent the sessions playing quietly on the floor around the therapist's desk and feet. In one of the more boisterous sessions he appeared to dramatize or recapitulate one of the types of problems he presented to his mother. This involved going out of the office window onto the fire escape and refusing to come in until the therapist went out after him. Defiance was here mingled with threats to himself in the form of a flirtation with falling or jumping over the railing. This behavior would be extremely vexatious to anyone with any responsibility for him. As the therapist returned Tommy to the office he commented that he wondered if Tommy did similar things at home, and if it could have something to do with the reason his mother wanted him to come to the clinic. Tommy smiled a knowing smile of assent.

In connection with attempts to interpret the provocative and at the same time dangerous aspects of this behavior in which he had an adult save him, Tommy protested that he "didn't fall" and spoke of children playing on jungle gyms. The therapist again pointed out that adults frequently did not give children enough credit for their readiness for independence, adding that when children get hurt adults feel guilty and sorry, and that this also sometimes has something to do with why children do dangerous things.

In the next session Tommy expressed thoughts of wanting to be with his father on a trip to their summer place. He said that he could cook for himself, swim, and catch fish to eat, but his father and mother were afraid for him to stay alone.

The following session was one in which he spent most of the hour on the floor around the therapist's feet. He had frequently wanted to leave the office early, especially when interpretations were offered. This time he lingered around the door when it was time to leave, coming back to the office once after the therapist had dismissed him and sent him downstairs.

In the next session he told a tale about climbing a telephone

went into detail as to how he and his friends shoot birds to get feathers for the arrows, then use the bows and arrows to kill more birds.

He also told of their playing in an old garage owned by a man "who died four hundred years ago." Tommy and his friends had first entered by breaking a window. From the inside they shot at ducks. When the therapist undertook to get further elaboration on activities in the old garage, Tommy stood up, insisting he wanted to go back to the waiting room. Coaxing could not relieve him of the need to leave the office, so the therapist acquiesced, saying he wished Tommy would not run away and, further, that he realized boys had a difficult time with adults interfering so much with their freedom.

Tommy went down to the waiting room where he got acquainted with a youngster about his age named Stanley with whom the therapist had an appointment for the following hour. He came back to the office with this patient. This acquaintance later developed into a combination of rivalry and friendship, as Stanley usually had an appointment immediately preceding or following Tommy.

Tommy was always neat and well dressed. On his next visit he was wearing new trousers, and when the therapist commented upon them Tommy came around the desk to stand by him for closer inspection. As he looked around the room he noted a replica of a coiled rattlesnake made from modeling clay by the young patient with whom he had become acquainted on his previous visit. He paused, looked at it intently, then, approaching it cautiously, reached out and snatched away the fangs, and, with a quick and decisive grasp, squeezed the mouth shut. He wanted to know who had made it and guessed immediately that it was the work of his new acquaintance. Tommy then recounted the first of a series of fantastic tales dealing with his taunting of authority figures and his adequacy to cope with danger. He asserted that he caught snakes, proceeding to tell a tale of his having caught a rattlesnake in his tent at camp. When he found the snake, so went the story, he hurried and cut a forked stick which he placed over the snake's neck until it expended all its poison. Then he killed it, skinned it, and cut open the rattler to see what was inside. The therapist commented that the story seemed to have two points that concern a lot of boys; namely, how dangerous things function, and how to control them.

Tommy had previously asked for finger paints upon seeing the paintings of other patients, but the therapist was temporarily out of them. A new supply had been purchased and was now on the desk. Tommy turned his interest to painting and quickly went about putting the materials in a state of readiness. When he reached the point where he was actually ready to smear the paint he was quite hesitant. He touched the paint very lightly with his index finger, then sat for some time with his finger extended in the air. The therapist tried to make some suggestions as to how Tommy could go about painting, but finally realized that Tommy was acting inhibited because he didn't want to be observed. The therapist then turned away, saying that Tommy could paint something without being watched; whereupon he proceeded to work with vigor. The therapist carried on a running conversation about the painting, meanwhile keeping his head turned. Tommy said he was making a lake, the one where he spent his summers. He referred to various buildings, fishing sites, and the place where he walked into the water. When he had finished and was ready for the therapist to look, there was only a heavy mixture of green and blue paint smeared over the entire surface of the paper. There was no attempt to represent anything except a water surface.

He repeated in the next session the same type of smearing, calling it a lake. When the therapist tried to draw him into conversation, Tommy wanted to leave.

On his next visit he was carrying a cap pistol. He snapped it a few times as he came to the door, but did not snap it while in the office. He would not respond to efforts to draw him into conversation about it. The therapist indicated that he realized that Tommy did not like to have questions asked. Tommy launched into an account of how he sailed planes from the roof of his house when his mother and the next-door neighbor were away. When they were at home, he could launch them only from the upstairs window, which was not so much fun.

He told a tale of fantastic proportions about stealing, in company with other boys, road flares from a truck garage. They would light one, place it on a plank, and let it float down the

river while the cops went from house to house trying cessfully to find who had done it. They kept a supply h away in a tunnel and took them out on special occasions Halloween night they lit them and "threw them in wind stuck them on walls of houses, and on trees," giving the po and firemen "many, many headaches." The therapist comment on how older people are afraid children will hurt themselv or other people without intending to and how this concern sometimes makes children want to do more daring things; also, how boys imagine, and sometimes do daring things on Halloween because they want to get even with adults for forbidding so many things.

This was followed by several sessions in which Tommy brought picture cards dipped in paraffin and asked the therapist to compete in a game for which Tommy made the rules, often changing them to suit the occasion. The game consisted of tossing the cards against the baseboard to see who could make them fall closer to the wall. The therapist sat on the floor with him to play this game. Tommy was inconsistent with regard to his choice of who should win. At times he would change rules or resort to inaccurate measurement so that he would win, and at times would do the same in order to have the therapist win.

The pictures on the cards consisted of an assortment of baseball players, cowboys, and Indians. These pictures as such did not seem to mean much to him, nor did he care. He would not discuss them beyond pointing out one cowboy movie character and saying that all the cards with the Indians were the "brave" ones. He later managed a series of meetings with Stanley to play this game after each had seen the therapist. Tommy's mother, in the meantime, had begun letting him come by himself to the clinic after school.

At this point Tommy had been seen once a week for approximately four months. The ending of his school year was near. Though his report card showed some improvement and there was a prospect that he would be promoted, he still was getting poor marks in conduct. His older sister had indicated to their mother that Tommy seemed to get into less trouble with other childen going and coming from school and during recess. His mother was planning, through the clinic, to send him to a summer camp for

line pole where he sat with small green apples and a slingshot. When the woman across the street tried to call the police he shot an apple through the open window, hitting her hand each time she picked up the telephone. He hit the police car as it went by; the policemen looked all around, not knowing from where the apples came. When he climbed the pole, so went his account, he took a key with a string tied to it and tested the wires to make sure they were not alive. His mother's version of this episode as she recounted it to the social worker was simply that a neighbor threatened to call the police when she saw him trying to climb a telephone pole.

One further tale of fantastic daredevil adventure and defiance of authority was recounted in one of the remaining sessions before he went to camp. According to his story, along with two girls and a "small boy," he had found a haunted house in which a tramp lived in the basement. They broke into the house and found money hidden at various places. The tramp came out of the basement to see what was going on and Tommy threw a knife at him and drove him back into the basement. From the basement the tramp shouted: "I'll beat your brains out if you don't get out of here." Tommy and his friends will investigate to find out who he is and, when he is asleep, will tie him up and continue to search the house. They have already found an ax which they will use to chop a hole in the floor and peep into the basement first.

He then became somewhat confused and contradictory in the story, talking about their having climbed on the roof to gain entrance through a trapdoor and of his lowering his knife on a string first to "test" and see if it were safe to enter. He then lowered himself into the house with the understanding that if he did not come out before the others had counted ten, they would know everything was all right and should enter. The cops saw them emerge on the roof and came to chase them away. Tommy threw a knife at a cop and it "went through his shirt on the side." The cop threw his gun at Tommy; he circled wide in the chase and the cops lost his trail. Then he circled around and came back and picked up his knife and the gun.

The only element of reality that his mother could supply in relation to these stories was that there had been some talk among the children concerning a notion that a particular old house was haunted. It was assumed that the tales were, among other things, a testing of the therapist's tolerance for fantastic flirtations with danger and with unreality. The defiant and danger aspects were interpreted with an added hint that the accounts had some similarity to imaginative-type stories.

In the final session before Tommy was to leave for summer camp his thoughts and expectations about time to be spent there and with his family at their summer place were discussed. He fantasied going boating, and sleeping in a tent as he drew the layout of the grounds at their summer place. He brought along a small toy boat which he asked the therapist to help him repair. He was reluctant to leave the clinic at the end of the hour, wanting to explore the building.

When Tommy's mother contacted the social worker in the fall, she reported that Tommy had enjoyed his stay at camp. She added that he was almost a model child in behavior when he first returned, but just before he had left he was irritable and unruly; jealous of his sisters, he tried to incur their disfavor in the eyes of his parents by tattling on them.

During his first week in school he brought home papers with good grades and completed work. His mother was feeling very encouraged, noting the many ways in which he had changed. She was especially amused by his attempt to use words somewhat beyond his understanding, but very much pleased. To her it was a token of his attempt to grow up. He was promoted to the fifth grade.

When the official report of his stay at camp was in, however, it was less encouraging. He had frequently come into conflict with the rules, had not developed friendships with his companions, and had been negativistic toward the counselors. There was an unqualified statement that any application for his enrollment in this camp again would be unfavorably received.

The course of treatment in the following year saw most of the problems implied or explicit in the preceding sessions develop to a high pitch and great intensity. His relation to parental figures became acutely exaggerated in certain elements of the behavior around the therapist; his aggressive behavior was intensified to the point where its more basic features emerged. His concerns and anxieties were displayed in their more general and focal aspects. He continued to dramatize his feelings and problems with only minimal verbalization. Fantastic tales waned and were replaced by fantastic behavior.

On his first visit after summer vacation he was extremely quiet and subdued, giving perfunctory answers to questions about the interim since he had been seen. He asked whether Stanley was still coming to the clinic. He measured his height on the wall where he had had the therapist mark it before vacation. He hid a straight pin in clay and played a game of hunting for it. He talked about making darts at home to throw at targets.

On his next visit he brought a bean shooter and shot at various objects in the office as targets, including paintings done by Stanley, and finally at his own painting of the lake. In returning to play with clay, he stuck himself on the pin he had hidden the previous time. He reacted with intense feeling, insisting that he had not put the pin there, but that the therapist had deliberately hidden it so that it would stick Tommy. He referred to it as the "death pin." He briefly attempted some finger painting, then spent considerable time at the washbasin washing his hands and playing in the water. He would not leave it at the end of the hour, insisting that his time was not up but that the therapist was only making an excuse to get rid of him.

The following session began a series in which he abandoned restraints. He threw clay at the walls, ceiling, and light fixture. The malleability of the clay saved the office from damage, but when his fury had subsided, the litter and disorder were reminiscent of a somewhat violent storm. Comments on his anger and his testing the therapist only intensified the display. Tommy refused to clean up when this was suggested near the end of the hour, but came back to the office with Stanley, whose appointment followed, shocking him when he showed him the debris. Variations on this session continued a few times. His mother reported that he had, on one occasion during this period, soiled and wet his bed, saying that he thought he had had a bad dream. He instructed the therapist on precautions to take with respect to the windows in the clinic building on Halloween, as he and his friends were getting prepared with a tremendous stock of flares. He added that he was not afraid of the cops, that he had tripped one last Halloween, making his gun go off. One tale of fantastic exploits outside the clinic was related in this period. According to his story, he and some friends had a system for swinging from a rope tied to the limb of a tree on to passing trains. Sometimes they stopped trains by waving flashlights at night. Once, when the engineer was away from his post, they started a train and took it some distance along its route before the engineer knew what had happened.

Within a few weeks this phase of behavior had passed, being followed by a concern with fire and smoking. He began by building "forts" or "factories" from clay and asking for a lighted cigarette to imbed in the clay to represent smoking guns or smoking chimneys. During this development he always assured the therapist that he would clean up the office at the conclusion of the session. As he became more concerned with the fire as such, he would make a bowl-like structure, ask for cigarettes, which he would crumple into it, and set fire to the tobacco. To this he would sometimes add paper and get a flame going, then roll the edges of the clay inward and smother the fire. Then, frequently, he would roll the clay into a ball with the remaining charred material inside. As he became more engrossed in the fire play, he wanted to see even greater flames and would light a paper and watch with intense excitment as it flared up, or would light the end of a pencil and blow upon it until he was exhausted, trying to keep a glowing ember alive. The whole procedure seemed to enthrall him.

After a few sessions of this type he passed to more interest in lighting and smoking cigarettes. His earlier lighting of them to use in his play was followed by actually smoking them. In one of the early sessions in which he was taking draws from a cigarette he wanted his height and weight checked. In the first session in which he sat down to light a cigarette and smoke it through he began by sitting in the chair and swinging his feet like a small child, as he told about seeing movies at the boys' club, then about target practice with a "real twenty-two." Following these accounts he asked for a cigarette, crossed his legs, and sat back to smoke it, flipping ashes on the therapist's desk. He later modeled some ash trays from clay which he then used despite the fact that there had been a tray on the desk all the while. He commented that he had gotten a good report card and that he had a good teacher this year. Apparently he had a young woman recently out of training, whereas he had previously had older women. Before the end of the session, however, he lit the end of a pencil, and while blowing on it intently swung his legs vigorously from the edge of the chair.

In the session that followed he brought Stanley to the office with him. Stanley's appointment now immediately preceded Tommy's so that they met in the waiting room. Tommy asked for a cigarette, which shocked Stanley. This was then followed by a discussion of smoking with each questioning the other and volunteering information about smoking among their associates and how it was dealt with at school. Stanley told Tommy that if he smoked he would be a little "shrimp." This was a very sensitive area for Tommy as he was small for his age while Stanley, approximately the same age, was quite large. After some competition in a target game, Tommy ordered Stanley around in connection with some activity with clay, calling him "slave." Finally each constructed a "fort" at opposite ends of the desk and began "firing" clay. Stanley was hit in the face, at which point he screamed and withdrew, sobbing. With some comments to both, and then to each separately, the therapist had Stanley leave, at which point Tommy wanted to leave also.

The next session was rather calm, with Tommy asking for a cigarette. As he smoked, he spoke of a place where he went with a group of boys, "all ten years old," with one of them posted as a spy to keep watch. A group of "bad boys" had a place nearby, sometimes engaging Tommy's gang in fights. The bad boys "steal from stores."

Occasionally, in sessions that followed, he wanted to throw clay and set fires, but this behavior was replaced by other preoccupations, to a great extent, after a few months. Two boisterous sessions followed the one in which he had alluded to the activities with the gang. In response to interpretations he introduced the themes of control over fire and of his sense of personal inadequacy. The latter he did through comparison of his abilities to that of other patients on the basis of their productions. He became especially interested in some cartoons of an adolescent patient, commenting: "I can't draw or paint." The play with fire was now accompanied by his keeping a cup of water from the basin near at hand with which he would put out the fire. On one occasion he put lighted cigarettes in a cardboard box and threw it, saying that wherever it fell it would start a fire. Finally he suggested that he would be content if the therapist would provide him with a candle that he could light while he was in the office.

His next preoccupation was with the disassembling, repairing, and manipulation of some puzzle boxes that were stored in the office. These boxes had been constructed for use as psychological test apparatus during the early days of the clinic but were no longer in use. He worked with them very quietly and patiently. When he was particularly successful he might say: "See, I'm smart," or remark that he had seen a safe in a clinic office which he could rob as easily as he figured out the puzzles. Once, when he seemed to be unsuccessful and frustrated, he beat his head, saying: "What's wrong with me?" He expressed the thought several times that he would bring some carpenter tools to build a recessed safe in the wall of the therapist's office in which he and the therapist together could keep their money. He frequently kept a lighted cigarette in an ash tray beside him as he worked. Once, when he heard footsteps in the hall, he exclaimed that it was his father coming and hid under the desk, where he sat on the floor smoking, remarking: "I hate my father." He recalled that his father had visited the clinic and, therefore, since he knew where it was, might come any time. For several sessions he maintained this attitude, seeking places where he could hide and smoke. Before leaving he would wash out his mouth.

This series of sessions dealing with the puzzle boxes began near Christmas. One of his favorite tools was a penknife from the therapist's key chain. This suggested an appropriate gift, so the therapist gave him a similar one. When Tommy received it, he showed mixed feelings. He examined it and was obviously pleased, but put it aside for a while with the embarrassed comment that he didn't know the therapist was going to give him anything. Finally, when he decided to use it as he engaged himself with a puzzle box, he gradually eased himself around the desk as he worked, until, at last, he sat on the therapist's lap.

The following session Tommy brought a comic book. He sat silent for a long while, reading and ignoring the therapist. The next session began with his firing a cap pistol as he entered the office, but when he was ready to leave he searched for a drawer in which he could hide the puzzle box from other patients and instructed the therapist to watch over it. He took some stage money from his pocket and put it in the box, then, drawing his gun on the therapist, told him to hand over his money so it could be put in the safe with his. The box had a combination-type lock. He left by way of running upstairs to the next floor and coaxing the therapist to chase him. He disregarded the therapist's command to come down because his mother was waiting. In the meantime, the therapist had a session with another patient, and when it ended Tommy appeared at the office door telling the therapist where he had been hiding. His mother and the social worker had searched the clinic but were unable to find him. His mother had resigned herself to sitting in the waiting room, as she assumed he was still in the building.

The puzzle-box sessions were followed by an intensified concern with hiding and smoking, with an occasional burning of papers or threat of setting fires. He persisted, over a period, in attempts to defy prohibition of a dangerous daredevilish manner of ascending the stairs. He would rapidly climb them by holding to the railing and walking the narrow overhang at the outside. The slightest misstep would have meant a long fall.

Two critical and focal developments emerged in connection with the smoking. First, he would strangle and choke on the smoke. This provided an opportunity through interpretations for the therapist to undermine his need to smoke in imitation of older people, and to give him reassurance in accepting more realistically the status of a small boy. Second, he produced clear representations of masturbation in the hiding and the smoking behavior. Hiding, of itself, became a preoccupying interest. Some sessions he shut himself in a dark closet where he would stay quietly, or describe to the therapist the glow which a ring he had acquired produced in the dark. Cigarettes and matches were forbidden in the closet. Finally, one day as a compromise, he agreed to stay out of the closet if he were permitted a cigarette. When given the cigarette he proposed that he and the therapist have a race to see who could smoke faster. When the therapist complied, Tommy closed his eyes tightly, bounced up and down rhythmically in his chair, and became increasingly excited as he puffed away. The therapist was able at this point to deal with masturbatory concerns and to indicate to Tommy again what was implied in some of the earlier sessions.

The session in which this took place was followed by one in which Tommy brought "Lone Ranger" comics, sitting on the therapist's lap as he read them. This, in turn, was followed by one in which he immediately asked for a cigarette, then produced a newly acquired ring in which the set opened to become a magnifying glass and a tiny ball-point pen. He would write his name with the pen, then demonstrate how it could be read through the magnifying glass. This was taken as an occasion to talk with him further about smallness and growing up, and to deal with his concerns about masturbation and its effects on growth and normality. From this activity he shifted to play with assembly materials from a mechanical-aptitude test. With attempts on the part of the therapist to bring the session to a close, Tommy would persist in his activity, saying: "Don't hit me!"

Sometime previously Tommy had shown interest in model planes he had seen in other offices, the therapist agreeing to buy one for him to assemble. When on entering the office on this occasion Tommy saw the carton containing the plane he literally danced with glee. As he began opening the carton he remarked that he did not think the therapist would get it; maybe he would forget it. When he saw the plane, he said with delight that it was exactly the kind he wanted and remarked that his mother would not get him one that large because it cost too much.

First he worked quietly on the floor. Then he decided he needed to look at the instructions and placed all the materials on the desk in front of the therapist. As he worked away, occasionally asking the therapist to hold a piece secure while he cut, he hummed and sang *They Wouldn't Believe Me* and *Off We Go, into the Wild Blue Yonder.*

He continued to work with complete absorption in the task through the next session, having brought some additional pins and instructing the therapist to bring some new razor blades for cutting. He talked of cousins whom he had never mentioned before. Cousin Eddie, a college student, was going to study to be a doctor. Cousin Jack didn't like school so he went in the Army and went to school. Now he wants to go to school some more when he gets out. Cousin Eddie wrestles with Tommy every Friday night when he doesn't have to study. He lives next door.

Tommy delayed and resisted the ending of the session. He wanted to take the plane home and finish it. Since the therapist wanted to prolong the more controlled sessions he promised that Tommy could take it home when it was finished. By the next session, however, Tommy was arguing that it would be too big to take on the trolley car when completed and that he wanted to show it to his cousin Eddie. He promised to bring parts of it back, so that the therapist could help him with it each week. He was permitted to take it home, and when he returned again he reported that he had completed it.

He was carrying a new gun his mother had given him, but it was not the kind he wanted. He had also learned of a type of plane he wished he had rather than the one the therapist had given him. He wanted to return to hiding in the closet. The therapist would not permit it. Tommy turned to play with clay, modeling a piece into which he could pour water to have it run out two holes. The therapist's comments evoked fantasies dealing with sex differences, and Tommy continued by elaborating on an imaginary swimming pool where people swam without suits – "Men only. Women on Saturday." Boys go "bore holes and peek at the women"; also, they go in the water, but "the women don't know it." He covered the eyes of men in a picture on the wall by sticking clay over them. Reference in interpretation was made to the previous manifestations of sexual concern. He was reassured as to the normality of such curiosity.

The session closed with Tommy asking for four cents to buy caps for his pistol, which the therapist granted. This was followed by Tommy's saying that he expected to get a paper route and deliver papers.

The next session began with Tommy talking about his plane and his wish that he had a gas motor for it. He asked the therapist for money to buy the motor. Ways of getting money were discussed with him. The therapist agreed to contribute a specified amount if the remainder could be obtained from Tommy's father, Cousin Eddie, Tommy's own earnings from his paper route and tips earned by delivering grocery packages. After expressing the thought that his father would "kill" him or say he was crazy, Tommy agreed. He figured how much of this money he and his younger sister already had, but thought his mother would not let him spend it.

The following week he reported that his cousin had agreed, his father made it conditional, but Tommy had not raised his part. He suggested, then demanded, that the therapist supply the difference. The therapist repeated his willingness to fulfill his part of the bargain but no more.

Several turbulent sessions followed in which Tommy stamped the floor, pounded the desk, tried to throw things, threatened to jump out the upstairs window at home in reaction to this unwillingness to grant him the money immediately. The therapist talked to him about the attitude and manner in which Tommy was trying to obtain the money. This behavior was interpreted to him, especially the tantrum aspects and the threat of self-destruction, as a means of forcing a show of affection, while the therapist offered that this was neither necessary nor realistic.

Tommy could only partially and reluctantly accept the idea of waiting for the financing of the motor to work out. He turned to trying to force the therapist to give him money in other ways. The therapist had given him small change for pistol caps. Tommy began spending his carfare for various things, and then demanded that the therapist give him money to get home. He would resort to threats of destructive behavior, such as throwing clay and cutting the desk, or he would try to go on the fire escape. The therapist restrained him frequently while repeating interpretations of Tommy's behavior and seizing every opportunity possible to direct Tommy's interest and solicitations to his parents, especially his father, and to his cousin. At times the therapist would restrain him by a playful procedure that Tommy came to enjoy, that is, the therapist would lift him high into the air. Tommy would become interested in trying to touch the ceiling, the overhead light, or in swinging from the doorway lintel.

He asked for cigarettes a few times in following sessions, but once burned himself with a match and another time shifted the cigarette and tried unsuccessfully to light the wet end. In one session, while smoking and sitting in quiet talk with the therapist, he asked if the therapist would give him a cigarette holder. The therapist told him he would do so when he was old enough to smoke and recalled interpretations of the smoking. Tommy wanted to know if he could smoke when he was sixteen. The therapist agreed it would be more appropriate than smoking while a little boy. Tommy protested that he would not be coming to the clinic then. A suggestion was offered to the effect that maybe he would come back to let the therapist see how much he had grown up and how things were going. This seemed to please Tommy, and at the end of the session he wanted to measure his height against previous marks on the wall and to check his weight on the examining-room scales.

Remaining sessions were generally more calm, lacking in intense display. He spent considerable time working with mechanical assembly material. He frequently did not want to leave when the hour was over, protesting that it was not time to go, or running from the office and hiding in the clinic, asking that the therapist try to find him.

Plans were made to send him to a different camp for a month the latter part of the approaching summer. Through the previous fall and winter his school work continued to improve and his mother reported that he was making friends with boys his own age. She was having difficulty in getting him to come home on time when he was away at play. He periodically would want to sit on his father's lap in the evening although at times Tommy carried it to a point where his father became annoyed with him. He sought every opportunity he could to go with his father when he was driving around on business.

In the spring months there were episodes in which both parents lost patience with him. They feared he was returning to his old difficulties. This paralleled the period in therapy leading up to and following the purchase of the plane. He baited his sisters, provoking fights. He wandered from home, not letting his parents know where he was going. He broke the plaster in his room and threatened to jump out the window. His father's attempts to control his own temper failed, on one occasion banging Tommy's head against a door. When he was assured a motor for his plane, his mother reported, the situation improved.

His mother complained to the social worker that Tommy was too self-centered. He boasted and bragged continually about his

achievements. She gave as an example the time when he repaired a lamp plug. After accomplishing this successfully, he turned to his father and pointed out how well he had done it. He commented that he had told his father how to do this repair job. His father was not in the least amused by this. Taking it very seriously, he was quite sharp with Tommy, saying that he, the father, had told Tommy how to make the repairs.

The social worker received the impression that both parents continued to be quite strict with Tommy. For instance, they refused to tell him the definition of words when he asked, but insisted that he look them up in the dictionary. Mrs. Hawkes at this time commented on the fact that she was trying to be more lenient with him, but had the feeling that she always had to give in to him rather than his ever making compromises.

His stay at camp this year was quite different from that reported the previous summer; for example, he tried to please the counselors by offering to do chores. He posed somewhat of a problem, however, in that he wanted to stay with them rather than engage in his scheduled activities.

Mrs. Hawkes decided that she would let Tommy try starting school in the approaching fall without continuing at the clinic, and, if things should become too difficult, she would bring him back. She called later to report that he was not doing extremely well, but that the more serious aspects of his behavior had improved. She felt he no longer presented a serious problem at home or at school.

Harold Bernhardt

EGO RESTRICTION IN A CHILD

HAROLD WAS REFERRED to the clinic by his schoolteacher because he was failing in the second grade and had to be demoted to the first grade. He was "too good" in his behavior but could not do his school work. He could not read or count and passed in blank papers. In the first grade he had a kind woman teacher who was badly crippled with arthritis. She gave him candy and did not punish him but said he was "just unable to absorb learning." The second-grade teacher seemed, in the estimation of the father, to be critical of Harold and more strict with him. She observed of Harold that he seemed "afraid to learn." He made no progress in the second-grade work and was soon sent back to the first grade. His new first-grade teacher said that Harold did not concentrate and did not play with other children. At home he had not learned to button his clothes or tie his own shoes.

Harold was described as a pudgy seven-year-old with blond hair, large dark eyes, and a limping gait. His father accompanied him to the clinic on the first visit. He began to tell the social worker Harold's troubles in a complaining way with Harold still in the room. Harold made no response but went docilely with the social worker when she led him to another room to play. His father told the social worker that Harold was not only failing in school but was very lazy at home. He never wanted to do anything and did not show any enthusiasm even about going places with the family on pleasure jaunts. He was afraid to play with other children, and ran when his little brother threw things at him. His father spent a great deal of time trying to teach Harold school work; Harold seemed to understand, but a few minutes later knew nothing about what he had been taught. His mother reported later to the social worker that Harold was slow about dressing himself. He did not care. She said it was as though, if he did not get dressed in one day, it would be all right with him to wait until the next day. His mother considered him a poor eater and said that he was always complaining about minor aches and pains and spending any money he could get for cough drops.

Harold was the middle child, with one brother three years older and one brother three years younger than he. The older brother was rather passive and had some difficulty when he first went to school, but it seemed to straighten out and he was doing quite well by the time Harold was brought to the clinic. The younger brother was extremely aggressive in spite of punishment. Both brothers bossed Harold, and the younger beat him so that Harold was afraid of him.

The focus of concern of both mother and father at the time they came to the clinic was whether or not Harold was mentally defective. His mother thought it strange that people could think mothers were happy, since their life was filled with worry. She worried about her children a good deal, especially about their physical health. Nevertheless, she was impatient with Harold's frequent complaints and vague aches and his tendency to spend all his money for cough drops. The younger brother had asthma which became severe when he had a cold. The mother worried about Harold's limp. His limp had no discernible physical basis, but she could not accept medical opinion on this.

The parents and all the children were obese. The family was scrupulously neat. The parents tried to provide better things for their children than were provided them as children. They supplied them with an abundance of food, toys, and clothing beyond what one would expect at their economic level.

In spite of their fondness for their children they were very much concerned about their being well behaved. They had strong feelings about right and wrong, not distinguishing between minor infractions of rules and more serious ones. They used yelling and strapping as disciplinary methods when the children did not obey or seemed too mischievous. Fighting or making a noise had been quite an issue since the doctor had said that being nervous or exposed to noise would aggravate an ear condition which the mother suffered. Father did most of the strapping, saying that his wife yelled instead, often so loud that the children ran out of the room.

The mother reported that her method of child training was to allow the children to "learn by experience." Instead of telling them not to touch a hot radiator, she would tell them to touch it. They would be burned and so learn not to touch it again.

The mother has always stayed in the home with the children while the father operated a service station in the small town where they have always lived. Both mother and father gave the impression of being reasonably intelligent. At the time they brought their son to the clinic they were both in their middle thirties. The mother had completed high school and would have gone to college except for the lack of money. The father had had to leave high school before graduating to go to work.

The mother had had impaired hearing since the oldest child's birth. She was planning to go to the hospital for a fenestration operation when Harold first came to the clinic. This operation and repeated treatment were unsuccessful, and she continued to use a hearing aid. The father assumed a good deal of responsibility for the children because of the mother's illness.

Her hearing became worse after Harold's birth. She did not breast feed him for fear of making his older brother jealous. He did not eat well and was thin until he was three years old. The mother considered him a bad baby because he did not eat enough and she had many struggles trying to force food into him.

At eleven months Harold had begun to talk and walk. In the twelfth month, while the mother was bathing Harold, he and his older brother struggled for possession of a rubber nipple. The older brother accidentally turned on the hot water and badly burned Harold's heel. He was unable to walk for two months on account of the burn and refused to try to walk for several months thereafter.

Harold was trained to use the toilet by the time he was two years old, but had a brief period of difficulty again at three following the birth of his brother. His mother says toilet training was not a problem because she did not force it. There was a period when he presented difficulties because of a propensity for stuffing small objects in his nose, but finally stopped this when he was frightened about a penny that got stuck in his nose and had to be removed by a doctor.

After the birth of his younger brother, Harold's mother was ill from severe hemorrhages, her hearing was worse, and she felt unable to care for the children. Harold and his older brother had chicken pox and then whooping cough when their mother returned home with the new baby. She avoided them in an attempt to save the baby from infection. The baby, nevertheless, did catch whooping cough. Whether from this or some other cause the younger brother developed continuous respiratory difficulties and had asthmatic attacks from an early age. After his brother's birth Harold began to stutter and to be generally uncommunicative.

Later in the same year Harold had his tonsils removed. There were no physical complications but no prior explanation of the operation was given him. Because of crowded conditions in the hospital, he was placed with the women in the maternity ward. His mother recalls his asking when he was going to get his baby. While he was still three years old he was hit on the head with a chair leg by a child in the street and had to have stitches taken to close the wound. When he was four he had another such accident resulting in a cut over his ear that required stitches. During this time, too, he began to wander away from home. Three times he was brought home by the police, having been picked up as a lost child. His mother finally tied him to the porch railing with a rope to prevent his wandering.

Harold's stuttering gradually subsided so that only a rather indistinct babyish quality remained by the time he went to school. His extreme uncommunicativeness remained. By the time he was six and attending school, he had withdrawn from associations with other children in the neighborhood and was afraid to go out to play. His mother and father attempted to handle this by planning to be out of the house for a walk with the younger brother when Harold came home from school, hoping this would force him to go out and play with other children. However, they always found Harold sitting in the house alone when they returned.

Treatment

Harold was in treatment at the clinic for four years. Visits were once a week except when appointments fell on holidays and during summer vacation. Turning to the content of his therapeutic sessions we are interested in what he was symbolically trying to say to his parents through his slowness, his limping, his pains, and his inability to dress himself. We are interested in what he thought of himself and the meaning his experiences had for him and, finally, what connection his school behavior and inability to learn had with these general problems.

Harold was seen during his first year of treatment by a male therapist. His early reactions to the therapist give a dramatic picture of his feelings about people and the inhibiting fears that underlie them. One should remind himself that the behavior described is that of a seven-year-old who is in the second year of school.

At the time of the first appointment Harold was found kneeling on a couch in the waiting room looking out the window. The therapist introduced himself and Harold extended his left hand very feebly. He walked up the stairs, and down again when he left, with great care, very slowly, while holding on to the banister and placing his feet very carefully, one step at a time. His gait in general was clumsy and shuffling.

He kept his coat on during the session and was not talkative. When he spoke, it was in a very high-pitched voice, softly modulated. Although he seemed shy, when encouraged to activity he tried to smear the therapist while playing with finger paint. It seemed very hard for him to verbalize and he could not say anything about why he was coming to the clinic, so the therapist explained about clinic visits and the therapist's role with him, but it did not register.

The first thing Harold noticed in the room was a dart gun. He picked it up and asked: "What is this?" as if he did not know. He handled it cautiously and carefully, shot it once, then put it down. The therapist remarked that it appeared as though it seemed dangerous to Harold. He replied: "Yes." The therapist wondered if Harold had a gun, and he said: "No." Did he ever see shooting? He answered: "Yes, in the movies." The therapist commented that this was not real, and Harold answered: "Oh, yes, it is; it really happens; they really are killed." The therapist again expressed doubt, but Harold would not accept it.

He would not engage in activity on his own but seemed to do anything the therapist suggested. Upon the suggestion that he draw, he drew a picture of a house in which all the shades were halfway down. It was bleak, with no further details. He took black crayon and made snow, saying that it was just make-believe. In response to inquiry about the snow he said it was one hundred inches deep, but then wondered how much that was.

With encouragement he used the finger paints but only with a brush. He repeated the drawing of the house, then an orange and red sky, and finally figures. The first figure had black hair and very large ears. He added arms and legs seemingly as an afterthought. This, he said, is a bad man, a murderer. Behind him he painted a figure which he said was a policeman chasing him. He would not elaborate on the plot but stated: "The bad man is you." The therapist remarked that it seemed that Harold was afraid of him. He did not reply, but spent the remainder of the session mixing paints and water, apparently exploring the kinds of colors he could make. When he left he said that he would see the therapist the next week and returned immediately and repeated the same remark.

In the next session his general manner was the same. He was awkward in handling the paints, doing a great amount of spilling. As he smeared the paints he seemed anxious about getting dirty, watching the therapist with quick glances. He picked up the dart gun and it went off accidentally. This startled him, and he put it down. A very noticeable mannerism was a long sigh, reminding one of the reaction associated with exhaustion.

He wanted to play checkers and played according to his own rules, letting himself win. This pleased him, and he remarked that his checkers at home were broken. He used the finger paints and made a house similar to the previous ones, saying a lady skeleton lived in it. He made a quarter moon but changed it to a sun, remarking: "The sun is sad because the lady skeleton lives in the house."

He frequently asked about the time and whether the therapist saw anyone else. He spoke of prolonging the time, saying that he wished he could stay for one hundred hours, adding: "How long is that?" The therapist offered him a stick of gum which he accepted, eating it rather than chewing it. Harold then moved toward the therapist, examining his tie clip and looking at him in a scrutinous manner.

Harold's hands got dirty with paint and he wished to wash them, prolonging the process. Then he switched to play with clay, deciding to make a sailboat. As he cut the clay into pieces with scissors he remarked: "Scissors cannot hurt." The therapist encouraged him to tell a little about his family, but Harold replied: "I don't know; I don't remember."

Harold arrived early for the next appointment, coming upstairs and knocking on the therapist's office door instead of going to the waiting room. The therapist was giving dictation to his secretary. He asked Harold to wait a few minutes. Harold asked later what the therapist was doing and why he had to see a secretary. He asked questions about the therapist's seeing other patients—who came next, who made various play products about the room, what the therapist did with other patients.

He was somewhat more aggressive and self-assertive. He talked more and took off his coat for the first time. There was still the sighing, and after a little activity he acted exhausted, having to rest periodically.

He decided to play a game of chess despite the therapist's attempts to discourage it because of its being a difficult game. He wanted to play apparently because other children played. The therapist tried to explain some of the rules but Harold quickly replaced them with his own, jumping and taking the therapist's men to win.

Again Harold was careless with finger paints, spilling water and paint around the room. He seemed to boss the therapist around in terms of getting things for him. He painted the same type of house as in previous sessions but asserted that it was in another street from where the lady skeleton lived. He joked about peculiar words that he made up which were more or less clang associations. He repeated such combinations as stinky-pinky, nilly-willy-billy, followed by talking about his younger brother whom he called naughty because he made their mother mad. His brother hit him, but Harold would not hit back. When the therapist commented that he must feel mad at these times, Harold denied it was true. The therapist remarked that he wondered if the younger brother was a stinky-blinky and Harold continued with verbal aggression against the brother.

While painting he made what he called the sun with a face and heavy eyebrows. Later he called it the moon and it was changed so it appeared highly suggestive of breasts. He spilled some red paint on his hand and wanted to get it off quickly. The therapist remarked that it had the appearance of blood. Harold spoke about the sun being so hot it warmed the whole room. He then painted an animal and converted it into what he said was his younger brother, calling him "stinky." Then he made it into a horse with a curled-up red tail. Finally he smeared the house and tore up the paper.

Following this he went to the blackboard, saying that he was doing arithmetic problems. He played the teacher. His problem was 3 = 3 = 3. The therapist tried to get him to change the equal signs to plus. To this he reacted by wanting to wash the blackboard, saying that he never got to do it in school because the teacher never asked him and he "never raises his hand." When the therapist said it was time for ending the session Harold said the therapist was only fooling.

As the trends initiated in these sessions developed through the remainder of the year, the aggressive aspects were prominent. He smeared paint, destroyed articles in the playroom, and played aggressively with water. He put soapy water in glasses and placed them in other offices, saying that people would drink it and be poisoned. At the same time he appeared frightened and frequently supplied his own retribution. Once when he made a smearing attack on the therapist he immediately got glue on his own hands. Then he wanted to wash up "so the teacher won't see it." Next he wanted to put paint on the therapist's hands to immobilize him so that the therapist "couldn't touch anything." The therapist commented on hands doing bad things, and Harold said: "Shut up!"

In school he had first inhibited writing altogether, and when he did begin it was messy, smeared, and marked over. His further association of writing as expressive behavior with aggressive behavior is demonstrated in an episode near the end of his first year in treatment. Harold asked to take several toys from the office home with him. The therapist gave him the choice of one. Harold would not compromise, ripped the blotter from the therapist's desk, cut it with scissors, and then rushed at the therapist with the scissors. When restrained he turned immediately to scribbling on the blackboard.

Harold became less fearful of the permissive therapist as the year progressed. The therapist always had candy for him and many times took him out for food. He ate more at home also during this year and became quite obese.

Over a period of time Harold made noises of inanimate things as he played or painted. He frequently said: "I'm a fire engine," then screeched like a siren. This type of behavior developed when the therapist took note of the hardly audible noises Harold would make and encouraged him in order to lessen Harold's inhibition. This quiet little boy frequently sat with his mouth wide open making a noise like a fire engine or steamboat as he rocked back and forth rhythmically in his chair playing with paints. At times he would demand food during this activity or shout for the therapist to get out of his way.

Frequently during this year Harold came to his appointments with his pants open at the fly. He continued to sigh after any activity, physical or mental. His careful, constricted gait loosened up considerably.

At the beginning of the second year Harold was transferred to a woman therapist. She was not a complete stranger to him at this time as he had had several sessions with her the previous year during which she gave him psychological tests.

When they met in the playroom he went quite willingly to her office and went inside, went over the play materials, remembering quite accurately what he had seen in the office at the testing sessions.

First he painted something indefinite which appeared to be either a red flower or a red flag. He wanted the therapist to wait upon him and take care of his needs, keeping fresh water, putting the brush in the water in a specified way.

After a while he wanted to go outside the clinic. He wanted to go to a ten-cent store where his previous therapist had taken him and wanted to be sure to take the exact same route that they had taken. He asked if his present therapist would be going away to the same place his previous one had gone.

In the store he could not make up his mind what he wanted, actually wanting many things rather than deciding upon one as the therapist suggested. As the time for the ending of his visit with the therapist approached he still vacillated. Finally the therapist made a decision among the contending items and bought a small live turtle. Once the decision was made Harold seemed quite content. After the clerk put the turtle in a box with holes in it she placed the box and turtle in a bag. On the way back to the clinic Harold became concerned lest the therapist would smother the turtle by holding it so it did not get enough air. He took it and carried it himself. He was afraid as he left it in the therapist's office until his next appointment that she would not feed it and it would die.

In the second session he duplicated the pattern of the first, except he made fewer references to his previous therapist. He made a dark brown painting which he again refused to comment upon. Then he wanted to go out and get another turtle. He picked out a larger one this time. While the clerk was preparing it to be transported she spoke of how turtles get to know and recognize people who are familiar. On the way back to the clinic Harold repeated the remarks with pleasure and interest.

The therapist was late for the next session and Harold reproached her, saying how long he had been waiting. He checked the food for the turtles and was concerned whether or not the therapist was feeding them properly. He wanted the therapist to go alone and purchase another turtle while he stayed at the clinic. Since the therapist would not do this he finally decided both should go. On the way back he removed the turtle from the box and carried it in his hand. He was quite rough with it, squeezing and crushing it. The turtle drew in its head and Harold became frightened, saying: "The turtle is holding its breath; if he holds his breath he will die." The therapist asked Harold if he ever held his breath, and he replied: "Of course, everybody does, all night when they are asleep." When asked if he were afraid he would die then, he replied: "No, because God takes care of you then. That's how we are able to wake up." As he played with the turtles back at the office he asked if the therapist had a boy. When the therapist said she did not, he replied that it was a good thing because he might stick something in the middle of the turtles' shells and kill them.

In the next session, as he gave the turtles a bath, he said that he had dreams of turtles in lots of water since his last visit to the clinic. He was quite rough as he bathed them, squeezing them, running hot water on them, and picking them up by the feet. The therapist reminded him that once his own foot got hurt. Harold replied that he knew it; it was when he was six years old. In a very babyish manner he added: "I was still just a baby." The therapist told him it was at one year. He looked uncomprehending for a moment, then agreed. He acted somewhat as though he could not hear.

From visit to visit the turtles continued to figure in activities in which he associated to his mother and brothers, especially the younger. Once, as he rolled marbles down an incline hitting the turtles on the head, he remarked that his brother turned the hot water on and meant to do it to burn Harold's foot. But then he said: "It was my mother, she didn't take care of me."

On one occasion he picked up the therapist's pen and squirted ink in the turtle bowl, adding some water from a nursing bottle, as he said he would like to see if it would kill them. Then he went to the sink where he turned on the hot water, letting it run until it was very hot and putting his hands under it. The therapist turned off the water, saying that perhaps Harold was trying to see if she would do what he thought his mother had done—not take care of him. He asked immediately whom the therapist was going to see tomorrow. She said maybe Harold was afraid she was going to see some child she liked better than Harold, as he was afraid his mother had liked his younger brother better. She then added that this was not true; the therapist liked Harold as well as other children she saw. Harold looked at the turtle bowl and said someone had taken the black stuff out. Then he looked at the therapist affectionately and said: "I know. You did." He began to hum a song and ended by singing the words "and a happy New Year."

There were other evidences of less negative feelings during this time. His mother said that when Harold complained of small aches and pains and said he did not want to go to school she would tell him that then he could not go to the clinic. He went to school in order to be able to come to the clinic. When he was sick and unable to come in, Harold told the therapist he had dreamed he was in her room "just doing the things we always do."

Even though he perceived the therapist more favorably, it was difficult for Harold to give up the services and gifts that had served to reassure him. Part of the reason for this became apparent in Harold's perception of himself. He had previously maintained to the therapist that he was the best boy in his family because "I never do anything." Now, in a more confident relationship with the therapist, he was able to reveal that he really thought otherwise. In the middle of the second year of therapy the therapist tried to get Harold to give up his demands to go out each time and buy a gift. She explained that buying gifts could only make him feel better for a little while, and if they could spend more time talking about the things that bothered him, she could help him feel better longer. He looked out the window to where there was construction work going on in the street and said: "How can anybody make anything out of that pile of dirt?" She was able to persuade him that there were other things in the construction besides dirt and that something useful was being made out of it. He consented to stay and talk.

Just prior to the time Harold's mother was to be hospitalized for another operation on her ear, he, always uncommunicative, seemed to pay less attention than ever to the therapist, acting as if he just did not hear her. The therapist asked Harold if sometimes his mother did not hear him. He said, sadly, he did not know. Then he became concerned about what he should do in the therapy hour. He did not know whether he wanted to go out and buy a present or stay in and paint. He painted a carefully drawn pink shell-like shape and then began to smear it wildly with brown and black paint. Becoming extremely anxious, he called to the therapist: "Get me another brush; it's dirty and it's breaking!" (The brush was not breaking.)

Later, when his mother was actually in the hospital, Harold said he did not know if she were there to have an operation on her ear or on her foot. This in spite of the fact that her ear was a preoccupation of the whole family. In a still later instance Harold made other associations between his hostile feelings toward his mother and his own difficulties. He told the therapist that his father had read him a book about babies. (It was a book about birth and sex written for children.) He said that he had learned how babies were fed inside the mother. He thought of the baby as being inside the mother's stomach and receiving the food directly. What he did not understand was how the baby got fed after it was outside the mother. He wanted to look at a copy of the same book, which was in the therapist's office, to see if he could find out about this. When he came to the picture of the mother with a baby at her breast he said in a pitying voice: "Does it hurt her very much?" The therapist said that sometimes a baby did bite its mother's breast as it got older, but the mother was not really hurt much; she could remove the breast for a minute and then the baby could go on sucking. The therapist promised Harold to discuss it more next time.

At the beginning of the next session Harold was interested in arithmetic examples another child had put on the blackboard. He demonstrated that he could do them except when a larger number had been placed under a smaller number to be subtracted he added figures to his answer to show a large remainder. He did not simply do what children often do—reverse the position of digits—but added several digits to the remainder to make it very large. The therapist asked if arithmetic was not one of the things that had been hard for him when he first started school. He made no verbal reply but erased the arithmetic examples and put in their place a large breastlike shape which he said was a rainbow. He used the colored chalk to fill it in but said he had to save the black for the center: "because it's always black in the middle." The therapist commented that maybe Harold was still worried about what they talked about last week. He said he "couldn't be," because he could not remember it at all. Then he used a wet sponge to erase the drawing, and as he watched the board dry he cried out in a disappointed voice: "Why did it dry up so quick?"

Some months later Harold drew an elephant on the blackboard. He started with a trunk and large projecting ears and then added the rest of the body. The elephant was lame, with one leg on each side shorter than the others. He began putting in the eye but decided that the trunk and the ears were too big. Suddenly he erased the whole thing and went out of the office to the physical examining room where he listened to his heart with the stethoscope and blew on it to see if his breath was still coming out. Then he weighed himself and was alarmed that he had lost weight. The therapist told him that what he had been thinking while he was drawing the elephant had made him fear for his safety and that he must feel such thoughts were bad. He made no reply but went back to the office, where he asked for clay. He made an elephant with it and put a fence around it, but he could not put the eye in it. Later he stabbed the elephant's stomach and opened it. The therapist commented about babies being inside mothers and wondered if Harold had seen someone who looked big and was going to have a baby. He said he had not; he was too small when his brother was born to know about anything like that. He reiterated that he did not know how babies were born despite the fact that his father and the therapist had been discussing this with him a short while before.

Not seeing and not knowing had previously been themes that had come out in his productions, as well as the not hearing. The danger of seeing had seemed to be involved in his behavior when he wanted a magnifying glass as a gift, but when it was offered him he would not take it.

Apparently the exercise of the power of seeing had become inhibited in a very generalized way. From the beginning of his school work he was reluctant to look at his book and perceived the forms of letters poorly. After his reading and spelling were much improved he still could not spell the names of members of his family and did not know his mother's first name.

His expectations about learning seemed to be related to knowing his own bad impulses or knowing sad feelings. Once when he was playing word games with the therapist he became concerned that she was winning. She pointed out that he had in his hands cards to make the word "sad." He said he knew it, but he did not want to make that word. He was waiting for the letter "p" so he could make the word "sap" instead. Even when his school work was much improved, feelings of depression about school were evident.

Gradually through the four years of treatment Harold abandoned his diffuse fearfulness and was able to relate his fears to his own thoughts and activities and accept the therapist as a helper. He eventually was able to bring gifts to the therapist instead of demanding them. He enjoyed games with complicated rules and took delight in the mental activity.

After his second and third years in treatment he went to a camp operated for children with psychiatric problems. The first summer he was teased as the fat boy with the high voice. The following summer he became a leader. At the end of the fourth year he went to regular camp where he took his place among normal children.

When Harold was tested during his first year of treatment he scored clearly above defective level, but his performance showed many signs of his inhibitions. He scored an I.Q. of eighty-five on the Stanford-Binet Form L. At the end of his third year of treatment he scored an I.Q. of one hundred three, which is an average score, but was probably still not at his upper limit.

He did not repeat a grade except the year he started treatment. His school work gradually improved, and one year after termination of his visits to the clinic he was doing well, making mostly A's and a few B's, and only one C. He had friends, and was active in sports. He became tall and large for his age but no longer obese. His parents felt pride in his achievements and there was more warmth in the feelings between the family members.

Gerald Bittinger

ADOLESCENT SCHOOL FAILURE

As a youngster Jerry had liked school and had gotten good marks, but since the fifth grade his interest had waned and his marks progressively declined. He managed to get promoted each time but now, in his senior year of high school, he was failing two of his courses. He and his mother were warned that unless his performance improved he would not graduate. His teachers complained to his mother that he clowned around and distracted the entire class. They stated that he did not pay attention and concentrate on his work; he would not try.

His mother realized that things were not as she would like them with Jerry, but had hoped they would straighten out with time. Now she felt he had gotten himself into an unnecessary crisis and took steps to try to avert the dreaded outcome. She tried to help him with his assignments, but this ended up with him in tears and her screaming at him. Obviously this did not help, so she abandoned it. She and his stepfather deprived him of his radio, allowance, and the use of the car, but he maintained a nonchalance toward such punishments. "Nothing bothers him," is the description she gave of his reaction.

Jerry's school predicament, while pressing and of immediate concern, was not the only problem on his horizon. His mother indicated that she was concerned about his playing with much younger children, and what she called his "secretiveness." More careful questioning brought out even more symptoms of interest psychologically. He stuttered, but she felt this was only a minor difficulty and stated that he was able to control it now, so that it was hardly noticeable. She also stuttered as a child, she added, and did not stop until she was about twenty-five years old. She also mentioned that he had attacks of asthma, but felt that the condition was better than when he was younger and now presented no problem of any consequence.

She indicated that she had "not been too concerned and had not noticed" his stuttering until Jerry's aunt, her younger sister, had pointed it out. His aunt also indicated to his mother in recent years that she considered Jerry an unhappy boy and advised her to seek psychiatric treatment for him. His mother consulted his school about bringing him to the clinic a year prior to his coming, and was advised against it, as they did not think his problems were "serious," reassuring her that he would eventually "snap out of it." However, a year later, with his outright failure in school, she reconsidered her sister's advice and consulted the clinic.

When an appointment was scheduled for Jerry she told him she had arranged to take him to a place "where he could get help with his English," which was one of the subjects he was failing in school. On his initial visit he dutifully told of his difficulties with English and considered that they arose primarily because of the teacher's "going too fast." He added, however, that he had been in a special class from the seventh grade until this year and that he did not understand the subject matter. This was a speech class for stutterers. Discussion of his stuttering also brought references to his asthma, which he regarded as a current problem.

Jerry was described as a compliant child, and for this his mother was grateful, because she was forced by circumstances to be away from home so much. When he was six weeks old she returned to work and left him with his grandmother and grandfather where she could visit him on weekends. This arrangement continued until he was ten years old, at which time she remarried and Jerry came to live with her and his stepfather.

Jerry had been a full-term baby and delivery normal. He was breast-fed for six weeks but did not thrive on his mother's milk, so was put on a formula. He was a feeding problem for about four or five months and did not develop into a good eater until he was about ten years old. He talked at one year, walked at one and a half years. Toilet training was started at six weeks but was interrupted when he was with his grandmother, as she did not believe in early training. His mother then had a great deal of trouble in training him. He would sit on his toilet chair for hours and do nothing, then soil his diaper immediately when taken off. Training was not accomplished until he was two years old. Occasionally he wet the bed until he was fourteen or fifteen years old. He enjoyed sucking his forefinger, and his mother tried many devices, including an aluminum mitt, before this ceased.

Jerry has always been thin, underweight, and wiry. When teething he got an abscess in his ear with every tooth. He had a tonsillectomy at two years and measles, mumps, and chicken pox at about five years. When he was four he started having two or three severe asthma attacks each winter. When he had an attack he would get very panicky and cry out for his mother to call the doctor. She would not do this, but would try to quiet him first. According to her report, the periodic attacks continued until he was about thirteen, at which time he received inoculations for hay fever and had no more asthma attacks until one just prior to starting treatment. This, she said, happened when he slept in a different bed after giving up his bed to a guest who was visiting the family.

Jerry's father was a musician who traveled widely in moving from his seasonal engagements. His earnings were good, but he was irresponsible and a spendthrift, so that Jerry's mother had to work. When she became pregnant with Jerry during the first year of marriage, she and her husband moved into the house with her parents. She started work soon after Jerry's delivery in order to keep from financially imposing on her parents. When her husband worked in the vicinity, he continued to live in her parental home. The first few years of marriage were so unstable and insecure that she asked for a divorce after three years, but her husband was adamant and asserted his intention to buy a house and settle in one place. Sometime later, however, he informed her that he had become a father through an illicit affair. He wanted her to accept the child and care for it, offering to move her out of her parental home into a house of their own as an inducement. She was extremely upset, as she had never suspected his being unfaithful, but it made the basis for her marriage difficulties clear to her. After talking it over with her family and friends she decided to get a divorce. He was chagrined and made things difficult for her. In recounting this she said that he thought she would do anything because she loved him. Playing on this hunch he appeared at the court proceedings, and his behavior resulted in a great deal of publicity for the case. She was so embarrassed and upset that she decided to resume her maiden name, not thinking at the moment of the awkward situation she was creating, as Jerry retained his father's surname. Jerry was five years old when these events took place. After the divorce his mother continued to work and her parents took care of Jerry. She saw him only on weekends and sometimes less frequently.

Jerry was not told the story of his father. His mother suspected that he may have heard gossip about it, but never discussed it with him. She thought this was upsetting to him and she wanted to tell him, but said she did not know how. His surname had been changed several times, but he was legally adopted by his stepfather and consequently has his name. His mother's only attempt to deal with these realities with him was to leave pictures of her first wedding in a desk drawer in the hope that he would see them and ask about them. This he did. She told him that the man in the picture was his father and that they separated as people do when they do not get along together. He apparently did not try to question beyond this. He commented that he wondered why his father had never been to see him or sent him anything. His mother was very much afraid that in future years Jerry might get into his father's circle of friends or actually meet his father. Jerry's final adoption was accomplished only within recent years. At the time of the hearing Jerry was present and listened, but asked no questions, and nothing more was said.

Jerry's mother described her present husband as a very methodical, well-organized, dependable person. She remarked that he was different from her in that she was impulsive, doing things and thinking about them afterward, and that he was different from her first husband because of his dependability. The first husband was good-looking but cared only for himself. He always had the best for himself, including tailored clothes, but never had money for the support of her and Jerry. The second husband takes pride in his home.

In further discussion of her second husband she commented that they had been married seven years and only recently had he started to talk more freely and become more open about things. She said that they had of late gotten into discussions that were really arguments, but that she liked it this way. He was brought up in an adult household; his mother was nearing menopause when he was born. His father died soon after the birth. This she related in trying to explain why Jerry and his stepfather did not understand each other. She felt that the stepfather never had a childhood, as he played alone and was trained very early to be a very proper sort of person and abandon the activities of a young boy. In the beginning the stepfather tried to discipline Jerry but was too strict, with little understanding of a young boy's behavior. Jerry played his mother against his stepfather, and the situation was not good. When the mother took over, things improved. Jerry was said to refer to his stepfather as his father outside the home, but at home he called him by his first name. His mother spoke of an undercurrent of competition between Jerry and his stepfather.

The household currently consisted of Jerry, his mother, his stepfather, and his stepfather's mother. The latter seemed to resent Jerry's coming into the home at the time of the marriage. She would always ask where he was going and what he was doing. She and Jerry's mother had disagreements about his eating habits. This they did not discuss, but managed to contradict each other in the attitudes they expressed directly to him. When Jerry's mother was to be away, she would instruct Jerry to eat something when he returned from school because she felt he needed the food. His step-grandmother would forbid this, and later his mother would privately tell him to disobey her and eat anyway, or suggest he do it without his step-grandmother's knowledge. His mother fears that this had contributed to the "secretiveness" she dislikes in Jerry.

His mother spoke very warmly of her own parents. In discussing Jerry's life with them, she commented that he liked them very much, saying that the maternal grandmother was nervous, but Jerry liked her, as she would give him practically everything he wanted. She beamed as she spoke of the maternal grandfather and the fact that he was easy-going, nice, and placid, and that Jerry still called him "Daddy." She later felt that she was too naïve in her first marriage and had given Jerry a bad childhood which she would like to correct if possible. She feared that Jerry's adolescent behavior had elements of his father's irresponsibility in it. She also mentioned that she wondered if he felt as she did when she stuttered. Her embarrassment was painful, and she felt as though her throat were tightly bound, but added that if Jerry felt this way he never mentioned it. As she recounted this there was a sort of tic of her throat muscles.

Jerry went to private kindergarten when he was three and a half years old. When he was four, he was eligible for a public kindergarten and was transferred. This early enrollment was his mother's way of trying to relieve the maternal grandmother of some of the care. She said that she herself was so preoccupied with her own troubles at this time that she had very little to offer Jerry the little time she was with him. He was five years old when he entered the first grade. The grandparents moved several times during his first few years in school which entailed him changing schools each time. Then when he was ten he moved again in order to be with his mother and stepfather, and started in the fifth grade. The standards were not so high as those of his previous schools so he was able to pass without studying. He continued in this school and was in his senior year when first seen at the clinic. At the marking period immediately prior he received an "A" in Art and in Applied Chemistry, "B" in Public Speaking, but failed History and English. He strongly disliked the History and English teachers.

Jerry at one time was interested in becoming a professional baseball player but did not make the high-school team. When he failed to make the team he worked very hard preparing a playing field where he practiced with much younger children. When his mother saw him play she felt sorry for him and thought his ineptness was due to shyness. When she did not see him play, he would boast to her how well he played.

He was a tall, rather handsome dark-haired lad. His mother

once referred to him at the clinic as "my baby" and corrected herself with "my six-foot baby." Because of his height he was asked to try out for the school basketball team, but he did not make it. He and his mother both attributed this to his asthma. She described various devices which he had for use in exercising his hands and arms, saying that he spent time each day alone in his room exercising. During the time he was coming to the clinic his mother gave him money to buy a set of bar bells.

She said that each time someone came to school to talk about a vocation Jerry became possessed with thoughts of pursuing it. He was excited about the Coast Guard when someone talked at the school about it. She said that she pointed out to him that he probably would not be eligible because of his stuttering and asthma. He told her that the asthma was nothing, and that he could stop the stuttering whenever he wanted to stop. He expressed interest in becoming a radio announcer, and at one time thought maybe he would attend a professional baking school. His shifting interests puzzled his mother and she inquired at the clinic as to whether this tended to happen frequently because, when she was growing up, she always knew exactly what she wanted.

Jerry was described as usually very quiet, talking very little at home. He once was very helpful about the house, but became less willing to take responsibility for chores. His stepfather frequently checked to see if Jerry was falling down on his job. His mother checked on him occasionally. Jerry resented being lectured by his stepfather, but tried in many ways to please him. The stepfather was inclined to be abrupt and gave him no encouragement. Any critical remark made by Jerry, especially in regard to privileges other children had and he did not have, was likely to hurt the stepfather's feelings. Usually, if Jerry wanted to do something and was not permitted, he got angry but did not "show it." His mother remarked that his face "just goes blank." He laughed readily and showed his feelings more up until he was about seven years old. Then he changed and became glum and secretive about his activities in so far as possible.

After Jerry entered treatment he was seen for psychological testing. He was very serious during testing sessions and was described as reserved and lacking spontaneity, except when he was asked for a demonstration of freehand sketching which Jerry had indicated to the examiner he liked to do. He stuttered frequently and was somewhat erratic in his test performance. He scored just above average on an intelligence test, with very little difference in his success with verbal and non-verbal, or performance, test items. The Rorschach Test called attention to, among other things, a markedly hostile element in his fantasies which was dealt with by repressive means and a negativistic type of reacting.

Some of his stories to Thematic Apperception Test pictures are quoted as he rendered them because of their dealing with his current concerns, or alluding to matters that probably occupied an important place in his fantasies.

When presented a picture of an older woman and a young man, usually interpreted as a mother and son, he gave the following story as his explanation of the picture:

> "On July 17, 1948, a young man had just graduated from high school. On finding that he wanted to go to art school he only had one problem in the way of going there, and that was he was almost eighteen and that he would be drafted soon. The question in his mind [stutters] should he be drafted: should he go to art school or should he join the Navy. This brought much thought to the boy's mind and after many hours of figuring he finally decided that the best thing to do would be to join the Navy. Since his mother wanted him to go to art school, another problem arose: How would the boy's decision affect his mother? He finally thought the best thing to do would be to go down and tell her his idea. After figuring around for about an hour he finally called his mother into the living room and told her his decision. After much thought the mother who loved her son very much finally agreed to the idea and today the boy who joined the Navy is now Lieutenant Commander and has a very successful life."

To a picture of a man in trunks climbing or clutching a vertical rope with his hands and feet he gave the following story:

> "Well, let's see. At the age of seven little Johnny decided he would become in future years the world's champion weight

lifter. For two years he saved money on his paper route until he had enough money to buy a gym set and after he joined the gym club. He started at the age of nine and a half and trained for twelve years doing such things as pushups, rope climbing, setups, knee bends, and weight lifting until he had become so great that he was chosen in 1938 to go on the United States Olympic Team. He competed with many stars from all over the world in the field of weight lifting. He came through and was the World's Champion Amateur Weight Lifter in the Olympics in 1938. Johnny now looks back to when he was a boy and often wonders how he became a great strong man when at first he was a little, skinny boy [laughs] in a country town. He is now the world's greatest professional weight lifter. That's me."

The picture of a boy contemplating a violin on a table before him evoked the following interpretative story:

"The violin was made by Stradivarius in Italy in Florence. He had his shop at Florence or Genoa. One of the best instruments; has a very pleasant sound. The boy is probably a poor boy in the slums of New York. At the age of six he turned on the radio one day and heard a concert from the RCA building and heard a lovely instrument known as the violin. He decided then and there to take up violin and someday to become a great concert violinist. At the age of seven he had saved enough money to buy a secondhand one in a pawnshop and at first was discouraged. After many years of hard practicing his love for the violin grew until at the age of twenty he had saved enough money to travel to Boston and audition with the Boston Pops Orchestra where he soon went far ahead in that field and became a concert master and later became leader and is known today as a famous violinist, Joe Schmoe."

A picture of a woman lying on a bed with her breasts partially exposed by the drawn covers and a fully dressed man standing in the foreground with his hands over his eyes and forehead gave him inspiration for the following:

"All New York City was looking for the worst killer in years who had strangled many people. One day a husband came home from work late at night to find that his wife had been killed. He vowed that he would get the killer before he died and with close co-operation from the police he was given a permit to hunt the killer down. After three years he finally caught his man in a bar in St. Louis and brought him back to New York only to find that he was the wrong man. Meanwhile, the police had found a letter in the wife's bureau drawer saying that she wanted a divorce from her husband, but the husband would not give it to her; and with this evidence the police suspected the husband of the murder and got him finally to confess to the murder of his wife."

Jerry was seen twenty-two times for treatment sessions at weekly intervals, except when appointments were missed or fell on holidays. These appointments extended from late fall, through winter and spring into part of the summer. In addition, he was seen by a speech therapist during the summer and the following fall.

In the initial interview he blamed his teachers for his failures in school, said that he stuttered when he was "nervous," which he was able to elaborate further as "feeling afraid." In commenting on his asthma, which he still felt to be a handicap, he said that he was allergic to all animals, except dogs, and "especially cats." He dated the beginnings of both stuttering and asthma symptoms at the age of ten when he first went to live in the country. This was the time at which he returned to his mother and her new home with her second husband. She dates the onset of both symptoms between the ages of four and five years of the period when her first marriage was disintegrating completely.

Jerry also expressed concern about what he would do when he graduated from high school. He would like to go to the Coast Guard Academy because he "has always liked water," and told of his cruising in a small boat with his grandfather. He said that he prefers a small boat to a large one. He also mentioned that he was interested in art and was thinking of going to art school. He told of doing sketches for the school yearbook and posters for special occasions. He stressed the fact that his grades in art were good.

He spoke of being too light to play football and of his pleasure in teaching a group of small boys to play football. In referring to his family group, he spoke of his stepfather simply as "Father."

As treatment proceeded, Jerry tended to cling to rationalizations around his school problem. The English teacher, a woman who was well past her youthful years, he saw as stern and demanding of perfection, with no understanding of youthful limitation. This in spite of the fact that during the spring months when, in response to the therapeutic efforts, he made some effort to do his work she gave him an incomplete instead of a failure. Only when no alternative was left did she fail him. The history teacher, a man, apparently liked athletes and gave them good grades while Jerry, without athletic ability, had to share the leavings, which could only be a failure. In his course he chose to sit with the athletes while they whispered jokes and he laughed in appreciation, which only resulted in his dismissal from the room. While his behavior and relationship to this teacher were being discussed in the treatment sessions, Jerry went through a variety of futile maneuvers to win his favor guided by an unshakable belief that only an athlete could pass. For instance, he drew cartoons of the athletes in class with the notion that when the teacher took them away from him, the reaction of the teacher would be one of sudden pleasure and approval.

In coming for his treatment appointments he was usually early but was likely to be late following any session in which the face value of any of his positions seemed to be challenged. In spite of the fact that his mother was asked to correct her original presentation of the treatment as "help with his English," and of discussions in treatment sessions of the fact that he seemed to present a number of problems with which he would like help, he referred, in his most negativistic phase, to the sessions as "classes." He was always, however, very polite and friendly in attitude. At one period he missed two appointments with rationalizations such as: "My train was late and I had not had any breakfast or any dinner last evening, so I thought you wouldn't mind if I stopped to get something to eat. Then it was so late that I thought you probably had started another class, so I went to a movie that I hadn't had a chance to see."

He inquired in interviews if weight lifting were not indicated to help with body building since he had not gained any weight in two years. He also asked for support in his wish to join a boxing group at the "Y," but when he actually went to join he arranged only for swimming instruction, later asking for the therapist's concurrence in getting a punching bag with which to practice at home.

Throughout the period of treatment, from time to time, Jerry demonstrated his excellent cartooning talents. Usually this grew out of discussions of current activities in school and he would demonstrate or reproduce drawings which he had recently done. One of the early favorite subjects was a currently famous pitcher in professional baseball whom he usually represented in a determined and hunched attitude with exaggerated mouth, bulging with tobacco, waiting for the catcher's signal. He drew, also, an inadequate, insignificant-looking baseball player fielding a fly ball from which the cover had been knocked, with many strands of loose string trailing from it as it sailed through the air. The player, excellently portrayed in action, appeared as though the catch was going to be successful and dramatic. Later, he dealt with the same theme, using a scrawny football player charging down the field clutching a bucket to his chest while a pass did zigzag antics through the air, but somehow appeared as though it would, as if by magic, drop into the bucket. His most repeated cartoon subject was a hockey player drawn in such a way as to give the impression of his skating toward the observer at great speed, with club raised high over his head and an enormously exaggerated mouth with large teeth bared. During hockey season he went out for the team for a while but did not make it; so he quit.

There were several cartoons dealing with school life. One contrasted "yesterday's teacher" with "today's teacher." "Yesterday's" was represented by a very masculinized woman with a baseball bat over her head, glaring eyes, and enormous teeth, saying: "Okay, Joe, I'll have to belt it into you." "Today's teacher" was portrayed as a girl in sweater and bobby sox, smiling and saying: "Now look, dears."

The acceptance of his art talent, which Jerry sensed in the therapist, led him to solicit work in the art department of newspapers. He would arrange appointments at such times that he would have to arrive late for or leave early from therapy sessions. There was also a period during which he would visit a radio announcer. Once during a bus strike, however, he had to cancel his appointment by telephone, stuttering so badly that the therapist had considerable difficulty in understanding him. As the summer season approached, Jerry considered what he would do, since it was established by this time that he would not go to summer school to make up his courses. He considered first that he and a friend would rob lobster traps and sell their loot to restaurants. Next, he thought maybe they would dig for clams in places where it was prohibited and sell them to restaurants. Finally, he became interested in a job in a shipyard, which he actually obtained.

His mother's reaction to the effects of the early treatment sessions was that she was glad to see him showing his feelings at home. He became more self-assertive, she remarked, and when he was angry did not just become glum, but would leave the room and slam the door. She was pleased with an increase in social activities and the fact that he spent more time with friends his age. He asked her opinion on matters which he had never discussed before, but she was not always pleased with the result of this new attitude. For instance, he had two social affairs scheduled for the same evening, one a school dance and the other a party being given by a church club of which he had been elected president. He wanted to go to the school dance, but she and his stepfather thought he had a responsibility to go to the club party since he was president. After discussing it they left the decision up to him, and he decided to go to the club party. His mother then became concerned about the fact that maybe he was too easily led into this and that she was to blame if he did not have a good time. Later, she discovered, however, that he appeared briefly at the club party, then went to the school dance. She was very angry, referring to him as untrustworthy.

Jerry's mother accepted and followed his gains through treatment without becoming too distressed with the fact that they were limited and undramatic. She tried to correct her appraisal of him. For instance, she commented, after he had been in treatment for a short period, she noticed his stuttering more since attention had been called to it. She detected early that he had decided he would not graduate because he did not have his picture taken for the yearbook as did other seniors. When she asked him about the matter, he offered what she recognized as blatant rationalizations. She became quite encouraged, however, when later in the spring he seemed to make a serious effort for a period of some weeks which resulted in some improvement in grades. She did not blame his difficulties on his teachers. She pointed out, for instance, that the English teacher, about whom Jerry would blurt out hostile remarks if his mother inquired of her, was not an unpopular teacher with other students. All his teachers knew his mother and stepfather and communicated freely to them. At the very end of the year, when it was apparent that Jerry would not graduate, the teachers asked his mother to the school where they advised her of this and suggested he be sent to a private school where he could make up his credits and graduate.

Through the spring months his mother noted with interest his attempts to find a girl friend. She gave accounts of how he would call a girl at least three times and talk to her on the phone before finally getting up enough courage to ask her for a date. All his efforts were only "one occasion" affairs, until he finally settled for a series of dates with a fourteen-year-old high-school freshman whom he reported in therapy session as a sister of his best friend at school.

Early in the treatment his mother became concerned lest the therapist had discussed the matter of Jerry's paternity. She then decided she would rather have the therapist talk to him about it. She was advised that the therapist would not talk with him about it until after she had. Finally, she decided that this was a matter that she probably had more feelings about than Jerry. Her final appraisal of Jerry's contact with the clinic was that he seemed much happier and that her increased insight into his behavior would enable her "to be more patient with him."

At the beginning of the summer he was referred to a speech therapist on the clinic staff. This therapist, a woman, employs a technique of her own devised along lines of her psychodynamic understanding of the symptom. A part of her procedure consists of "biting" and "chewing" exercises administered in a rather authoritarian manner. She also has a patient yell rather vigorously to her from an opposite side of the room.

Jerry responded to her very positively and was much impressed with the fact that she told him his stuttering was "in his head" and not because he "moved to a certain place at a certain time." Jerry had apparently referred to, or reproduced, part of discussions with the therapist in which circumstances surrounding the onset of this symptom had been explored. Jerry continued to come to the clinic for speech therapy through the following fall after his treatment interviews were terminated in the summer.

He entered a private school in the fall, with his grandparents paying the tuition. This latter pleased him very much. With the passing of his crisis neither he nor his mother was interested in his continuing psychotherapy. He successfully completed his high-school course the following year. He was noticed by his teachers as "a boy who stuttered a little when he was excited." His asthma was not quite so severe and he was able to participate in sports with moderate success. He entered college to pursue a course of study in which he majored in art with some courses specifically oriented to commercial and industrial work. He has been able to accomplish academic work without further failures.

Roberta Hackett

EMOTIONAL COMPONENTS OF A SOMATIC SYMPTOM: I, EPILEPSY

ROBERTA WAS FOURTEEN when she first began experiencing strange sensations which would come over her suddenly and make her unable to speak. Presently she would feel all right again. A few years later these experiences became more frequent and severe. She noticed that something familiar would come to mind as a sort of warning each time; then, all she could do was stand and stare, unable to speak, even though she was aware of what was going on around her. A further increase in severity began in her twenties, and she began having convulsions with these attacks. When she learned from a doctor that she had epilepsy she resolved that she would try to live a normal life anyway. So in her thirties we find her married and the mother of two children, but quite accustomed to responding to a recognizable premonitory experience, or aura, that lets her know she is about to have a seizure. She has learned to respond to the warning by preparing herself so she will not get hurt.

In her twenties the seizures occurred with an average frequency of one every four months. They have been more frequent in recent years, ranging from five to ten per year. Each lasts about nine minutes and she comes to in about fifteen minutes. During her two pregnancies she did not have any seizures.

She was accepted for psychotherapy with confirmed clinical evidence of epilepsy. Numerous E.E.G. studies have shown abnormal records with excessive bitemporal slow activity and sharp waves from the temporal lobes, especially the left. She had been seen periodically for anti-epileptic medication for several years before she began psychotherapeutic treatment. She was standardized pharmacologically on mesantoin, four tenths of a gram daily.

The first seizure, at age fourteen, coincided approximately with menarche. Both frightened her and especially made her scared to go to school. She was afraid the teacher would call on her and she would be unable to speak and would be punished. Likewise, with her menstrual periods she aroused the anger of the teacher because if she had cramps at the moment she was called upon, she could not answer.

She recalls that she was playing with dolls at the time her first menstrual period began. She noticed that she was bleeding and thought she had cut herself. She spoke to her mother about it, and she says the only information her mother gave was that she should not allow a boy to touch her, else she might become pregnant. She still voices strong resentment against her mother for not giving her more sex information.

In recalling her childhood she speaks of having had temper tantrums which were "like seizures." She would tell her mother she wanted a drink of water and then would not drink it. She would repeat this two or three times, and then, finally, her mother would refuse to get the water, at which time Roberta would have the temper tantrums. She says: "I would holler until I got things." Tantrums also occurred during the period when she was twelve to fifteen years of age in response to her mother telling her to go into the house when out playing with friends. At the time she began going out with her boy friend her mother would tell her to come home early, and this, too, she remembers as arousing intense anger. She would often get angry at her mother and shut herself in her own room. Even though she felt angry inside, she added, she would not hit her mother. She always wanted to be close to her and to kiss her. When she was twelve to fifteen years of age her mother would tell her she was too big for such things and not to act like a baby. She states as her opinion that the age from twelve to fifteen is the most difficult, "when a child is trying to grow up." She laments that when she tried to be close to her mother, her mother would push her away, adding: "She would push gently, not push me on the floor."

Sex was always a "hush-hush" topic to her mother. She would tell Roberta to figure things out for herself, never giving advice, except not to let boys touch her or she would get pregnant. The sight of blood always made her mother feel sick. If any of the children cut a finger, her mother would bandage it and then would have to go lie down on her bed.

Her mother often nagged Roberta to do things around the house, yet would not let her cook because she would dirty the stove. When Roberta was going with her future husband her mother would stay up and fix them an evening snack. Once during this time her menstrual period was three days late and she told her mother because she felt she had to "tell someone," even though she had not had intercourse. When Roberta and her future husband were making love she would think of her mother upstairs and how she was trusting her. Her mother did not approve of Roberta's choice of a husband. After the marriage her mother suggested that Roberta wait for a year before having a child. Her mother was married only ten months when Roberta was born and felt that this was too soon as she had not had time to have fun. Actually Roberta waited six years to have a child, and her mother objected to her having a second on the basis that it was too much trouble. Her mother has never liked the second child.

Actually Roberta does not see her mother often since marriage even though they live in the same city. She describes her mother as having always been "cold" but is more so since Roberta has had children. She says that if she could understand her mother she feels she would not be sick with her seizures.

Although her mother did not give affection, her father did, and when he did, Roberta said that she would "eat it up." In recent years she has gone to visit him occasionally where he works. She refers to him as an alcoholic, but he has held the same responsible job for a long while. She feels that her mother's lack of affection causes him to drink. Her father always used to get drunk at Christmas and New Year's and would sing songs on the front porch to the annoyance of the neighbors. Roberta gets "goose pimples up and down her spine" even now when she hears Christmas carols. When he is drunk he "talks funny." The food falls out of his mouth, and he talks as if he had a "hot potato in his mouth." She always feared that when he was drunk he would do something to her mother. Sometimes he goes to the bars for companionship, so that he can "talk with the boys." Roberta relates her father's behavior to her own craving for affection and says that her need for affection is why she is so active in attending various club meetings.

Roberta has three younger sisters. One is four years younger, one six, and one eleven years younger. The next younger seems to have been the mother's favorite and she and Roberta have always gotten along poorly. Roberta complains also that she cannot understand this sister. For instance, they will make an appointment for luncheon and the sister won't show up. This disappoints Roberta, especially if it is a celebration, such as a birthday. The youngest sister is her favorite. She was probably a change-of-life baby. Roberta recalls the birth and remembers being sent next door when the doctor arrived carrying a lot of instruments. It was a cold and snowy day. Roberta later played dolls with this sister and would refer to her dolls as babies. For the most part, however, the other sisters played together, and Roberta was more or less alone.

In adolescence Roberta was never really interested in boys. She did not like such things as "mugging parties," and preferred to go to the Girl Scouts and "not think about sex." When she was sixteen a boy touched her on the breast and this boy was her future husband. At age seventeen she once went parking with a girl friend and a man. She was sitting by the door and the girl friend in the middle. The man touched her breast and Roberta was petrified at the thought that this would make her pregnant. In relating this to the therapist she stated that the man touched her on her breast, "inside like this," which she demonstrated by inserting her hand into the front of her dress. During the parking episode the girl friend and the man "went to town in the back seat." She could hear noises associated with the sexual act and feels that she would have run home if she had known the way.

She used to stay in bed late on Saturdays and masturbate all morning. At the time she was going around with her future husband. She did not know "what a man looked like" then, and so did not connect masturbation with sexual intercourse. After she was married she was at times indifferent toward sexual intercourse and "it was more fun to do it myself." A doctor told her that what she was doing was masturbating. Currently she states that masturbation has not occurred "for some time." When she feels sexually excited now she tells her husband and they have intercourse. Yet as she spoke of this in the interview she sat rigidly in her chair and twiddled her thumbs. The thought (to masturbate) "doesn't come to me at all now." However, she often feels "restless and itchy," especially before her menstrual period. She calls her period her "friend." When she has the restless and itchy feeling she does not like to be alone and in response to the feeling "eats everything in sight." She does not mind the sight of blood but will vomit if she sees anyone else vomit. She feels tired and sleepy with her periods, and since her first pregnancy she has not had cramps.

She met her future husband when she was sixteen, began going steady with him at twenty, and six years later, following a fracture of her arm, he proposed to her at the hospital. A few months later they were married. During courtship they "played with fire" but did not have sexual intercourse. They would "kiss all over" but she would "freeze up" when he wanted to kiss her on the breasts. She "knew what he was like," meaning sexually, before they married. She stated that the marriage ceremony changed very little in their relationship. She remained a virgin for five months after marriage because her husband "was so gentle" and intercourse so painful to her. She went to a doctor and he "cut it," meaning that she had a hymenectomy. She commented: "What is it down there—a film of tissue or something? The doctor put a big long thing in me. It looked like a duck's bill or a duck's mouth—then I was okay." She describes her husband as being a great kidder when they are visiting other couples, but is a strict disciplinarian with her when they are at home. His kidding consists of deriding the man and making overtures to the wife. He sometimes has the woman sit on his lap in these situations, but Roberta adds that she is not jealous.

She repeats frequently that her husband is a strict disciplinarian. He says that he wants her "to be on her own two feet." She feels that this is good in case he ever has a heart attack. She asserts that her husband is not a "milk toast"; "he is not the type to kiss my feet." He wants her to do bargain-basement shopping and nags her to do the housework. She feels that he nags about other things, including sexual intercourse. They sleep in separate rooms and intercourse usually occurs on the livingroom couch when the children are asleep upstairs at night or outdoors playing during the day. They frequently have television on at these times. She feels that she could "love him to death" without sexual intercourse and gets very angry if he wants to kiss her breasts.

Her first child, a daughter, was born six years after the marriage. When she had difficulty getting pregnant a second time she went to an osteopathic hospital for treatment. She was treated by massage and liked the "personal contact," after which she got pregnant. She wanted a son as a second child so her daughter could grow up with a brother. The second was a son, born two years after the birth of the daughter.

Although she had no seizures during either pregnancy, she did after the deliveries. She lost interest in sexual intercourse after each and for a period of months masturbated frequently. She felt tired and depressed after each child was born and found it difficult to take care of them. She had no desire to breast-feed either one of them, considering it too much trouble.

Both children do well in school. The daughter idolizes her father, even though he gets angry and shouts at her. The son is very active but described as "no bother." She was very eager for both children to reach school age so they would be away during the day. The daughter has remarked on the fact that her grandmother does not show much love. Roberta comments that she feels her mother, her daughter, and her husband are alike while she and her son are alike.

She feels her children should be brought up differently from the way her mother dealt with her. She says it is best to trust and encourage them and satisfy their curiosity. She told a story of a little girl who did not have her curiosity satisfied. This little girl asked why she did not have a penis like her brother. "The lady said the doctor cut it off, I mean that's the way it was when the doctor brought the baby." The story continues with the little girl cutting off her brother's penis and his bleeding to death. To prevent such things, she says, children's curiosity should be satisfied.

Most of the social life of Roberta and her husband centers around couples' clubs, usually affiliated with a church. In addition, Roberta belongs to various women's clubs. She states that she "likes to socialize" and craves love and affection, "especially from women." In spite of her liking to be with women she prefers men to women. She feels that men are not hypocrites, are not jealous, and do not talk behind her back.

Her symptomatic course during treatment is of special interest because it presents striking variations that seem to be related to the therapeutic situation and what transpired there. She was seen in treatment as a part of more comprehensive research study dealing with psychological factors in epilepsy for which she agreed to be a subject. During this time there were no changes in medication and E.E.G.'s taken at regular intervals showed no essential change. During this time there were no events of importance outside the treatment situation to upset her and disturb her routine life. Consequently, the sequence and content of the fantasies and emotions aroused in the treatment process and the events to which they relate are of considerable interest for an understanding of her seizures. During the first eight months of treatment she had sixteen seizures; during the next seven months, when she had rather clearly shifted into a distinctly new phase of treatment, she had seventy seizures. With the resolution of some of the problems with which she was struggling at this time the seizures again varied, increasing at times and then leveling off again to the point where she could go several months without having any.

When treatment began, she spoke of her mother's menopausal baby and the fact that she herself had recently had hot flashes, and wondered if that meant that she was pregnant. She spoke scornfully of her husband being around the house so much (his job permitted him to work there often), and of how he was always keeping an eye on her and bossing her housework. She spoke with aversion of her sexual life and with particular distaste of any contact with her breasts, in which she occasionally felt pain. She avoided sleeping in the same room with her husband as much as possible on the grounds that she might disturb his sleep.

A considerable amount of material during the early months of treatment brought out complaints about the husband, and about sexual advances she had received, such as from the man who had touched her breasts in a car, and her father-in-law who had the same predilection, and of husbands of friends who have made advances to her. During this time she showed considerable interest in the therapist, spoke of how nice it would be to work for doctors, inquired about him from the E.E.G. technician, looked up his address in the phone book, and spoke of how similar his soft voice was to that of a husband of a girl friend who attracted her and with whom she thought of having an affair. Her seizures during this time either occurred during the evening of the day of her interviews or while watching television programs about illicit love affairs. She dreamed a number of times that a man was talking softly and tenderly to her and that she was planning to have intercourse with him. "But I always wake up and nothing happened." She asked her therapist: "What are you doing Saturday night?—I am only kidding"; then said: "If I had my life to live over again, I would like to be a medical secretary." She mentioned a television program about a psychiatrist, and commented: "I don't know whether it happened in that play or not, but in other stories the woman falls in love with her doctor." She quickly added: "I am not falling in love with you or anything like that." She then related how a girl friend once worked in a hospital, and that the doctor there told her that he loved her. She also mentioned that sometimes she feels anxious prior to her interview. "I feel as if I want to have a seizure while I am sitting waiting for you."

For some months prior sexual relations with her husband had improved. During this time, however, she was concerned about the possibility of his death.

A new phase of treatment now followed, in which her transference became intensified. Under pressure of her pregnancy fantasies and her increased demands for real gratification from the therapist which could not be satisfied she was thrown into intense conflict and simultaneously her seizures increased markedly. This phase was entered with an interview, at the time of menstruation, in which she recounted her premarital activities with her husband and her passionate feelings toward him, then asked if a virgin could become pregnant. She understood the therapist's reply to mean that it was possible.

The following week she reported several seizures and the fact that she had felt somewhat "restless and excited" since the last interview. The restlessness "felt as if I wanted to have one." Asked to elaborate, she said that somehow her "system would be better" if she could have a seizure, adding: "It almost seemed as if my system needed it." She was afraid that the therapist would be "disappointed" at the recurrence of seizures, because "I guess doctors like to see their patients do well." The following week she reported more seizures occurring the evening and day after the interview, and related how her daughter loves to sit on her husband's lap, how affectionate her own father was toward her, the fact that she thought about her therapist the night after the interview, and asked if he had any children.

A new note in her relationship to the therapist enters in this interview. She spoke of how her mother repulsed her efforts to be close to her between the ages of twelve and fifteen, and of her temper tantrums during which she lay on the floor and kicked her feet. She told of a friend's husband who has epilepsy. His wife is afraid he will lose control and do something violent during his attacks, such as injure the children. He is angry with his psychiatrist, fights with him, and thinks of quitting treatment. Since the patient has told the wife of how different her therapist is, couldn't he take the husband into treatment? Although she extols the therapist, the patient closed the interview by inquiring for the first time: "How much longer will I have to come here?"

The following week she spoke of the lack of affection from her husband and of how he wants her to stop treatment. She added that if she were to have seizures in the office, she thinks her therapist would take care of her. Maybe her husband is right, however, and she should stop treatment. She could stand on her own feet, but she still likes affection. When she gets over her seizures, maybe she could really stand on her own feet. After praising her therapist, she told him how angry she was at a psychiatrist she saw five years before. She then asked permission for a vacation and left, uncertain whether she would be in the following week. She did not come in, and a week later wondered when the therapist was going to take his vacation. Upon being told it would be at the end of the month, she replied that that was what she expected. She missed her next appointment, and the following week reported many seizures during this interim. She again asked if the therapist had children.

Upon the resumption of treatment following the therapist's vacation she showed impatience with the time of her appointments and complained of the difficulty of getting up for them. She wondered again if she was entering the menopause and added that her stomach felt heavy as when she was pregnant. She visited her dentist and described the sensation after the novocaine wore off "as similar to when you begin to feel life." Mentally, she said, she is feeling much better, but she is worried whether she is not now becoming physically ill.

Her husband said that treatment is not helping her. She now loves him and has passionate feelings toward him as when they were just married. She now knows when she is going to have an attack because she gets "a funny feeling from within." She noticed the same feeling when entering the door of the clinic for this appointment. The feeling is like she is "handling something like eggs and nobody else is around." "Last Thursday night after I was in here," she remarked, "I felt very passionate toward my husband while I was having intercourse."

Her attacks increased on Thursday night and Friday following this interview, and she called to arrange for an earlier appointment with her therapist. She later reported that at the time she had these seizures—a batch of four, five, and one—was "at the height of my temperature, and when my temperature dropped my spells broke." The patient here is referring to ovulation which is followed with temperature charts she takes daily as requested in connection with physiological studies on her case.

At this appointment she explained to her therapist that she called because she thought there was something physically wrong with her, saying: "There is nothing wrong psychologically." She felt "fatigued" after her attacks, adding: "But this seemed to be a rather relaxing, pleasant feeling; I have it now talking with you." She asked further personal questions about the therapist and angrily stated that her curiosity is never satisfied. She added that she doesn't want to deflate the therapist's ego, but she also thinks a lot of her husband and that she is now in love with him. She then told the following story about her daughter. She opened it with a remark that one should give children information about sexual things. Her daughter once saw the patient and her husband walking around the house with no clothes on. Her daughter explained that now she understands that she is like her mother and that her brother is like her father. The patient then compared her behavior in satisfying her daughter's curiosity with that of another woman, and gave the story of the little girl who cut off her brother's penis. She concluded the interview by wondering whether there wasn't something physically wrong with her and whether she shouldn't see some other doctor about it.

The following week she was asked if she has tender feelings toward the therapist, and was reminded of the fact that she once spoke of liking men who spoke gently and softly to her. She replied that she might have, but actually she prefers a man like her husband, adding: "He may be rough and gruff, but he is all man." She continued that she doesn't know what the therapist is like away from the interviews. At times, however, she felt that the therapist was "kind of wishy-washy." Perhaps what she wants is a "little action."

The following week she reported that she had had no seizures with her last menstrual period. Instead, they occurred a few weeks ago at the height of her temperature, "when a woman is supposed to be hot." Her seizures are now similar to her original ones at age fourteen when she was at school. She has a "familiar thought" that warns her of the approach of a seizure, which she can't remember, but adds that the thought doesn't occur any more. When asked what thought, she replied, "the thought to masturbate."

She did not keep her next appointment. The following week she unleashed a tirade against the therapist because two weeks ago he had said that she was fond of him. She said that she is disgusted and angry at him. She doubled up her fists and shook them at him. When she gets excited feelings in her vagina now, she says, she asks her husband for intercourse.

The patient within the course of the next two months talked about a heavy feeling in her abdomen, indigestion, lower quadrant pains, tenderness and pain in her breasts, "such as women feel when they are pregnant," a weight gain chiefly around her stomach, and "a feeling of life." She asked her gynecologist if she were pregnant. At the same time she denied any desire for pregnancy, arguing that she had lost weight, that she had been looking forward for years to the time when she would be free of her children, and that each of her previous pregnancies had been followed by a depression. She expressed great relief at the appearance of each period. For example, one time, she stated, her period was supposed to come on a certain day, but instead came two days later, during which time she had felt terrible. Her head felt as "big as this room." She felt depressed and noticed there were some twinges of pain in the lower quadrant, and thought that she might have some kind of disturbance "down there." Her periods started around noontime and then, she said, "everything broke and I was all right. It was like a miracle, I felt so much better."

She accused the therapist of having "put the idea of pregnancy in my head." She complained that her head was all knotted up, that it felt like exploding, and that she wanted to cut it off. She told the therapist of how a doctor had examined her some time after the birth of her son and of how beautiful, he said, she looked inside, like a woman who had had no children. Prior to marriage she had longed for an illicit pregnancy. A few weeks before Christmas she dreamed about an eastern star which she identified as the star in the East which heralded Christ's birth. During this time she showed increasing anger toward her therapist, and continued her direct disparagement of him. She asked the gynecologist to refer her to a doctor who would treat her physically and spoke constantly about stopping the interviews. Her thought about the physical basis of her difficulties finally crystallized as "something lacking, not in my head but down below."

Such, in brief, is the central content of her interviews during the second phase of investigation, which witnessed the eruption of an unprecedented number of seizures. The sequence of events, the major fantasies which dominated her, and the emotions which overcame her seem clearly to interrelate.

One further increase of seizures occurred during a period of months when she was dwelling upon her belief that there was a physical basis for her seizures which she felt to be opposed by the therapist. She noted that her seizures during this time were accompanied by a scream. The preceding, or warning, "thought" changed so that, in addition, she had "a rising feeling—like a volcano." She expressed the idea that the volcano meant she is "getting cleaned out" and that her seizures will cease with menopause.

The latter part of this last year of treatment brought forth tirades against men, comparison of their independence with the submissive and dependent status of women and, finally, explicit dealing with her wish to be a man. With the recognition of this feeling and the working through of some of its ramifications in her relationship to her husband she announced in one interview that she had experienced the first orgasm she had ever experienced during intercourse. She remarked, when speaking of her husband showing anger toward her on a later occasion, that she could not feel angry so soon after such a beautiful experience. She went through ovulation and menstruation at this time without seizures for the first time in eighteen months. Her comment was that she thought her sense of lack had been replaced by sexual desire.

The following month she had no convulsions, but did have three automatisms. Since then the incidence of her seizures has remained on a greatly reduced scale. As in the past, their occurrence is still correlated with periods of frustration and disturbance in her emotional life.

Roland Beechberger

EMOTIONAL COMPONENTS OF A SOMATIC SYMPTOM: II, ASTHMA

AFTER MANY YEARS of suffering from asthma and having extensive study by specialists who tried various medications without success, Roland was recommended for study and treatment in a program where psychological studies were made and psychotherapeutic treatment instituted. At this time he was thirty-seven years old, single, unemployed, and living with his parents. He was receiving cortisone injections regularly but was convinced they made his asthma worse, and he was "doubtful and discouraged" with the prospects of being helped by doctors. He had, as a consequence, imposed upon himself a life of comparative isolation and inactivity in his attempt at adapting to and controlling his symptom. Two years previously he had given up employment as a commercial artist and prior to this had adopted a very restricted life socially.

His first asthmatic attack occurred at the age of two while he was hospitalized for diphtheria. Because of the asthma he stayed in the hospital for six months, during which time he had a tonsillectomy. At the time he was discharged he failed to recognize his parents, cried, and did not want to leave the hospital.

Subsequently his attacks were infrequent and soon passed. Then around the age of five they became increasingly severe, lasting longer, and occurring more frequently. At thirteen and fourteen they reached a peak of severity when he had a series of "convulsions" during which he lost consciousness. Finally, when he was hospitalized with one of these attacks, a diagnosis of "drug poisoning" from his current medication was made and it was discontinued. Extensive tests were made and he was started on hyposensitization injections which he then had regularly for a period of years. By the time he completed high school he was having much less asthma and refused to take further injections. Within six months his asthma had ceased and he was free of it from the age of eighteen for ten years, until attacks began to reoccur while he was in the Army and led to his discharge. For several years afterward his asthma was kept under control through medical care and medication. Then it became worse, causing him to lose much time from work. Finally he had a severe attack in which he was hospitalized for a considerable period during which cortisone and ACTH treatment were instituted. Following his release he did not feel like returning to work. He felt his medication was making him worse. He withdrew to the isolation and restriction in activity in which he was living two years later when he began the program of study and treatment from which this account is written.

From childhood on Roland always regarded his asthma with shame. He felt no embarrassment that his family should know, as this could not be avoided, but tried to keep knowledge of it from all others. As a child a "tightening sensation" all over his body would warn him of the approach of an attack and the return of his appetite signaled the passing of an attack. He would eat, vomit, and then the attack was ended. Later he found that he could "work off" an attack by exertion—chopping wood, rowing, or playing actively. Between attacks he would "try to forget asthma," to equal or outdo other boys in sports. His later attitude was that attacks were brought on by exertion, hence he was afraid to work. Actually, he felt that a combination of physical factors set off attacks—fumes, pollen, dust, and fatigue. Waiting in heavy automobile traffic was capable of bringing on an attack, which he attributed to the fumes. Smoking could make an existing attack worse, as could panic. He tried to control panic during an attack by slowing down breathing and deflating his chest.

Roland's mother was a very active community woman, belonging to many organizations. She was troubled with asthmatic attacks about twice a year, but according to Roland "would not let them interfere with her activities." She worked in an office where other workers were much younger than she, but in the estimation of her son, though sixty, she "looked younger and younger each day."

When Roland had attacks during childhood and adolescence he would sit up in a chair wheezing all night. His mother would sit up with him, getting "sympathetic asthma" from watching him. She would kneel by his chair and pray not just for the attack to pass, but that he would survive. At the time of these attacks his father would move to the most distant corner of the room, completely withdrawn from the situation. One of his series of "convulsions" during early adolescence occurred at the breakfast table when only he and his mother were at home. He got a "cold feeling" in his jaw and felt his jaw pull to the left. Then he "blacked out." His mother later told him he was pale, sweaty, and rigid for fifteen minutes. When he came to, his mother wanted to call a doctor but he screamed: "No!"

When Roland was fourteen his father, who was forty, developed tuberculosis and went to a sanitarium for seven years. He was discharged as cured but retired from his work without going back. His wife went to work outside the home and he did the housework. At the time his illness began he had risen to a responsible position in a bank. In his early sixties he suffered a series of strokes. After each there was considerable impairment for a period, but eventually he would recover to his approximate prior condition. His morale concerning his health was bad after his earlier illness. He was said never to have been able to handle illness, his own or that of others. In this connection Roland referred to his father's behavior during his, Roland's, asthmatic attacks.

As a youth his father was interested in becoming an artist, but he incurred an eye injury in an accident which caused him to change his plans. His brother threw a rock at a bottle, the glass splinters hit and became imbedded in his father's eye. After this he was able to see only shadows with this eye. In recounting this

Roland remarked: "Thank God my eyes are okay." The father was a track star in school. After graduating he immediately went to work for the bank where he was working when he became ill. Though unable to paint because of his eye injury, Roland's father maintained his interest in art. He cultivated friendships among successful artists, occasionally doing some oil painting himself, but expressed his interest mostly through art collecting. Roland ridiculed his father's water-color collection, and his father told him to be careful as it would come to him some day.

Roland's uncle, his father's brother, became a successful commercial artist. He earned an impressive income throughout his entire career, even though he was alcoholic. Roland's father idolized the artistic works of one of his brother's teachers. The uncle, however, would not let his nephew, Roland, work with him. And when he retired, instead of thinking of Roland, he turned over his clientele to a young woman, described as highly skilled, who carried on with his work. The uncle died shortly after retiring.

Roland had a sister three years older and a brother two years younger. His brother was jaundiced at birth, was sickly, and had many childhood diseases. He had pneumonia several times, managed to survive, but is of "borderline intelligence," according to Roland. Roland blamed his mother for not training his brother properly and for not securing special schooling for him. He asserted that had this been done the brother would have been of at least average intelligence. The brother was described as having a good disposition and as being easygoing. He has held a steady job as a messenger boy for the past ten years. His interests and ambitions were indicated as being simple and limited– attendance at movies, ball games, and watching television.

Roland tried to dissuade his sister against acting upon her religious preoccupations and to influence her from becoming a nun. He told her she was "too nervous" and persuaded her to express her religious interests through church work and work with children. In recent years she has had two operations for malignancy, including a hysterectomy. She has remained single, never having had any very ardent boy friends. She was described as never having been close to her mother.

Roland always did well in school despite the irregularity of his attendance. He was interested in sports and competitive games but was ineffectual because of his small size. "Asthma stunted my growth," he lamented. He was extremely frail and stunted in growth all through childhood. At fourteen he was less than five feet tall and weighed fifty pounds. He "started to eat better" following the "convulsions" during adolescence. It was at this time that he started taking hyposensitizations injections. He gained weight rapidly and became very active in such things as riding his bike for long distances.

After graduating from high school he enrolled in art school where there were two hundred and fifty girls and about ten boys. In many classes he was the only boy. There were never more than one or two others. He decided that he would "concentrate" on his class work and ignore the girls. This resolution was put to a test when he first attended a "life" class where there was a nude model. He wanted to watch the reaction of the girls but refrained and launched himself on the task. He always tried to find himself a place in a corner somewhat apart from the girls.

He was particularly troubled by the arrangement of the toilet facilities for boys at the school. The door had open spaces at the top and bottom and was located off the main smoking room. Because of the presence of girls in the smoking room, he would not use it, instead, he held his urine until lunch recess when he could get to other toilet facilities. One day he was stricken with pain in his abdomen and was sick on his stomach. A doctor rushed him to the hospital with a tentative diagnosis of appendicitis. "Fortunately X rays were taken" and the trouble was found to be a renal stone which he passed after six hours of intense pain. He attributed the stone to the fact that he had held his urine.

After graduating from art school he could not find a job in commercial art as he wanted, his uncle offering no assistance. He finally launched what proved to be a period of being extremely active living, taking two jobs. He had already "put his foot down" and refused to take further injections. While holding two jobs he got very little sleep but was free of asthma.

By day he worked as an office clerk and afterward worked a night shift as a service-station attendant. In addition he began dating girls, this, too, without moderation. He would drive about, go dancing and to movies. His manner of living caused his mother great concern but he ignored this. One of his girl friends he described as an insomniac. He would meet her after work and they would go out drinking together. In this they were competitive. She, however, he said, was stronger and could also drink more than he. They would sit in the car in front of her house until daybreak, as she would not go in. He spoke with amusement about his mother complaining to him about "keeping a nice girl out until such hours" when actually it was the girl's own doing.

After a year or two this overactivity was interrupted by an early draft call at the beginning of the war. Before he was drafted, however, he had taken a physical examination in application for enrollment as an air corps cadet. This he passed but was turned down because of his having had a renal stone, not on the asthma difficulties as he feared. "I should sue the air corps," he remarked, implying that if he had become a cadet he might not have had a recurrence of asthma. When he was later called up for a physical examination in the draft and reported his medical history he was accused of trying to dodge the service. He was promptly accepted and assigned to the air corps. On the basis of aptitude tests he was given training in a technical specialty to which his previous training was in no way related. He took pride in performing his responsibility with efficiency, as he did not want "flight failures to be my fault."

When he was sent to a northern outpost he found his duties at times wearing. He was not in combat but emergencies required long hours without sleep. He saw plane crashes and noted that except for a sudden alteration in plans he would have taken a plane which crashed on a particular flight. When his duties were not rushing there was very little opportunity for recreation. Natives were unfriendly and there was a strong undercurrent of hostile feeling between the United States and other troops stationed there. Drinks were cheap, and he and three other men from the barracks spent evenings in a bar. Frequently after drinking they would decide to roll up in blankets and sleep in the woods rather than return to the barracks.

Once when he was on night guard duty under floodlights, bullets whizzed by him from out of the darkness. He turned off the lights and fired into the area from which they came. A widely held notion among the soldiers was that natives would take shots at them occasionally. He assumed this to be a native and intended to frighten him in return. He was threatened with court-martial for his action in turning off the lights. Nothing finally came of it; he assumed the reason to be that several other guards had been fired upon.

During his second year at this outpost he was hospitalized with an upper respiratory infection which led to wheezing and then to asthmatic attacks. Later he was sent back to the States, because his asthma was getting worse.

He was assigned duty as an interviewing clerk, a job he did not like because soldiers felt he was threatening to take soft berths away from them. While at this station he had two buddies as roommates who had had close calls with death. He was impressed with their constant wish to return to flight duty.

His asthma continued to get worse, and he was discharged on this account, this being near the end of the war. For the next three years his asthma improved under medical care and medication. During this time he took some college courses in business administration, following which he had several jobs involving sales representation. He said that he failed in all the jobs, adding that he was not "thick skinned" enough, as he was too concerned with the good of the customer. From these experiences he remarked that he could write a book on "how not to succeed, though ambitious."

He eventually found work in a label factory where he could use his training in commercial art. After a year or so his asthma became worse and he missed a great deal of time from work, feeling that he was being affected by the fumes in the factory.

In the meantime he had made a Sunday visit with his family to a shore town a short drive from Baltimore where they had frequently spent weekends and vacations when he was a child. He became fascinated with the place and soon thereafter bought a cabin in an isolated area overlooking the water on one side and a marsh on the other. He and his father went there on weekends to fish and enjoy "roughing it" while Roland also did some painting. Being near the water did not help his asthma but, nevertheless, he spent every weekend there the year round, having withdrawn all interest from social life and having "stopped chasing skirts."

One weekend while at the cabin he had a severe attack. He felt his throat tighten, could not get his breath, and then lost consciousness. He came to. His father found him and called an ambulance. On the way to the hospital he lost consciousness again, thinking, as it occurred, that he was dying. He was unconscious for three days and in pain for weeks afterward. He remarked concerning this experience that others pray to God at such times and get peace, but he damned God and got peace with morphine. He was puzzled about this attack because it came at a time of an approaching vacation and he was looking forward to fishing and "roughing it" through the week.

When he got out of the hospital he could not bring himself to go back to work. He became apathetic, dreamy, and described himself as having "stared at the walls" for hours. He felt very irritable, and isolated himself by staying at the cabin. His appetite, he said, became "phenomenal." He got a "nice fat neck, nice fat rounded chest, and pot belly," but there was no improvement in his asthma. The doctors tried many treatments, including ACTH and cortisone. He felt their efforts only made it worse. While on cortisone he "wheezed all the time" and in addition "developed a beautiful bursitis of the right shoulder" and arthritis.

Even though he did not feel that life at the cabin helped his asthma he did feel that going back to his home in Baltimore made it worse. This he blamed on the "house dust," and continued his program of generally restricted activity as his most satisfactory way of preventing severe attacks of asthma. Much of the time his father was with him at the cabin, doing the cooking and housework. Since the father was in bad health and liked staying at the cabin, the situation could be justified to the family in terms of the two ill members being out of the way of the working members. Much of the time he felt peeved at his father because each evening the father wanted to go to the village bar and chat with the natives. Roland was bored with this, but since his father could not drive he went with him and sipped beer. Roland had given up drinking because it seemed to make his asthma worse.

His mother and sister did not like to stay at the cabin because they did not care for the isolation and because of the lack of modern conveniences. Neither did they like the crowded living in one room. He later undertook further building and improvement in the hope that they would spend weekends there.

Roland liked swimming and fishing. Swimming as such did not affect the asthma but did cause him to breathe hard and others thought he was in distress. His asthma, however, would get worse immediately when he came out of the water. Surf casting became an interest which engaged a lot of his time. He related that when he told people about the "big one that got away" they thought it was only another fish story even though he knew it was really true. His father holds a record of some years standing for the largest catch for the town.

After a couple of years in which he lived mostly at his cabin, without working and in general inactivity, Roland began psychological treatment. He was described at this time as well tanned, of medium height with dark hair and large, bright eyes, showing a watchful apprehensiveness when first interviewed. He was inclined to clear his throat frequently and was given to an occasional sort of explosive chuckle. On first meeting he was disposed to force a sort of air of lightness.

His early sessions with the therapist reflected underlying feelings about doctors and the fact that his condition had not yielded to treatment. After giving an account of his symptoms in the first session he wondered if the therapist had seen a particular television play in which a psychiatrist was treating an unpleasant woman while having the fantasy of being married to her and poisoning her. In interviews which followed he dealt with themes of doctors making patients worse, of fears of doctors—through discussing his "drug poisoning" experience, of feelings that he was getting to be an "old man." Yet dependence upon doctors and the fear of needing help and it not being available were very strongly expressed. He passed remarks intended as humorous about his therapist being "demoted," went through periods of clearly negativistic lateness to appointments. On the other hand, he also wanted to please the therapist and gain his approval. Early in the series of sessions he brought samples of his art work to show him. He tried in various ways to compare himself with the therapist, for instance, in recounting his interviewing experience in the Army, remarking on the resemblance to the psychiatrist's job. He asked personal questions about the therapist's private life, at times making comparison to his father. He asked many questions about smoking in relation to his asthma, asserting that the smell of pipes and cigars make his mouth feel dirty and asking if the therapist was like his father, who is critical of smoking but smokes himself.

He spoke of having nightmares as a child in which he was walking naked down a street, and repeated dreams in which he was falling off a cliff.

Following assertions of his disbelief in prayer and critical remarks about his mother's praying during his childhood asthmatic attacks, he spoke of confession with different feeling. As a kid he "loved" to go to confession. He also enjoyed church ritual and felt better after attending church. He puzzled in this connection about a friend who lived with a woman with children without being married to her and still went to confession.

Some months later he announced he was celebrating an "anniversary" and offered a "confession." He said that he had had trouble all his life with bed wetting and that it had ceased some fourteen months previous, soon after he began psychotherapeutic appointments. At home he had always wet his bed practically every night. When he was away from home or in the hospital, he did not. In the Army he did wet it sometimes, but other soldiers had the same difficulty and seemed to dismiss it as the result of drinking too much. On return from the Army it diminished at home for a while but then returned. He confided that the therapist was the only one who knew about this outside his immediate family. He added that his enuresis was the chief reason why he was not married. He was so ashamed and fearful of embarrassment from the symptom that he turned down a job with a good future when he graduated from art school because it required that he live among strangers in another part of the country.

When he was scheduled for psychological testing his asthma became worse. As associations to the scheduling of tests he recalled his examinations for the draft. He spoke of the way in which the psychologist had stared at him and the way in which he was asked blunt questions relating to homosexuality. He spoke of his embarrassment at being naked among naked men.

His performance on intelligence tests showed superior ability. He was asked to give stories to Thematic Apperception Test pictures on several occasions as part of an extensive program of study of his case. Some of the stories he produced are offered for their content, as this relates to certain important feelings and guiding fantasies in his life. The first three stories were all given as his interpretation of a picture of a boy sitting and looking at a violin on a table before him. The first two were given fairly soon after he began treatment, the third when he was in his second year. Note the variations in mood, the handling and outcomes of achievement strivings, and the roles in which the father and mother are cast.

First administration

"The young boy is studying the violin with distaste. His mother has gone out to do the family shopping and he is supposed to complete his practice lesson by the time she returns. By the time she does return he'll be talking baseball through the window with his friends and he'll have to stay in for an extra hour. I suppose it is a picture of some prodigy like Beethoven."

Second administration

"You want the past first? [Examiner replies that patient may do so if he wishes.] Young Yehudi's father had been a famous violinist. He did not remember his father well for he had died when he was very young. His mother was still very much in love with the memory of the dead man and as a consequence had instilled in her son the desire to emulate his father. The boy had begun his lessons on the violin at a very early age, as his mother desired him to gain fame as a child prodigy. The young boy did not resent this. Rather, he always tried to his fullest to achieve success with the instrument. Now at the age of ten years all the better instructors in the country had informed his mother that while he had achieved great mechanical success with the violin he would certainly never be a virtuoso. His mother is now working at any job she can find in an attempt to accumulate enough money to further the youngster's studies abroad. She is determined not to believe the opinions of his instructors while he, on hearing their verdict, has become greatly discouraged and does not desire to play again. Within the next two years, by contacting friends of her dead husband's, the mother will achieve her desire in obtaining instruction for her son abroad. He, while there, will no longer apply himself to the instrument but will eventually achieve success in some other field."

Third administration

"Well, the young boy is looking at the violin which has just been given him by his father. It is the finest gift his father could give—it's a family heirloom as well as being an exceptionally fine instrument. The boy has been studying violin since early childhood and consequently has never had the opportunity to decide whether or not he really wanted to be a violin player. Playing the violin has been the tradition in the family and were it not for the fact that his father's arms had been badly mangled in an accident he would not have hoped to received this as a present for many years to come. He feels very rebellious at the moment for the burden that has been thrust upon him, the family pride being so great he has been constantly cautioned about how seriously he must take his studies. And now that he has received the family's prized possession he knows that he must devote more attention than ever to his studies. . . . Now we have to look into the future. The boy attained concert ability in his early teens and was hailed as a great success locally, but the burden of living up to the family tradition became increasingly odious to him so that on attaining the age of twenty-one . . . he forsook the concert stage and became a taxi driver."

The following was given as he looked at a blank card and was asked to imagine his own picture and create a suitable story for it. Note again the characterizations he ascribed to the father and mother and the feelings and fate of the son.

"As a boy Ted had frequently accompanied his father on his hunting expeditions. His father had been very proud of his old-fashioned ways and vigorously maintained that young Ted would not be big enough to shoot a gun until he was old enough to earn the wherewithal to buy it. Even though he was greatly disappointed at not being allowed to shoot at the birds and other forms of game he still enjoyed the trip into the woods each fall, the unusual meals, and the good clean fun of camping under the stars. On his sixteenth birthday Ted's mother, despite her husband's orders against it, presented Ted with a gun for a present. Overcoming his anger his father finally agreed to teach him to shoot and by the time the season opened young Ted was an excellent shot. As had been the custom over the years father and son went into the woods that fall for their annual hunting trip. To the father's chagrin young Ted outshot him three to one. Being [laughs] of a very harsh nature his father, who had always prided himself on his woodsmanship, decided that henceforth he would accompany his cronies on hunting exhibitions . . . ah, expeditions rather . . . where he would be sure to shine. Two years later young Ted while driving home from school was seriously injured in an automobile accident. His vision, while not totally gone, was insufficient for future shooting. Ted and his father once again take their trips into the woods every fall and enjoy themselves immensely, the father because of his excellent woodsmanship, the son because of his approval of nature as it is."

The following was given as he studied a picture that is usually interpreted as a family scene on a farm. A young woman is in the foreground with books in her arms. A man is plowing and an older woman, often seen as pregnant, stands off to one side. Note the mood and vacillations in feelings engendered by facing a world beyond the family limits.

"Jesse has just come home from the spring semester at State College. Her welcome has been considerably different from that which she had expected. The family has always lived in a rather remote area and what little schooling was available was of a very primitive nature. Jesse said she neither talked nor acted like her contemporaries on the campus and found school a rather lonesome place and had looked forward a great deal to her summer with the family. It was quite a shock to her on her return to find she no longer talked the same language or had the same hopes and dreams as her family. She's very disheartened at the moment, feeling herself a 'cast out' both by her family and the people of her age at college. The yearning for the soil has been bred into her bones by the generations of farmers in the family, and yet she cannot see living in the future as her family does, and their not-too-good-natured teasing about her superior schooling and mental attainments has convinced her that she can no longer call her father's farm her home.

"After a very uncomfortable summer with her family Jesse returned to college in the fall with the determination that she must fit in with her classmates if she hoped to have a happy and successful life. So with some misgivings and a great deal of discomfort she gradually adopted their way of life."

As treatment progressed Roland began to make changes in his life situation. During the first year he started working as a free-lance commercial artist. He obtained steady assignments which increased to the point where he earned a livable income. His mood was less frequently pessimistic and at times he felt quite optimistic. Much of his time continued to be spent at the cabin with his father. He did all his work there. As the second year of psychotherapy got under way he became interested in enlarging and improving the cabin. In this undertaking he did all his own work, seeking advice from acquaintances who could give him technical information and the benefit of experienced judgment.

His social life remained restricted. However, he did go to a few parties but was critical of all the girls he met. These parties tended to be occasions where there were one, or, at most, a few girls and a greater number of men. An old girl friend returned to town and he saw her for a few times but would not involve himself again.

His attitude toward his father in early interviews was sharply critical at times. He did not have patience with his father's fears for his own health. He felt his father was too easily upset if a routine was disturbed or things were not as he happened to want them. He threatened an ultimatum against going to the village bar with him.

Later the content of his interviews reflected an inclination to want to reassure his father. He began encouraging him to more activity. His father gave up drinking and Roland saw him more as "mellowing" and becoming easier in the relationship.

With the closing of a two-year period of weekly sessions Roland was showing no inclination to want to discontinue his treatment. He had made considerable improvement in his general outlook on life and adjustment to his sickness. Asthma symptoms still occurred but with less frequency and severity.

Elizabeth Fearchild

PHOBIA IN A MARRIED WOMAN

MRS. FEARCHILD entered psychiatric treatment with the complaint that she was afraid she was losing her mind. This fear was especially acute in busses and subways. She was fearful about crossing the street at times, because of a feeling that she would be killed. She was also afraid to cross bridges because of a fear that they would collapse. She was so incapacitated by her fears that she avoided taking busses and subways to work and tired herself with the long walk.

These difficulties became intensified ten months prior to beginning treatment when her husband almost died of internal bleeding of a gastric ulcer, but actually can be dated back fourteen years, to the time her mother died of cancer of the pancreas. At this time she lost considerable weight, became quite thin, felt no interest in life, and was troubled with fears of losing her mind. Then after six months she took to drinking and going around with many men, indulging in what she refers to as "high living." After about four years of this she married her present husband "out of pity, not for love," and her fears gradually reappeared and have continued with very little variation until her present condition developed.

She met her future husband when she was nineteen years old and he was twenty-nine, but did not go with him regularly. She was still going with him two years later when her mother died, but she found him uninteresting. He is described as having always been a sick man and she wonders if she was attracted to him because "misery likes company." She says he practically forced her to marry him by telling her he would die of hemorrhages of his stomach ulcers if she did not marry him. One day he collapsed with hemorrhages and let her know immediately. She was trying to "wean" herself away from him by going around with other men but he begged her "on bended knee," saying his life depended upon it. She felt she had to marry him, adding that one never saw such a reluctant bride.

Elizabeth was familiar with illness and death. Many members of her family had died as she was growing up. She described herself as feeling "all alone" and "frightened" at the more recent death of her mother and "didn't know what to do." She had a remaining brother and sister, but had not been so close to them as to some of the siblings she had lost through death.

She indicated that she had known loneliness through several hospitalizations herself. At the age of four she fell and hurt her knee. Apparently it was not treated properly, as complications developed which required several operations with long hospitalizations between the age of five and thirteen.

Elizabeth, now thirty-two, is the youngest of six siblings. She was a menopausal baby, seven years younger than her next sibling. The oldest brother died of tuberculosis at the age of eighteen, three months before her birth. Next was a brother whom she idolized. She describes him as having been gentle, kind, and strong. He came out of World War I "gassed and a nervous wreck." She states that he then "worked too hard" and died of tuberculosis in his early thirties, when she was eight years old. He had a son of whom she was quite fond who died of meningitis in his youth. Next in the family was a sister who was described as gay and feminine. Elizabeth states that she "loved life" and was a beautiful dresser. Her trouble was that she "burned the candle at both ends" and did some heavy drinking. She went off to New York and came back a "broken butterfly"—thin, pale, and quiet. She told Elizabeth, who was fifteen years younger, never to "burn the candle at both ends," but to live right. She went away to a sanitarium and was treated for tuberculosis, but soon died. When her mother went to the sanitarium to visit she would come back and tell Elizabeth that her sister said "tell her to be a good girl." Elizabeth was seven when this sister died, leaving only the next older sister, twelve years her senior, and the youngest brother, seven years older.

Elizabeth was her father's favorite. He had a very harsh temper with the boys and blamed them for their illness. He would get angry at Elizabeth's favorite sister over her behavior and manner of dressing and tell her she looked like a prostitute. He had limited education but was considered intelligent. He liked Shakespeare and poetry. He would read to Elizabeth. He took her to such places as the zoo on Sunday and to the circus. He would bring a big bundle of food and say to her: "What you don't eat, I will eat." He died of cancer of the rectum at the age of sixty-four, when she was ten years old. She remembers that he refused surgery even though it was urged in the opinion that the case was hopeful.

Her mother suffered from mental symptoms after Elizabeth's birth. Among them, a horror of trolley cars. The mother is described as a strong and wonderful woman who never complained. As an example Elizabeth refers to the composure with which her mother met the situation of all the deaths in the family. She was, however, strict and superstitious. She would do things by the phase of the moon and would impress upon Elizabeth that "you must not hurt people or you will be punished." She was ill two years prior to her death at sixty-four. Elizabeth had to carry the burden of caring for her as the remaining brother and sister found excuses, but also justified their attitude with the contention that Elizabeth owed more to her mother than they since the mother had given so much time to her when she was sick as a child.

After the mother's death Elizabeth lived with the remaining sister. The sister's husband is an alcoholic and she is described as having phobias about germs and a compulsion to wash her hands. She is the only living relative whom Elizabeth can visit. She feels a great deal of dependence in relation to this sister, but also strong resentments. Elizabeth broke with the brother over his second marriage, but continues to see his first wife. She describes him as a "preacher type" who finds fault with her, saying: "You could have done this, you could have done that, you should have been an artist." He makes a lot of promises and then will not carry them out.

Because of her difficulty with her leg and the great amount of time in the hospital and in casts until the age of thirteen, when her walking was restored, Elizabeth received special tutoring. She apparently developed considerable interest in art. When she returned to regular school she felt self-conscious. She terminated her schooling at the end of high school because of her mother's illness.

Menarche occurred when she was twelve. She was afraid that it was some kind of illness. She states that at thirteen she saw her brother embracing a girl friend and practically became "hysterical," she felt so "humiliated." She was afraid that playing "post office" would cause her to have a baby. At seventeen she was quite upset by an older man who offered financial assistance to her if she would have an affair with him. It was the following year that her mother became ill, and it was also the year in which Elizabeth fell in love with a boy who wanted her to go to college. She states that she had to give up this boy as she had to care for her mother.

During the period following her mother's death, while Elizabeth was so lonely and anxious, a friend suggested that she get a job. She needed the support of this friend who went with her to make applications. Her first offer was work as an elevator operator and she felt equal to it. She started work, and soon was feeling better. She became friendly with another operator, a girl, and liked her very much. One morning as they were talking in the dressing room the friend told her that she was getting married. When they went to the elevators, the friend opened the door to an elevator, the elevator was not there, and she fell down the shaft and was killed. In recounting this Elizabeth remarked: "It might have been me. We took any elevator, not a particular one." She started drinking heavily and lost her job. She could not forget the moaning and crying of the girl as she lay at the bottom of the shaft. Finally she "got hold of herself" and obtained a job in an office where she worked for nine years, when her current symptoms got worse and she quit. When she started in treatment she went back to ask for her job, was told it had been filled, but that she was "not strong enough" to do it anyway.

Her marriage has been a continuous experience of frustration. She and her husband live with his mother, who owns the house and dominates her son. He tells Elizabeth that his mother comes first and he will always live with her. In a more conciliatory attitude he tells her that he is close to his mother because he has been so sick.

She recalls that a few months after the marriage she would arrive home to find that her husband had eaten dinner with his mother. He "flies off the handle" and behaves in an infantile manner. He will strike her, and has done such things as throw a pitcher of iced tea at her. They have many arguments over her dog. Shortly before the recent severe hemorrhage he had been cross with the dog. Apparently her action, in spite of the fact she feels she "went to pieces," saved his life at this time. After she rushed him to the hospital and the doctors felt he was already too far gone, she found another doctor who operated. She "prayed and prayed" that he would live, and she felt "very humble" when he finally pulled through. He asked for her just before he went under the ether and just as he came out. The nurses told her this meant he loved her. She was very pleased. She stayed by his bed seventeen or eighteen hours a day. As he recovered he would not talk to her and became very cold and irritable. She wondered if he felt she had babied him. As she looks back she wonders if the whole thing was punishment for her not loving him from the beginning. Since this time she has hated him.

From the beginning of the marriage she felt her mother-in-law "did not approve" of sex. Her husband wanted twin beds and she consented, but he never made love to her. Their bedroom was next to his mother's and everyone slept with the doors open. Occasionally he would close their bedroom door at night and tell her to be very quiet and he would hold her. This made her angry. They had sexual relations after his mother left for church on Sunday mornings. Elizabeth once referred to this as their date for sexual relations, and he acted so guilty and embarrassed afterward that she felt she was "no good."

A few months after his hemorrhage they had a flurry of arguments and she started seeing the old beau she gave up to marry her husband. She says that he was eager to show his affection and "proud to show her off." A month after beginning the affair she found that she was pregnant. Her husband demanded that she get an abortion. Her sister, not knowing the pregnancy was illicit, threw up her arms and said: "If you are pregnant by your husband, go out and get an abortion. It would be better to be pregnant by an old bum in the street rather than him." Only the old suitor was not upset. He wanted her to leave with him. She now found herself cold sexually toward him but pretended response because she was afraid he would get angry. He went away to a job and she was to follow, but after a two months' pregnancy she aborted spontaneously and did not follow him. She feels that if he should return she would be cold to him, but "deep down" knows she would give in to him if she saw him again.

When she first began treatment she spoke of her fear of losing people and recounted the various losses she had suffered. She expressed fear of losing her husband and her one remaining girl friend. She told of a dream in which she was riding in an old-fashioned trolley, drawn by horses. There was an old man driving. She got out but did not know where she was and felt "all mixed up," then a wild horse came charging down on her with teeth bared. She got on the little safety island but figured that would not do much good. As she looked around she saw large numbers of Roman pillars standing as in a forest and she ran to these for protection. Variations of this dream with a wild horse charging toward her were reported several times.

In some of the early interviews she dealt with the theme that she had tried hard to please the therapist but felt she had failed. She recounted a dream that she felt meant she was not co-operating. In the dream she came for her appointment and the secretary told her the doctor was out and would be back shortly. He gave the patient a bowl of macaroni, and told her to count the macaroni. When the doctor came back, he asked her how many there were, and as she had not counted them because she thought it was a childish thing to do she did not answer the doctor.

She spoke of feeling afraid to speak to men, even the little cop at the corner who tries to be friendly. She stated that she was afraid to dance because maybe she would faint on the floor and everyone would know she was a mental patient. She noted that she has resorted to romantic daydreaming about men she sees. She cited, for example, that this had happened recently when she saw someone she did not know, but who reminded her of her favorite brother, so strong, gentle, and kind.

She broke into tears as she spoke of the fears of busses and subways, saying that she did not know whether the therapist realized the crazy thoughts she had, like the fear that she would scream. When asked what would happen, she replied: "I would faint and then I wouldn't know what happened." As discussion of these experiences progressed she spoke of seeing men who looked at her as though she appealed to them. Once, when she was waiting for the bus on the way to her appointment, a man she knew rode by and nodded. When he stopped at the traffic light, she saw that he was blushing. She became panic-stricken and felt like running.

The theme of how worthless and helpless she felt was expressed in relation to not having a job. She was afraid to ask for one for fear of being rejected. She thought she was being punished for wickedness following her mother's death. Then she had affairs with many men but always had to have drinks before she could engage in sexual activity with them. Her mother had warned her that her sister's death was a result of being bad. She considered at times how she might have been to blame for many of the deaths in the family, including her mother's.

When treatment had been in progress for about a year her mother-in-law pressed her to get a job "because a wife should help support her husband." She became depressed about it, saying that his family do not realize how sick she is. She would like to "leave the house" but is too sick. At times she dwelt on the matter of wanting to get well so she could be independent and leave her husband, but would conclude frequently with a remark such as she supposed "half a loaf is better than none" and that people get married "for better or for worse."

Once she and her husband were invited by neighbors to go to the beach, but she became frightened and stayed home. Her husband came back and told her how wonderful it had been and the names of beautiful women he met and how pretty they looked in bathing suits. She reported to the therapist that she did not "sleep a wink" that night because she felt so jealous and frightened that he might want someone more gay and attractive than she.

The following session she was lamenting how he never kept his promises and how he and his mother planned things without her. When he had pleaded with her to marry him he had said that she would always come first and that, while he loved his mother very much, his love for her was different. She remarked that she had to compete with his mother for his affection and had lost, adding: "I wish sometimes I could just get up and leave him, not for another marriage or a lover, and many times I have thought about it, but now I can't. I can't hold a job or anything."

Over a period of months she thought her husband was thinking of getting her committed to a mental hospital. He mentioned maybe she needed shock treatment. He complained that she had been in treatment for more than a year and was not trying to get well, pointing out that people in the movies have breakdowns and are helped in a few months.

She thought of getting a room and living alone. Then she asked her husband for the two of them to get a place of their own. He spoke of the fact that he worshiped his mother. She tried to express her feelings about their living arrangements, and they got into heated argument. He accused her of just "bleeding her husband" again.

Some time later she did get a job. Her spirits sank very low and she was troubled because she felt so frightened with men around. Her husband and mother-in-law did, however, seem to be nicer to her, which surprised her. Shortly after this they planned a tenth wedding-anniversary celebration at which both the husband and mother-in-law seemed to have a good time.

During this period, which was the second year of treatment, her husband was being seen in the clinic. This seemed to bring some further relief. In the meantime she had heard that her old beau was married. When she talked about leaving, he now showed some sympathy and confessed that he knew their living arrangements were "hard for her." When recounting this she asserted to the therapist that she had a feeling of tenderness for her husband, but "not romantic excitement." He brought her a box of candy and took her to the movies saying that it was "their turn" and not his mother's. When they got home Elizabeth suggested sexual relations. He became angry and said that was "over," but later came back to her, asking her to manicure his nails.

She was having discomforting feelings on the bus and on her job, but unless men really flirted with her, she could tolerate these fleeting fears and tell herself they were "silly nonsense." Finally, she and her husband did have intercourse, and she was able further to verbalize to the therapist her fear that if she had a baby she would die. When treatment was terminated after two and a half years she seemed to feel in a rather triumphant mood in that she could face her job, the busses, and subway without panic and was hopeful for her future with her husband.

Mary D'Amore

ACHES AND PAINS IN A GIRL WITH HYSTERICAL PERSONALITY

MARY, AGED TWENTY-TWO, was referred to a psychiatric clinic after extensive medical study of her case failed to establish a basis for her headaches and other pains and disturbances which had become worse during the previous six months. The headaches had troubled her periodically since she was sixteen. Recent removal of a maxillary cyst had not helped. At times she was troubled with nausea at the same time as the headaches. The headaches were left frontal and persistent, lasting from one to three days. She also suffered from pains across the upper chest and on occasions had low back pains which radiated to her thigh. The findings from X ray, E.E.G., and other studies over a period of time were negative for all her symptoms.

Her most frequent symptom was headaches. Sometimes they occurred every week with little respite between the attacks, and at times there were intervals of several weeks when she was free of them. Often they started in the morning about an hour after she got up. Sometimes they started when she was at the movies or out socially. When they came on, she always wanted to go home and go to bed in her room. During the time she was in high school the pain came in the back of her head, but in recent years changed to the front. No one else in her family was troubled with headaches. Her father had arthritis in his neck at the time she was of high-school age.

The other pains have not occurred so often. Her chest pain, which was concentrated mostly in the left breast, sometimes occurred along with the headaches, sometimes independently. She could not associate anything with the onset. It was different from pain in her breasts during menstruation. Repeated studies showed no discernible organic basis.

The back and thigh pains, sometimes accompanied by nausea, were most likely to occur when she was at parties or while dancing. These symptoms seemed to occur more frequently during menstruation.

Two things of great significance to Mary had happened not very long before her recent increase in frequency and intensity of symptoms. Her father was in the hospital seriously ill with pneumonia and she had broken her engagement.

Mary lived at home with her father, mother, and younger brother. Her brother was three years younger and a sister four years younger had died at the age of three of pneumonia.

Mary did well in school work and was considered a popular and attractive girl. After graduating from high school she started working as a secretary with a large company. She took a secretarial course because she felt she should start working and earning money even though her father was a good provider and completely devoted to his family.

Her father was a man of strict standards, having been brought up in the Old World culture. Mary always emphasized in speaking of him that he was a good man, in spite of the fact that he took a few drinks on rare occasions. She was always frightened of him at these times.

She stressed how they confided in each other and that he always asked her advice after that of her mother. They "told each other their troubles freely." She described him as kind, generous, considerate, but always added a note as to his sternness and strictness. He made no compromises with his notions on how a young girl should conduct herself. When Mary was in high school and wanted to go out with boys, he would not hear of it. Even after she started working, he would not let her receive phone calls at home. This led to arguments, but, she added, they were "close and good friends" despite the arguments. He wanted to select a suitable husband for her and could see no reason for dating someone you did not intend to marry. This Mary attempted to solve by meeting boys outside the home.

Her mother always tried to comfort Mary after these arguments, but she stressed that Mary should obey her father because he was "nervous" and because he was her father, frequently adding a note about the saddened home through the death of the young sister. Her mother knew of Mary's meeting boys outside the home and urged Mary always to come home early so that her father would not know.

Her brother also went to work after high school in an office job in which he had continued. Mary spoke very fondly of him, saying that he was "good" to her and the whole family. She described him as helpful and solicitous, doing whatever she wanted without complaint. After she argued with the father, her brother would try to comfort her.

Mary liked to go out with girl friends to meet boys and go dancing or go to the movies. From the age of seventeen she argued with her father that she should be permitted to have boys come to the house to visit her or to pick her up when they were going out. Once, when he met her on the street with a boy she introduced him to her friend. When she got home, her father was upset and slapped her. Then she became more secretive in her dating. When she was nineteen, she met a man two years older and immediately dropped all her other boy friends. He was working as a clerk but had aspirations to be a writer. She was surprised when he presented her with an engagement ring on very brief acquaintance. She later reflected that she had not loved him but had accepted him because he was fun-loving and an all-round good fellow. The engagement lasted for nearly two years without her father knowing. When, finally, she invited her fiancé to her home her father went into a rage. Later he was reconciled and became quite accepting of the intended son-in-law. Her father took them shopping for furniture and paid the bills. The fiancé spent much of his time in the home. Mary described him as "very understanding" of her headaches. Frequently they would have to change plans or return home when out for the evening and she would go to bed because of a headache or pains and he would stay and talk with her mother.

Mary said that it was only after they were shopping for furniture that she thought seriously of marriage. She began to feel annoyed with his "staying around the house" so much. She began to see him as demanding, jealous, and possessive, and quarrels and arguments ensued. She broke the engagement, but he continued to come to the home and she to go out with him.

Mary took a vacation trip to visit a girl friend in a distant city. She dreamed one night that her father was dead. She was seized with panic the next day when she received a phone call from her brother saying that her father had been taken to the hospital. She hurried home to stay with her mother and be near her father. He eventually recovered but Mary's symptoms became worse and she began her many visits to the doctors only to have them fail to bring relief. After some months she was referred to the psychiatric clinic.

During this time her former fiancé was continuing to call, and she went out with him "out of pity." He had been so considerate and helpful during her father's illness.

When seen in the first interview at the clinic she was described as a well-dressed, attractive blonde, appearing somewhat shy and blushing. She stroked her hair during much of the first interview. She would not look the young male therapist in the eyes but stole shy glances at him periodically.

When asked, she recounted her experiences leading up to the referral in which many things were tried in the attempt to find the cause and deal with the symptoms, but all to no avail. She stressed that she had had the difficulties for six years and that she ordinarily did not "run to the doctors" each time she experienced them but that they bothered her so much within recent months that she had to seek relief. She spoke of the removal of the cyst and her disappointment in its failure to help the headaches. She said that recently her mother had told her that she had been hit in the forehead by a car when she was nine years old, and that although the doctor had said there was no damage, her mother thought this was possibly the cause. A check of her forehead disclosed no scar and later extensive E.E.G. studies were all negative.

She thought probably the cause was "nerves." When asked what she meant, she referred to becoming upset very easily. In response to further questioning she related how having to see the boss for permission to leave work for the clinic appointment had made her nervous. She was "ashamed" to ask the favor after being absent so much because of pains.

She spoke of the handicaps she suffered from her symptoms —that they had caused her to break her engagement, and also had prevented good times with her girl friends. She complained of dissatisfactions with her former fiancé who was still her boy friend, as she did not date anyone else. She spoke of the dream before her father's illness. Also of a more recent dream about her brother in which he had had his leg broken in an automobile accident, remarking that he had just gotten a new car. She then proceeded to relate how fond she was of her brother.

A week later, when she was seen for the next appointment, she appeared smiling and friendly. When asked how she felt she reported that she was still suffering from a severe headache she had had for two days and had not been able to go to work. Her brother had taken her to the beach, but this had not helped; neither had aspirin. Again she expressed her disappointment at not being helped by doctors and of her forced conclusion that it was all "nerves." This she did not like, because it meant she was a "chronic complainer." She had been thinking and could not remember anything that had happened that could have upset her in recent months except her father's illness. Since she had had the aches and pains so long she concluded that this could not be the answer. She had thought that if nerves were the cause that perhaps she should go away from home, but she wanted to be with her family. When she had gone away to other cities to visit girl friends, she had not been troubled with any symptoms. When asked about her family, she said that they were all "very nice" to her.

She was twenty minutes late for the next appointment. She came accompanied by a girl friend of about the same age who remained in the waiting room during Mary's interview. They had been away for the weekend visiting a mutual girl friend. She had had no aches or pains until this morning when she returned home. The former relation to the father and the details of their quarrels, the incident of his slapping her and the attempted consolation by her mother were discussed.

Interviews followed in which she spoke of the "loss of her desire" to come to the clinic. She said she could not think about her pains when she did not have them. She spoke of a girl friend who encouraged her in continuing with her appointments. This girl friend had also remembered that Mary had headaches when they were in the fifth grade. They recalled together that they had had a stern teacher that year and that the next year they had had a teacher who was well liked and Mary recalled she did not have headaches that year.

Her poor morale continued as she spoke about seeing a girl friend who had recounted her many physical complaints to Mary. This girl friend was getting married soon and Mary noted to herself that there were no complaints about the romance. That night Mary dreamed that this girl was getting married but was dissatisfied.

During the course of treatment Mary never came to feel that she really remembered the early history of her aches and pains. All she could remember that seemed to her to be far in the past was her mother's efforts to comfort her.

She could remember isolated instances going back over a number of years and reproduced most of them in current experiences while in treatment. She recalled that in high school she had frequently had to leave dances because of headaches or lower back and thigh pains and that this had continued to be duplicated in later experience especially if she was in a night club and drinking. She remembered getting a headache while being taught a new filing system in the office where she worked.

She recalled vividly that she seemed to get headaches under many circumstances when with her boy friend both before and after the engagement, also when she did not see him for a while and then upon reunion.

After she was in treatment for a few months she stopped seeing him for a period during which she tried out new boy friends. She went out with a handsome young man a couple of years her junior and he became affectionate, holding her hand and singing love songs in her ear but not getting "fresh." She got a headache, and he had to take her home. Later she went out with a man quite a few years her senior whom she had known as an acquaintance for a number of years. He took her to a night club and she was seized with a headache and nausea and had to be taken home.

At one point during treatment when she had been three weeks without headaches or pains she reported a dream in which she had been in labor in a hospital followed by a dream in which she had a baby girl. This led her to speak of her former fiancé as having liked babies. She continued the interview with listing his "good points" and "bad points." Later, when he was about to be drafted, she considered resuming the engagement, but when he did not have to go into military service she grew cold again.

In describing her experiences with boys she spoke of never permitting intimacies and as not getting any "thrill" from kissing. Her fiancé, she said, never attempted sexual relations with her, but there had been times when she had felt she wanted to but would not tell him. At times when they both realized they were sexually excited they would stop and "just laugh it off."

When Mary was seen for psychological testing she gave repeated evidence of themes expressed or implied in the interviews. Some of her Thematic Apperception Test stories are reproduced to demonstrate the characteristics of her attitudes and feelings when attempting to create stories involving relationships between people.

When presented with a picture that usually is dealt with as a father, mother, and daughter, she gave the following story:

> "This girl looks like a very nice girl. She's worried about somebody—probably the man there. Probably she is in love with him. She looks mad [the usual mother figure] because this girl is here. Probably they are here for the same purpose. I don't know.
>
> "This one [the mother] is very sure of herself. This one [the usual daughter] looks timid and shy—mad at this one. This one [the usual mother figure] has probably got him and will live happily ever after."

To a picture of a girl in a doorway with her face buried in her hands she gave the following story:

"The girl looks as though she had been out. She has been beaten up or is drunk, I can't make out. She's been in some kind of trouble. It's very tragic whatever it is.

"She probably went out and got caught by her boy friend or husband and is coming home crying because her boy friend or husband hit her. She did something she shouldn't have done."

To a picture ordinarily seen as father and daughter or boss and secretary she gave the following comments:

"It looks like two people at home. Probably husband and wife. It looks as though she has been waiting up for him. He's trying to explain. She looks mad."

To a picture of an older woman seated by a young girl with a doll in her hands Mary responded with the following:

"It looks like a mother and daughter. The little girl looks sad, heartbroken over something. The mother is trying to talk to her. The girl looks bewildered, sad. The mother is trying to tell her to be grown up, she shouldn't be playing with dolls. She's trying to teach her."

To a picture of a woman lying on a cot, covered except for breasts partially exposed and a fully dressed man standing in the foreground with his arm to his face:

"It looks like this man has been with this woman—had an affair with her. He's disgusted with himself and is going home.

"Or it could be a husband and wife. He's been up all night reading. His wife went to bed waiting for him and was very disgusted and fell asleep."

Mary remained in treatment for eight months, during which time her symptoms were present at times as indicated by some of the previous references. At other times she was free of them, more like she was before the time they increased to such a degree as to lead to the circumstances of her referral. She terminated treatment herself at a point where she seemed to be feeling good.

Immediately prior to termination she met a new boy friend,

the son of a man where she worked. She described him as being "very good" to her. He had just broken off an affair with one of the other girls where Mary worked. Mary felt elated and happy most of the time after she started dating him and was no longer interested in "talking about pains when she didn't have them." She told the therapist that at times she felt "afraid she would get hurt," that he would leave her. Then she would remind herself "but he hasn't." Whether her high hopes were realized is not known to the writer. A number of years have passed and she has not returned to the clinic with further pains and complaints.

Lionel Guttman

SEVERE OBSESSIONAL NEUROSIS IN A MAN

MR. GUTTMAN, at the age of sixty-five, visited a medical clinic because of lower abdominal pain which had troubled him for the previous four months. After diagnostic study he was referred to a psychiatric clinic for evaluation because of the lack of significant physical findings, his expression of anxious thoughts, and his mention of previous history of psychiatric symptoms.

When first seen in the psychiatric clinic he was described as not showing obvious anxiety. Instead, he seemed relaxed and pleased at having an audience for a recitation of his current and previous difficulties. He attempted to control the interview situation completely, showing little inclination to answer questions, unless they were directly concerned with what he was stating at the moment.

He spoke first of pains in his intestines which he felt from time to time in the lower right side. He referred to previous gastrointestinal and abdominal difficulties, adding that "all this really isn't important," as his actual trouble was an "obsessive-compulsive neurosis." When asked what he meant, he said that he had "obsessive thoughts." He then spoke of listening to the radio and wondering who was paying for the program. When he did not hear a commercial he got to thinking about who was going to pay for it and could not follow the program. He told himself that this was silly, that it did not matter, but he could not get the thoughts out of his mind and became very nervous. He also had other thoughts, he added, that kept recurring, and he asked himself why worry about such things, but could not dismiss the thoughts. He became evasive and did not want to elaborate but mentioned that one concerned the question of what happened when a young doctor was out on a case and encountered something which was too much for him to handle. He also was compelled to keep wondering if doctors who worked in clinics were paid adequately.

He then stated that he had had more difficulty with these thoughts since he had lost his job the previous year. "They are really obsessions," he said; "they are probably displacements." When asked to elaborate he said: "Well, something else, something more personal is bothering me." As for what this might be he did not know, but added: "You see, I get a thought, and then there is some sort of conflict there and that is where the emotion comes in." He then referred to previous periods in his life when he had had troublesome thoughts and was in psychiatric treatment.

He had, both recently and earlier in life, been in treatment from which, in addition to reading, he acquired considerable psychiatric vocabulary.

He was a robust, well-preserved, pleasant man, always tidy and well dressed when he came to the clinic. During the course of treatment he related that he had intended to apply directly to the psychiatric clinic but went first to the medical clinic because once when he was under a psychiatrist's care he had a perforated ulcer and wanted to make sure that this time there was no ulcer. He stressed that he really knew he needed psychiatric treatment.

At the medical clinic he described the pains on his right side as being like gas pains, stating that they were relieved by eating and defecating. No evidence of active ulcer was found although X rays revealed old ulcer scars. He complained from time to time of sudden loss of control of his bowels with defecation in his trousers without warning. Physical findings in relation to this were negative, including neurological examination.

His symptoms began at the age of twenty-eight and had waxed and waned since. The most recent onset followed the loss of his job, which was apparently due to a cutback in personnel. He had held the job for four years, after losing a wartime job with the ending of World War II.

A week after the loss of his job he first reported to the medical clinic from which in due time he was referred to the psychiatric clinic. During this time his only remaining brother and nearest relative was ill, and died. When Mr. Guttman had visited his brother he tried to "put his best food forward" so as not to let his brother know he had lost his job and "was slipping." His savings were soon exhausted, as he failed to find a new job. He was reluctant to seek any financial assistance, pawning various personal belongings. Only upon urging by a clinic social worker would he apply for old-age assistance allotments. He lived alone in a rooming house, resisting efforts of the social worker to arrange for him to live in a setting where retired persons lived and did volunteer work. He stated that he had always felt he should pay his own way and would not tell his nephew about his circumstances because he did not want the nephew to feel any financial responsibility for him.

Lionel was the oldest of four brothers and survived them all. Two died in their forties with tuberculosis and the remaining one died of cancer of the pancreas. He was not very close to any of them, describing the one who had recently died as "disagreeable, pessimistic, and discouraging," and as always looking on the dark side of everything. He expressed some fondness for the one nephew.

His father and mother lived to an advanced age; his father died at ninety of pneumonia and his mother died at eighty-five after a gall-bladder operation. He was reluctant to speak of his mother. His father he described as stern and foreboding, without warmth, while his mother was passive and allowed her husband to dominate the household.

He lived with his parents in Philadelphia, the city of his birth, until he was twenty-four years old. He spoke of his father as a lazy man who took his sons out of school and sent them to work to help support the family. Lionel went to work in a factory at fourteen for a very small wage. At nineteen he quarreled with his father about using his wages for family support and moved out of the house. He found it difficult to live independently of the family on his wages and became irked because of a small discrepancy in his pay and decided to get even by taking goods from the factory which he sold outside. He remarked that he "got tired of cheating landlords by moving to escape payment" and decided he would "cheat the company." He was soon caught and fired.

He tried to get other work in Philadelphia but had no other references and could not obtain any. After two years he went to Baltimore, where he got a job with a newspaper under an assumed name and with false credentials. He assumed the name of a former employee he had known at the factory where he previously worked who had left and since died without the company people knowing of his death. With much anxiety he waited until his assumed credentials were cleared. He later went to work as a floorwalker in a department store with his credentials from the newspaper. He was now twenty-six years of age.

A significant episode occurred when he had been in this job about a year. While about his duties as a floorwalker a girl from the perfume counter approached him on some pretext and suddenly, "with a wild look in her eye," threw her arms around his neck in front of all the people in the store. He was surprised and immediately took her arms from around him. Another woman employee took her away to the ladies' room and she was fired. Lionel was quizzed by his superiors with reference to his relations with the girls under his supervision. He denied anything more than friendship with any of them. The girl later died in a mental hospital. Lionel gave contradictory descriptions of her, once saying she was "beauty personified" and another time saying she was sexually unattractive.

Within a year after this episode he began to have obsessional thoughts of a sexual nature. He could not get rid of the thought: "What happens to girls who want and need sexual intercourse but can't get it?" He tried to deal with this disturbing thought by repeating over and over to himself: "They masturbate, of course," but this did not remove the thought. He believed it was these thoughts which caused his hair to turn gray.

He got the idea that he needed a suspensory. He gave as the reason his wearing a cutaway coat at work. He wore the suspensory, but without relief from the obsessive thoughts. He consulted a doctor, who advised more regular church attendance. Later he threw away the suspensory and then felt relieved of his obsessions.

In the meantime he had met a girl whom he dated a lot and had become quite interested in. Finally he confided to her his real name and the story of the assumed name. She was not disturbed by this and was willing to marry him. However, he says that he was fearful of reassuming his true identity and took flight from her, returning to Philadelphia.

He found work eventually as a salesman of medical books, in which connection he attended some medical lectures. A gynecologist spoke on eclampsia. This reawakened his thoughts about women. There was a dispensary for women near his route home. He felt compelled to walk past it and look in. He became so "confused and maladjusted" that he had to quit work. Later he took a job with a detective agency and went to New York. He stayed in this work for twelve years without further difficulties, except anxieties at times about being recognized as a detective at a time when it would be dangerous or embarrassing.

Then he suddenly had to leave his job in flight. This time because of panic with regard to his living situation outside his work. He began to get "one obstinate thought then another." The "fear of the unknown" threw him into panic. His landlady at this time was a widow with children. He and she were intimate and had sexual relations quite frequently. One evening the widow was sitting on the couch and he on a chair opposite. Suddenly he felt peculiar. "Something dropped within him" and caused him to go to pieces. His heart began to palpitate so badly that the widow had to send for a doctor. "It was like getting into a jungle of thoughts." His mind leaped back over the years to the medical lecture by the gynecologist. All he could think of was that he "needed that man" there to help him.

When he tried to recount this, he could not; he became so disturbed that he could not continue but switched abruptly to a discussion of the question of whether a mother should die and the baby be saved in a childbirth crisis. He believed the mother should be saved. The subject of the incident in the living room with the landlady was brought up with him again later, and he repeated the story and made the same switch.

This episode, according to him, was diagnosed as "acute anxiety neurosis with compulsive phenomena." He remembers that he washed his hands incessantly. He returned to Philadelphia, now at the age of fifty, and received psychiatric treatment for the first time. He developed a series of somatic complaints for which he was hospitalized several times during this period but he remained an outpatient psychiatrically. He had to have surgical repair for a duodenal ulcer. In due time his gall bladder and appendix were removed. His psychiatric treatment he terminated because he felt the psychiatrist was really not interested in him.

He spent considerable time and money in private treatment during these years, without finding relief. When in treatment in the clinic he characteristically carried a little black book in which he had numbers, dates, and facts about himself written down. Attempts at probing when considered advisable yielded resistance and an intellectualized set of statements in rather technical vocabulary. For instance, after referring to a specific obsessive thought involving someone's ability to pay for hospital treatment, he said: "A psychiatrist would say that that is a form of compensation," referring to an explanation that he was given before, that his "emotional excitement over such things is merely the expression of something more basic and hidden" in his nature. This "basic problem" he can't identify, but one psychiatrist suggested to him that he "has feelings he is not fairly paid" and was especially concerned with that thought. Any incident or situation "which had to do with paying or being paid had an abnormal fascination for him." This possible explanation he has had in mind for a long time but "so far the knowledge of it hasn't helped the problem."

One interview might deal mostly with physical functioning or physical complaints. For instance, he might characteristically remark at the opening of an interview that he "barely made it" in time to the toilet this morning, continuing with an account of difficulties in this regard since his last visit. The next interview might open with an account of his often-repeated obsessive thoughts with descriptions of the process in which he becomes involved in these thoughts: "The first thought was about who paid for a radio program. The second was about who the doctor was that the resident surgeon called in when he had a case that was too much for him. The third was about whether an obstetrician would save the mother or child first." Continuing without interruption, he might say: "The thought comes in at any time. If I try to fight it or ward it off, it becomes worse. If I let it alone, it runs its course and dies out to be replaced by another thought." He might speak intellectually about his "unexpressed aggression," or remark that "at age twenty-seven something went wrong with my mind—it was about sex."

Sometimes he complained that his childhood had not been discussed adequately in the treatment sessions, but with any attempt to pursue this he would immediately become resistive.

He maintained that he did not want to talk about dreams and rarely brought them to interviews. Once he told the following and asked the therapist to interpret but would not respond to attempts to obtain his own reactions or associations: A man's face appeared as if in a picture. This man he knew, a barber. This barber's wife died and he was left with eight thousand dollars all of which he "blew on drink." The patient felt sorry for the barber during the dream, since he was throwing his life away without seeking psychiatric help. Then the patient felt something around his ankle. At first it looked like a snake but later it was flat and of great diameter, more like a big flannel bandage. However, it was a snake because it held its head up. The patient suddenly found a stick in his hand and beat the snake off his leg, or pierced it; it was not quite clear to him which.

When this patient was discussed by the clinic staff, questions were raised concerning goals and expectations in treatment in relation to his age. His current difficulties with transition to retirement, feelings of being alone, inferior feelings from taking charitable or public assistance were pressing problems even though his concerns centered almost entirely upon his obsessive thoughts.

After several years of supportive contact with the clinic he was offered group therapy as a participant along with several other elderly men. This proved to be a situation he could not tolerate. He took an obstinate position against the others with regard to what he considered their lack of interest in "getting to the bottom" of their symptoms. Actually his anxiety became so great in the situation that he could not tolerate continuance of membership. He could not find any means of relating favorably with any of the other members and was referred to directly as "old woman" by them.

As he approached his seventieth birthday he still lived in the rooming house and continued contact with the therapist who advised him and gave him aid with reality problems while giving audience to his ruminations. His fears of "going to pieces" mounted as decline of his faculties became more obvious to him. As he noticed increasing difficulties in remembering, for instance, he was practically panic stricken. Obsessive thoughts continued along previous lines. In connection with radio and television he became more concerned with questions of technical function. A reference to "high-fidelity" or "stereophonic sound" or even "transcription" during a broadcast left him unable to stop thinking about "how it was done" and "who did it." A reference to the mode of transmission during a television program would cause him to abandon the program and be compelled to think how "something could be made" to accomplish this. He had recurring preoccupations such as what happened to women in Africa during childbirth when there were no doctors to attend them. He also wondered with regard to the local situation what would happen if a young doctor were attending a case in which childbirth was hazardous and could not get an older doctor in time. His thoughts have continued to rule him like an outside force with which he can make no peace.

Mollie Stein

ALCOHOLISM: I, CHRONIC ALCOHOLISM IN A WOMAN

Mollie made a most impressive appearance when she first began to visit the alcohol clinic of City Hospital. She was a massive, obese woman of forty, weighing about two hundred pounds, with a large square face free of any make-up. Her short-clipped hair was straggly and unkempt, in keeping with her generally disheveled appearance. When she smiled she disclosed many discolored, ragged teeth chipped from the many times she had used them in lieu of a more orthodox bottle opener. A large bandage covered the right hand she had accidentally cut in a fall while angrily pursuing her husband with a kitchen knife. Holding on to her other hand was her husband, a frightened little man not quite five feet tall whom she had asked to accompany her, because she was "scared." A heavy drinker for twenty years, she had been of late increasingly nervous and distressed and was now actively seeking help. Her speech, as she told her story, was vivid, colorful, and picturesque.

Mollie was the second of three children and the only girl in the family. One brother was three years older, the other two years younger than she. Looking back over the years Mollie felt she had been a "mistake," that she should have been born a boy because "a girl had no place in our family." During the week Mollie's father was a very quiet man who communicated only in grunts. Over the weekend, however, things were different, but her mother was a dominating person who could handle him under all conditions. Upon arriving home each Saturday he would turn his pay envelope over to his wife, out of which she gave him some money for the week and with some of the balance bought him liquor to stay home and get drunk there. This she felt to be preferable to his going out and getting drunk. On many occasions she made home brew for him and the two boys. Mollie, however, couldn't stand even the smell of it. Each weekend, when Mollie's father got drunk, he changed from his ordinarily quiet, passive demeanor to brutality, beating his children more often than not. Yet her mother could handle him, repeatedly pushing him back into bed until he finally would fall asleep. On the many occasions when her mother was out working Mollie would have to take her place, pushing a pillow under his head, getting him into bed, warding him off, or trying to keep him from putting his fist through the windows. Frequently in his drunken state on a Saturday night he would severely beat his daughter. But on the next day, sober and apologetic, he would cook Sunday dinner for her. Today Mollie's face still bears the scars of some of those beatings.

From an early age there was strong mutual dislike between Mollie and her brothers. But there was nothing Mollie could do about it. Whenever she tried to express her anger at them, they would beat her up. Should she succeed in doing anything to them, her parents would beat her. If one of her brothers wanted what was on her plate, she would be ordered by her mother to "give it to him—he is the boy—he is the favorite—we have to show him that he is." As time went on the older brother, who was bigger, became the more favored of the two. Since her younger brother was sickly and she was so strong, Mollie had to take him with her wherever she went and protect him. When he began to go to school she would have to fight most of his fights for him.

At first all three children would be sent out on the streets to get wood for the kitchen stove, but as Mollie got bigger, she alone was sent out "to do the dirty work." Her father would assign her to a certain section of the slums to collect the wood, and more often than not children from other families would be sent to the same neighborhood. A fight for the wood was inevitable. If she beat up the other children, she got the wood. Should they beat up Mollie, she would have to go home empty-handed, for which she was beaten by her father. Before long she became a proficient fighter who had gained the respect of the other children, "but I hated it myself."

By the time Mollie was thirteen she was as big as she is now as an adult. At school she was called "horsey" by all the other children. Even her father, when he was drunk, would kid her about her size. Because Mollie was so big her mother on occasion sent her to the barrooms to get her father when he was "missing." Not only was Mollie ashamed at pulling him out of such places but it added fuel to the teasing from other children.

An experience she had forgotten for twenty-eight years appeared in a dream during Mollie's psychotherapy. At about fourteen, while coming home from an outing with a group of neighboring friends, Mollie had gotten into an argument with a girl her own age. In the course of this Mollie had hit her with her fist. About a month later, on the next outing, she was told by another girl: "Oh, you know that girl you got in a fist fight with? She died the other day." For some time thereafter Mollie was sure she was responsible for the girl's death, despite being told it had been due to a fatal disease.

Both Mollie's brothers made fun of her during her childhood whenever she dressed up in a completely feminine way. They liked her better when she wore boys' clothes or pants. As time went on she invariably felt embarrassed when wearing frilly feminine clothes. Wearing lipstick or make-up would so embarrass her that she would cover her face with her hands. On occasions when her older brother saw Mollie out on the street talking to a boy he would hit her and send her home. In the evening he would tell the parents Mollie "was a bum" and had been doing "wrong things with the boys." As she recalled this, Mollie became vehement. "Actually I wasn't doing anything wrong with the boys, just playing or roller-skating, but he always accused me of doing something wrong. He had a dirty mind!"

In masculine pursuits, however, Mollie was more successful.

At fifteen she was swimming champion of North Chicago and the first woman to dive from the high railway trestle. Before long she was the local leader in all physical sports. Never much interested in school work, on her sixteenth birthday Mollie left junior high to go to work. Her first job was as a bus girl in the employees' restaurant of a large insurance company. After she had been there a short time one of the elderly executives became interested in Mollie. Having learned something of her background, he expressed a desire to adopt her and send her to a private school. However, when Mollie's brother heard of it he again became suspicious, and made her leave the job.

During the same period, unknown to her family, she was going out with an older man infamous in his neighborhood as a small-time racketeer with a history of many jail sentences. Among other talents he was a disreputable gangster and sometime bootlegger. Before long Mollie found herself pregnant. Though her family were upset when she told them they were adamant against Mollie's marrying the man in view of his police record and history of having led other girls astray. Nor was Mollie insistent upon marriage. Not only did she care little for this particular man, she did not want a husband at all. When the baby was born, he was given the family name and Mollie from the start lavished all of her love and attention upon him.

For the next five years Mollie lived at home, working to support her child and herself. Though this was in the depths of the economic depression she managed to get work, consisting for the most part of heavy manual labor. Soon thereafter she got an apartment for herself and little Richie.

When Mollie was twenty-two her mother died of heart failure. Tearfully Mollie told of her mother's death. "I can remember the exact day and the exact hour." Though her mother's fingers and toes had begun to turn blue her father had not called a doctor because he was afraid she'd be sent to the hospital. Despite his objections Mollie called the doctor, but on the following morning her mother died. "Everything went to pieces. I tried to step into my mother's shoes but I just couldn't." By this time both her brothers had become alcoholics, and Mollie found her mother's role too much to handle.

After her mother's death Mollie began to feel "lonely."

Though she had some time before lost enough of her earlier aversion to liquor to take an occasional drink, it was not until her mother's death that Mollie began to drink heavily. All she had in the world now was little Richie. At one point she got a job as a waitress, making enough to pay for someone to care for the boy during the day. But her drinking soon lost her this job. Six years after her mother's death, at the age of twenty-eight, Mollie began to have "black-outs." Though she drank herself to sleep, going to work the next morning with liquor on her breath, she never lost a day's work. When she was thirty, Mollie made her first visit to the emergency ward of City Hospital. "Blacking-out" on her way home from a bar she had fallen to the sidewalk, lacerating her forehead. After first-aid treatment she left for home, refusing to stay overnight lest she lose time from work.

By this time Mollie had given up jobs such as waitressing in favor of more strenuous physical labor, taking her place alongside the men. On the job she prided herself on being every bit "as good a man as they are." She was not interested in men as romantic objects but more as her equals in competition. There was no promiscuity on her part, indeed no interest at all in men. Life consisted of her child and her work, with liquor to help her fall asleep. Each night she left her fourth-floor hovel to work the swing shift in the shipping room of a local manufacturing company. Dressed in men's slacks and a sweater, she could take her place on the shipping platform "tossing boxes with the best of them."

At thirty-two Mollie visited the outpatient clinic of City Hospital, complaining of sharp abdominal pains, fatigue (particularly on walking up the four flights to her flat), palpitation, inability to sleep, and shortness of breath when exerting herself. Physical examination revealed some middle-ear deafness in the left ear due to an old perforated drum, and careous teeth; beyond this the results of her physical examination were essentially negative. As she told of eating only one meal a day, drinking fifteen to twenty cups of black coffee, and smoking two packages of cigarettes each night, with only a few hours' sleep in the morning and in the afternoon while Richie was at school, it was obvious that rest, less work, and more food and sleep would be the best prescription. Against the advice of the physician Mollie refused to remain in the hospital because Richie would be frightened not knowing where she was. Throughout the examination she had been a most resistant patient, being described in the hospital record at this time as being "of average intelligence but less than average co-operation."

Along with the beginning of her "black-outs" Mollie began to get into barroom brawls. It took but a few beers or a little whisky to make her belligerent. When in this condition she would get fresh with the other customers, after which she wanted to have a fist fight. It made no difference whether it was a man or a woman. Inevitably she would be picked up by the police and more often than not merely sent home. In the morning she would remember nothing of her belligerent behavior of the night before.

As Richie grew older, Mollie began to feel lonely again, and more and more sought solace in the bottle. On advice of the physician at the hospital she had changed her job to that of a charwoman working at night in a large office building in downtown Chicago. Because of her belligerent behavior when drunk some of her drinking cronies began to call her "Firpo." Rather than resenting this, Mollie was pleased. She so liked the name that she began to use it as her own when arrested. To this day many police and court records have recorded on them "Mollie Firpo" as her legal name.

Except for another visit to City Hospital three years later because of dysmenorrhea, Mollie remained in good health essentially for some time. Despite her drinking and fighting she did not lose a single night's work. From time to time she would be visited by one or the other of her brothers asking for drinking money. Her attitude toward them changed to one of pity, since she was now "a better man than they are." From time to time her older brother got into trouble with the law because of stealing. When free, he would live with one woman or another. "He always needed a woman to keep him company." The younger brother was more effeminate. With scorn Mollie told of her habit of calling him a "fairy" until he surprised her by getting married and having two children. Until his wife divorced him because of his drinking he liked to change the baby's diapers, wash clothes, and go to bed at six each evening. To Mollie this was what a woman did, and not right for a real man to do.

Mollie's drinking became worse every Christmas and on the anniversaries of her mother's death. On these "anniversaries" Mollie and her brothers would sit around drinking and crying as they talked of their mother. They recalled how good she was and how capably she could control the father and how now they were alone. The brothers and their friends still remark how much Mollie was like her father when she drank. Just as with her father, said Mollie: "Anybody who kids me along and is kind to me can stop me from drinking."

By now Mollie had achieved the status of a "local character." Friendly and hard-working during the week, she turned into a rough-and-ready fighter when drunk. Her normally picturesque language, combined with her willingness to take on all comers in a rough-and-tumble fight, helped spread her reputation. Even the police looked the other way from time to time to avoid a fight with her. Yet when she had been drinking Mollie seemed especially to seek them out, an extension perhaps of her childhood practice of throwing bricks at policemen because of "the way they used to beat up foreigners and drunks" or other helpless unfortunates. From time to time she would be brought to the police station, but more often than not was told to "go home and sleep it off." Despite this episodic behavior Mollie kept the friendship of her drinking companions and the local shopkeepers. Her good-natured generosity toward anyone in need of help when she was sober made it difficult for them not to like her.

This some protective attitude toward the weak and helpless kept Mollie constantly in trouble at her job. Whenever some of the women began to pick on one of their fellow workers Mollie felt compelled to step in as protector. "The next thing you'd know the other woman was out of it and there I was fighting again." Fortunately, the "fighting" here was verbal, resulting in nothing more than official criticism and the development of Mollie's reputation as a "troublemaker." And as Mollie went back to her job at such times, silent and tight-lipped, her mind dwelt on how everyone misunderstood her and how everyone was "ganging up" on her.

The feeling of loneliness that had slowly and inexorably begun to come back as her boy grew up threatened to overwhelm Mollie when Richie began to "go steady." Mollie felt he was too young to be going steady, the girl was no good for him, and many other objections, but to no avail. As he stayed out late Mollie began to drink more. She was now thirty-eight, and alone. Her increased beer drinking caused her soon to put on weight that bloated her features. She became self-conscious about her appearance, at times covering her face with her hands until she could reach the dim light of a barroom. There she could relax.

One year later Richie was drafted, and after basic training sent overseas. Now Mollie was truly alone. Her periods of drinking increased, as did her fighting. Though she did not drink very much at any one time, she drank more frequently. Her black-outs increased but seemed not to occur from the alcohol absorbed but to coincide with her losing her temper. When she heard or fancied she heard an insult, she became very angry, then "blacked out." It was during these black-outs that Mollie would fight. Sometimes during these periods she would fight a man who was more than a match for her. Though at these times she might get much the worse of it, a few days later Mollie would invariably look him up and apologize.

The police began to "book" Mollie more often. But though she often spent Saturday night in jail, escorted there by a vanload of police, she was never brought to trial. In the morning, when sober, she would go home. This was her pattern of weekend behavior. During the week, unable to sleep when she got home from work, Mollie would hit the bottle "to knock myself out."

At thirty-nine Mollie made another visit to City Hospital, this time for extensive burns about her hands and thighs. Having had too much to drink the night before, Mollie had passed out in bed, a lighted cigarette in her hand. Despite the severe burns she refused to stay in the hospital lest she lose her job. After repeated visits to the outpatient clinic Mollie's burns were finally healed.

The following year Mollie received a letter from Richie telling of his plans to marry when he got back to the States. For a while Mollie was beside herself. Now she would not even have his return to look forward to. In anger and spite she wrote him: "If you are going to get married, I will, too." Turning to Aaron, a small, frail man whom she had known for a few years, she told him she wanted to get married. Though a good friend of Mollie's, Aaron did not want to get married. But Mollie insisted and begged. Now that Richie was engaged she wanted to get married more than anything else in the world "to get back on Richie." The more Aaron resisted, the more Mollie pleaded. As Aaron later described it, she "nagged me to distraction." Unable to get her to accept his refusal, he finally hit upon what he thought to be a safe proposition. If Mollie could stay sober for forty days he would marry her. This, Aaron felt, was a gentlemanly way of getting out of it, since in all of his acquaintance with Mollie over the past couple of years she had been sober for no more than two or three days at a time. Mollie accepted this as a challenge. To Aaron's surprise she didn't touch a drop of whisky for the forty days—then demanded they marry as he had promised! "I'm a man of my word," Aaron said mournfully, slowly shaking his head, "and I married her as I promised, and it has been awful ever since."

Aaron was a bright man who worked as a draftsman in a local engineering office. Where Mollie was impulsive, Aaron was orderly and controlled; where Mollie was generous, at times to the point of extravagance, Aaron was aware at all times of making every penny count. In addition Mollie's addiction was countered by Aaron's total abstinence. Inevitably they soon began to irritate each other. Before long Mollie became disappointed in marriage, regretting her impulsive step. Gradually Aaron's little eccentricities had begun to irritate her as did his lack of sympathy when she was drunk. As Mollie described it: "He wants to be boss and so do I, and we just don't get along." Though she felt Aaron was understanding she took out on him all of the hostile reaction she felt but could not express toward Richie. Before long Aaron began to feel afraid of Mollie. Many times he would run out of the house when she had been drinking lest she beat him up.

During an argument a few months after they had been married Mollie stabbed Aaron with a kitchen knife. Though the wound was superficial, both Mollie and Aaron were frightened because of how close it had come to piercing his heart. They saw each other only a few hours each evening, since Aaron worked days and Mollie nights, yet even these few hours were full of strife. Whenever he saw the storm signals Aaron would go out "to the corner store," staying away until he felt it safe to come back.

On Mollie's part there was her increasing resentment of Aaron's "stinginess" and the scorn he heaped on her when she was drunk. She would nurse a remark of his for a long period, then get drunk and explode with all of her pent-up resentment. Later, added to this, was her displacing on to Aaron all of the anger she felt when Richie was married, six months after she herself had been. Not only was Mollie not invited to the wedding but she soon began to feel Richie was being kept from her by his wife. Mollie's drinking and belligerence quickly increased, and Aaron many times had to appear at the police station to collect his wife.

In addition to his fear of Mollie, Aaron was both fascinated and disgusted with her. Almost with awe he described how "everybody steered clear of her, even the police, when they saw her drunk. They turned and went the other way because it took at least five men to hold her." Before long Aaron could recognize the symptoms of her having been drinking. Her eyes would become glazed and her language would become coarse ("she has a foul mouth—she swears like a sailor"). Many times he would come home from work to find her on the floor, lying where she had just urinated. ("She's a monster!") When she was sober, he repeatedly told her Firpo had retired from the ring and he wished she would, too. But Mollie refused to give up the name.

At work Mollie would spend the early part of the night away from the other women, trying to "sweat it out" and control the jitters. Later she would appear among them as though nothing had happened. Though it soon became obvious to them that Mollie was drunk, they looked the other way because of her good work. ("Drunk or sober, I'm a better man than they are!")

Six months later conditions at home had deteriorated to such an extent that Mollie took Aaron's advice to visit Alcoholics Anonymous. For three months Mollie seemed to improve. She had a "permanent," began to lose weight, and soon preached A.A. to everyone. Then one night an old member, a woman who had been sober for four years, told Mollie she would never make it. Mollie's reaction was immediate and violent. Directed first against this woman, Mollie's anger then spread to the entire group. "You're nothing but a bunch of . . . phonies!" she shouted. She accused them all of drinking secretly. Whereupon she stamped out, going to the nearest bar where she proceeded to get drunk.

Two months later, after she had been married about a year, Mollie again visited the outpatient clinic of City Hospital, complaining this time of dysmenorrhea, nervousness, and depression. She ascribed her weight increase to "nervous eating." Except for early signs of liver failure there was no significant disease. Because of her history of alcoholism and her present depression Mollie was referred to the psychiatric clinic for possible disposition to the Alcohol Clinic. After being seen there a few weeks later, Mollie was told to return in two weeks to complete the preliminary interviewing.

A week before she was to return Mollie called the clinic to leave the message that she had been drinking, and had gone to an A.A. member to seek help, but instead had had to help the member. From her speech at the time of the call it was evident that Mollie was quite drunk. That same evening, after having consumed a half pint of whisky, Mollie became highly enraged at Aaron and "blacked out." Snatching a large knife from the kitchen table, she went after him. In desperation Aaron fled to the bathroom, locking the door after him just in time. In her rage Mollie plunged the knife into the door. The unexpected resistance caused her hand to slide along the knife, cutting an artery in her wrist. The next thing Mollie was aware of was the severe bleeding from her wrist. Helped by Aaron, she rushed to the emergency ward of City Hospital, where she told them she had cut her hand while trying to open a can. On the following morning Mollie again called the Alcohol Clinic, this time to tell them "the truth" about what had happened.

Because of her repeated homicidal attacks it was decided to begin psychotherapy immediately rather than put Mollie on a waiting list. When she appeared the following week, she was frightened at what she had done. In addition, she was distressed because her injured wrist was keeping her from going to work. Though she didn't like her job, it kept her from being lonesome and idle, two conditions that made her more prone to drink. On a few occasions she even tried to knit or crochet, but that only increased her frustration. Besides, if she were to stay home from work, she would "have to look at Aaron all the time"—and this was even more frustrating.

Ten days later Mollie returned, disheveled, anxious, and

guilty. With her was Aaron, whom she had asked to come along because she was "so nervous," and to corroborate her version of what she was so guilty about. After her last visit she had gotten drunk and decided to visit a cousin. While there, two women came to visit, one lame, the other pregnant. As they were talking, Mollie heard herself called "a no-good bum," the same term used so many times in the past to characterize her father. Fists flying, Mollie tore into the three of them, beating them until the police arrived. This time she was not told to "sleep it off," but was brought into court where she was given six months' probation. In telling of this Mollie seemed confused by it all. Though she could remember no anger as a child, drinking now brought back memories of how she had been mistreated. The slightest insult from anyone would cause her to lose her temper, black-out, and later find she had gotten into a fight. "Is there too much man in me?" she asked. No matter in which direction she looked she found only confusion and helplessness. And so in November, at the age of forty-one, Mollie began her psychotherapy.

Despite what seemed to be an unfavorable prognosis at the time, Mollie responded well at first to the authority of the hospital, speaking freely of her past. She immediately stopped drinking, but became constantly aware of the need to control her temper. She began to leave situations where she was in danger of losing her temper, reacting with "dry" heaves. She became afraid of what she might do to people if she did lose her temper, but was unable to control herself when her husband was around. Any injustice that came to her attention was enough to arouse her anger. At work Mollie began to avoid the others, afraid of losing her temper and her job. She felt they were spying on her and telling tales. Should she get into an argument with them, she was accused of being drunk. After she had been two weeks without liquor she was visited one day by her younger brother, his baby in his arms, trying to beg money from her. "He knows I'm soft on babies and he'll get what he wants." Despite her having told him on a previous occasion after he had spit in her face never to return, here he was again, asking this time for money with which to buy "milk for the baby." "I will give you milk for the baby and food, but no money," Mollie shouted. But he wept, begging for fifty cents. When she gave it to him, as she had all along known she would, she felt a terrible anger within her.

In telling of her troubles now, she again blamed them all on her husband who "doesn't understand me," "thinks I'm a big, fat drunk," and "I never should have married him." Sober now for a month, she was beginning to take pains with her appearance, looking better but feeling depressed. Once again she was visiting A.A.

A few days before Christmas Mollie and a woman neighbor got drunk together. When the inevitable argument began, Mollie this time called the hospital for advice rather than take the law into her own hands. She was feeling bad at the time, having found she was being sued by the two women she had beaten up some time before.

For the next two months Mollie stayed "on the wagon." More and more she expressed resentment against Aaron. She felt he was keeping track of her biweekly visits to the clinic. She was furious at his sleeping all the time he was home, not only not helping her with the housework, but also being personally messy. She resented his making her use her earnings for household expenses, at the same time not using any of his own. Anxious and jittery, she battled Aaron constantly, throwing at him whatever came to hand. Sometimes she even felt he really wanted her to be drunk. Nor did her hatred stop with Aaron—it seemed to include all men, causing occasional friction with maintenance men where she worked. However, though she had lost none of her hostility, with the help of the clinic she was trying conscientiously not to lose her temper.

During this period, however, as she talked to the therapist, Mollie began to feel different toward Richie's wife. She appreciated how well his wife was caring for Richie, and how responsible and sober her son had remained since his marriage. As she began to feel better, Mollie asked for a diet so she might lose weight and look better. Somehow she felt it would be easier to follow a diet given by the hospital than one she herself had chosen. After a few weeks she began to look much better. No longer did she hide in the barrooms until it was dark outside because her friends said she looked pregnant. Yet as she began to lose weight and have more respect for herself, she also began to worry lest her "enemies" say she must have been pregnant before and "gotten rid of it—that's what their dirty minds are like."

After the initially fast weight loss in the first few weeks she began to be impatient about how slowly she was losing pounds ("just like all alcoholics, I'm impatient"). She attempted to make up for the lack of liquor by drinking enormous quantities of coffee. She was determined to show herself and everyone else whether she was "a man or a mouse"—strong enough to keep away from alcohol and stick to a diet. But at the end of two months of sobriety, faced with a court appearance in the lawsuit brought by the women she had hurt, Mollie "broke out." When, a few weeks later, the trial did come up, Mollie was fined three hundred dollars. Though she accused the women of having lied in court, Mollie didn't feel too badly as she recalled the many times in the past she had been guilty and not fined—"it evens out." At the same time she wondered aloud: "Does it always hurt this much to be grown up? If you are going to be grown up and behave yourself, is this what you get for it?" How could she pay her fine and still have money to pay for the furniture she had given Richie? she worried.

At about the same time, in mid-March, Mollie became a grandmother. Because she had been drinking, Richie and his wife would not allow her to see the baby. For the next two months Mollie did not appear at the clinic although she did make another visit to the Emergency Ward after a fall while drunk. She began to drink heavily but sporadically, becoming increasingly vicious toward Aaron. In desperation he had moved to a rented room away from home. She became more and more destructive. According to Aaron, who had come for help, even the policeman on the corner would now run when he saw Mollie. Yet during all this Mollie still couldn't resist bringing stray kittens home, until now there were six. Even these, however, according to Aaron, were not safe from her when she was drunk. On one occasion she threw one of the kittens against the wall, killing it. A.A. had also been given up, Mollie again complaining that they were "phonies."

In mid-May Mollie showed up again at the Alcohol Clinic. To the therapist she blamed her continued drinking on inability to sleep. Awakened by bad dreams of rats, she would walk around the house and eat compulsively. As she talked of this, she remembered as a child hearing her mother saying enemies were "rats." Associating to this she talked first of an "enemy" at work, then of Richie and his wife. Richie was spending all his time with his in-laws. Many times he would call Mollie (on the telephone for which Mollie was paying the bill!) to say he was coming to see her, then not show up. Occasionally he would call to invite her to watch T.V., but when she arrived, no one was there. When the therapist suggested she might be angry with Richie's wife because of her own need for affection, Mollie muttered: "I would hate to have anyone know how much I want affection and how helpless I feel."

For a week after this Mollie was able to stop drinking. She was still distressed at not being able to see her grandchild but was able to endure her morning anxiety enough to keep from taking a drink. In the meantime Aaron was trying to "analyze" her when they were together, but before long, in mid-June, he was back at the hospital to get help. Mollie was smashing everything in the house, he cried, but only when he was around. She had been drinking for eighteen hours steadily, and he was afraid to go home. At his request he was given a note to slip under the door, telling Mollie to come into the hospital. She complied, but stayed on the ward only twelve hours, leaving to go to work.

For the next two months Mollie did not keep her appointments. Nor was she going to A.A. any more. During this period, however, Aaron himself appeared, deeply upset because Mollie was no better and concerned that the clinic wasn't more concerned about her "bad behavior." By now he was living at home, fearing that in his absence she might wreck the house he had paid for. Yet he could not get any sleep because he was so afraid to be found there when she came home from work. During this same period Mollie did appear one day, quite drunk, to explain that just because Aaron had asked her to she had not come in before. Finding that her therapist was on vacation, she refused to see another, though saying she didn't know why anyone would put up with her.

In mid-August Mollie reappeared at the clinic. Since her last visit she had been on a continued drunk, imbibing a pint a day in two half-pint amounts. She would walk to and from work with a pint under her arm, sneaking into the toilet of a nearby café to have a quick drink. Yet by avoiding the women at work she managed to keep them from knowing she had been drinking. On one such occasion, on the way from work, she met a woman at the bar where she had stopped. When Mollie returned from a trip to the ladies' room, she found her pocketbook gone, as was the woman. Furious and upset at the loss of her week's house money, Mollie hunted for the woman, found her, and "beat her to a pulp." Mollie then thought of lodging a complaint, although the police had already been called to quell the disturbance. Yet when given the opportunity by the police she refused. Angry as she was with this woman, she didn't have the heart to see her go to jail nor could she forget her own hatred for the police. Throughout this whole period Mollie was dutifully making the payments on her court fine and on Richie's furniture. Despite her drinking she had not missed a single payment.

For the next month Mollie was again abstinent. Sure that the hospital would have no more of her because she had "slipped" she was surprised at still being accepted. She returned to A.A., feeling more friendly toward the members and being told that they, too, had resentments but had learned to control them. Shortly before she had completely sobered up at the end of her last binge she had found another drunk sitting on a doorstep. Borrowing some money, she had delivered him to A.A. but refused to stay herself because she felt so ashamed of being drunk.

At the beginning of September Mollie began to get restless and irritable. On one occasion at home when Aaron had asked her for his cough medicine, "by mistake" she gave him the dog's mange cure. Prompt use of the proper antidote forestalled any ill effects. When he later accused her of trying to poison him, she called him an idiot for not first looking at the label. A few days later Mollie went on another drinking spree. This one lasted two weeks, during which time she made another visit to the Emergency Ward. While drunkenly hailing a cab she had blacked out, bruising her face and nose when she fell. As she lay there in the gutter the falling rain woke her, sobering her enough so she could get home by herself.

When she reappeared at the clinic, in mid-September, Mollie blamed her drinking on the bad dreams that were still keeping her awake. She was now dreaming of events of years before that had deeply bothered her at the time of their occurrence. Things were worse for her when she was alone at home. Even Aaron's presence now helped her sleep. When he was not there, she became restless, had bad dreams, and sought relief by drinking. It was the same way when Richie had been living with her. When he was home, she felt fine. "He could always make me laugh," but when he was away, she was uncomfortable. Yet she didn't drink much until he left her. When she felt lonely these days she drank, and then felt better though she stayed by herself. She was alone often now, since Aaron had taken to spending so much time away from home. She was still unaware that it was his fear of her that was keeping him away.

In October Mollie was put on Antabuse therapy. Almost immediately she began to report she was sleeping better. This change she ascribed to the Antabuse although this was not a medically recognized side effect. Because of her ability to sleep, she felt she now found it easier to abstain from alcohol. At approximately the same time that she began taking the Antabuse there was also a change in Mollie's home situation. Her older brother had come to her, fresh from jail on a charge of beating his mistress, asking Mollie to be allowed to stay. For a few days all went well, but as her brother began to help Mollie with the housework, Aaron became so jealous of their relationship that he tried to pay him by the hour. Immediately Mollie became protective, denouncing Aaron for his attitude. Before long the brother began to beg Aaron and Mollie for money, ostensibly for expenses while job hunting. When she found he was using the money to buy liquor, Mollie "became tough with him," refusing to give him any more money. Despite her brother's drinking Mollie continued to remain sober. During one especially drunken weekend she took care of him in the same way her mother had handled her father. Just as her mother had done, Mollie added a large amount of black pepper to a "last drink," relying, as her mother had, on the drunkenness, warmth, and added liquor to induce sleep. The next day, when her brother had sobered up sufficiently, Mollie "acted like a psychiatrist" with him, asking what he was looking for and what he hoped to gain by drinking. At the end of the day he offered to "think about" giving up alcohol, asking about the Antabuse that seemed to help Mollie so. As she told her therapist of this incident, Mollie bitterly contrasted the kindness she had shown her drunken brother with the hostile attitude of Aaron toward her when she used to be in the same condition.

Until the middle of January Mollie remained sober, the longest period of abstinence in many years. Though her hostility toward Aaron was greater when she was sober, her relations with others were improving. The brother remained with her and Aaron until early December, when he suddenly disappeared. Though Aaron objected strenuously, Mollie had continued to care for her brother all the time he had been at their home, drunk or sober. She seemed to get great satisfaction out of helping him. To Aaron's objections she had each time responded: "Where will he go if we throw him out? After all, he does very good work around the house."

Along with her improved relations at work, Mollie was developing more respect for herself as a woman. She began to wear make-up and had even given herself a home permanent. Before long she joined an adult education dress-designing class. There she found "some very nice women who are very friendly, don't know me, and don't care who I am or if I am a drunk or not." She felt accepted by them, and was pleased. At one point Mollie had even forgotten to take her Antabuse for a few days, yet she did not drink.

Even Mollie's anger was now being kept under control. In October she had visited a local dental clinic for the repair of her teeth. Just as treatments were about to begin she was told that the clinic could not do the job. In a fury she walked and walked. At the end of two hours she found herself at the Alcohol Clinic where she angrily poured out her tale. Yet she was proud of herself for not having gotten drunk, as she might have in the past. After many attempts the social worker at the Alcohol Clinic was able to make arrangements with another dental clinic. Despite many misunderstandings, during which Mollie threatened the dentists with going "on a binge" if they disappointed her, she was finally assigned to a young dentist ("he's the same age as my son"). For the next few months she looked forward to her sessions with him, proud of the experience she was furnishing him and delighted in her ability to horrify him with tales of her past.

For the first time in years Mollie had a sober Christmas. She was able to resist drinking even when taking her usual job as bartender at the employees' Christmas parties. Yet she felt both ashamed and afraid to admit her abstinence to her fellow workers. When asked if she were on the wagon she would vehemently deny it. "If I said 'yes,' they wouldn't leave me alone until I took a drink." She even fabricated the story that she was a "bedroom drinker" to keep from accepting a drink yet not lose her friends.

By the beginning of the new year Mollie had established much better relations with Richie and his wife. She began to feel they liked her. Many an evening she would baby-sit for them before going on her job. No more did she call them when she was drunk, berating them for the way they were slandering her. All was serene between Mollie and her "children." Though they refused her offer of financial help when Richie lost his job just after Christmas, she felt calm and content.

In the middle of January Mollie began to have a sudden craving for sugar, eating a whole box of candy at one sitting. She found herself collecting money from all her hiding places the way she used to collect money to buy a bottle of whisky. A few days later she found her husband was shoplifting small articles from various stores. Feeling she herself was being watched when she entered these same stores, she became so infuriated with Aaron that she again began to drink. On the day of her next appointment she called the clinic, obviously drunk, to say she'd be in on the following day. Instead, she continued to drink. Walking into a barroom in the midst of her anger, she got into a fight with a drunken customer, kicking him in the face before she was thrown out. A few days later, at home, Aaron gave her some Antabuse tablets after she had been drinking, telling her they were aspirin. That night, while at work, Mollie suffered a severe reaction. Calling the police, she had them take her to the Emergency Ward of City Hospital. After emergency treatment she left against the advice of the physician, refusing to allow any more thorough examination.

All during the next month and into March Mollie continued

to drink sporadically. She stayed away from the clinic, feeling too ashamed to appear. She even began to use back streets to and from work, lest her friends see her. Finally, in the middle of March, she appeared at the clinic, after having been reassured over the phone by her therapist that he wouldn't commit her to a state hospital. She was now tense, jittery, and depressed. A few days later she again called the clinic, very upset and obscene in her language. Over the phone she shouted that Aaron was again stealing and this was making her so angry she had to drink again. Yet in the same conversation, like a little girl, she asked her therapist how she sounded with her new teeth. Twice more on the same day she called her therapist, asking if she should leave Aaron. But her therapist refused to make the decision for her. Mollie continued to drink that day, becoming more and more furious at her husband. Finally she attempted to commit suicide by taking a number of Antabuse tablets. Again she was taken to the Emergency Ward, but on this occasion was kept in the hospital overnight. When seen the next day by her therapist, she was quite shaky and weak, but aware that her anger was the cause of her suicidal attempt.

When she next appeared at the clinic Mollie was accompanied by her dog. She was depressed, tearful, and slightly intoxicated. From time to time she would point at the dog, saying: "That's Mike, he's *my* dog." She had just about decided to leave Aaron, but was having difficulty finding a room where she would be allowed to keep all her animals with her. Added to all of this difficulty was another spat with Richie and his wife over Mollie's drinking.

Two weeks later Mollie reappeared at the clinic. This time she was cheerful and feeling fine. "Somebody needs me," she boasted, telling how Richie had come to his mother for help after having lost out on a job he had expected to get. Now he was willing to have Mollie help pay his rent. At the same time his wife was acting in a more friendly fashion toward Mollie. As far as Mollie could tell there was no longer any reason for her to drink. Nor would she have to visit the clinic for further help, she asserted. With a wave of her hand and a toss of her head, she sailed majestically out of the clinic.

It would be gratifying to be able to end Mollie's story here, at a point in her life where she was sober and self-confident. Unfortunately matters did not remain as fortunate as they had seemed to Molly. Within a few weeks she was back, disgusted with herself for having been drinking again, and at the same time angry at her therapist for having granted an interview to Aaron on one of his infrequent visits to the clinic. Aaron, she stormed, had no right to talk to her therapist, nor should her therapist say anything about her to Aaron. And out she went, headed in a straight line for the bar and her drinking companions. One week later she reappeared, much the worse for wear. Once again she vowed to give up drinking, deeply shaken by the memory of the squalid, vermin-infested surroundings in which she recently had awakened. Looking about her at her drunken, dirty companions, as she shook the roaches from her clothes, Mollie had thought: "My God, this could happen to me if I keep on drinking." And Mollie was determined she was not going to let it happen.

Patrick Michael Quinn

ALCOHOLISM: II, ALCOHOLIC EPISODE IN A MAN

PATRICK MICHAEL QUINN was fifty years of age when he came to City Hospital seeking help. His heavy drinking over the past ten years had finally cost him his job, leaving him with no income and a family of five to support. Feeling himself at the end of his rope, and unable to pay for private treatment, Pat followed his family doctor's suggestion to visit the free clinic. A thin, flat-chested, underweight man of average height, he gave the impression of obsequious gentleness. Before he had gone very far in telling his story, however, the strong resentment and suspiciousness underlying this superficial mask became quite apparent.

Pat was the youngest of three boys, and sickly and underweight ever since early childhood. He made frequent visits to the outpatient clinic "to build me up." In addition to the usual childhood diseases he had had diphtheria at the age of nine, and a radical mastoidectomy at fourteen. Because of his frailty he was a source of concern to his mother and a disappointment to his father. Many were the arguments between husband and wife because of her pampering Pat. When Pat was thirteen his father got him a job for the summer in the American Steel Company where he was a section chief. And each summer thereafter, while going to school, Pat worked at the job his father had gotten him. In the meantime one of Pat's brothers died suddenly of polio at the age of seventeen. The other brother, after having worked summers in the American Steel Company, was now a regular employee there. When Pat finished college he, too, went to work for the same company.

Pat's father was a good provider but was extremely strict and moral in his relations with his family. Because of his own lack of formal education ("a self-made man") he was determined that his boys should have a good education. At the same time he expected them to learn the value of money by handing their earnings over to him. In turn he would pay for their schooling. When Pat's brother finished his schooling he had to continue to turn his money over to the father, who would then determine how much should be returned for expenses. All the children had to be in by ten-thirty at night "or else!" During his senior year in college Pat had made all arrangements to take a girl to the senior prom. When his father heard of it, he refused to let Pat go, saying he was too young; all the pleading by Pat and his mother could not change his decision. At work Pat's father was a strict, paternalistic boss, highly respected by all levels of personnel. Though quite capable of "chewing out" one of his underlings for the slightest wrongdoing, he protected them when they got into serious difficulties. "I don't want you getting into trouble," he would tell them, "but when you do, come to me right away." It was inevitable that Pat would be known as "Tim's boy," indebted to his father not only for his job but for any advancements he might be given. "Big Tim's" record was used as a standard with which Pat's work was explicitly compared.

Pat's mother was a quiet, gentle creature who was unable to stand up to her husband just as her children later were. A few years after her first child was born she began to look to alcohol for escape. On one occasion, just after the birth of Pat, she ran away to another state, leaving her baby alone at home. When Tim finally found her, drinking heavily in a squalid rooming house, he managed to talk her into coming home with him. Back with her family she continued, from time to time, to drink heavily, despite Tim's being a strict teetotaler. Of all her children she was closest to Pat.

Many years later Pat's mother confided in him that his father had been arrested twice because of homosexual episodes with young boys. All that time she had kept the information to herself but now felt Pat should have this as a weapon. Pat was completely disillusioned. He was the only one in the company to know of this, as well as of his father's dominating ways at home, but could say nothing. It seemed as though each time Pat started to say something his father's record was held up to him and his reputation extolled. Nor could he shake their belief that his father had put him through college by telling them of the many scholarships he had won.

When Pat was twenty-eight his father retired, amid much ceremony and expensive gifts from the many employees of the American Steel Company. Now Pat was on his own, though still referred to as "Tim's boy." At thirty Pat married, becoming the father of a boy about a year later, and then a girl three years later. All was going well. Pat was happy, satisfactorily handling his increasing responsibilities at work, and deriving much contentment from his wife and children. Before long he was able to buy an expensive home on the outskirts of town.

In the meantime, Pat's brother had for some time been a heavy drinker. Now it was so interfering with his work that the company regretfully contemplated discharging him. Because of Pat's important position in the company now, this decision was ultimately left to him. And Pat had to decide "objectively" to fire his own brother because of drink. Pat himself had not yet had a drink, partly because of his father's attitude and partly lest, like his mother, he would not be able to stop.

When he was thirty-five he began to drink ale in an attempt to put on weight. At first, unable to stand the taste of it, he had to have a sandwich with it before he could get it down. In this same year he became involved in what Pat later vaguely referred to as "unethical dealings" for one of his superiors. When exposure came, the superior committed suicide but Pat was able, with much maneuvering, to cover his own trail. The experience was quite disturbing to Pat since he was well aware that there were two main sins the company wouldn't stand for, alcoholism and dishonesty.

The next four years were the war years. Since the company was involved in defense work, Pat soon had many more responsibilities and much more work. At times he had to work around the clock in order to get the steel delivered on time. The strain under which he was working, particularly the added responsibilities, soon brought an increase in his drinking. He began to change from some ale with his meals to drinking whisky by himself at home in the evening. By the time the war had ended Pat was drinking during the day. Since he always drank alone, he was able to keep his superiors from finding out about this.

The following year Pat's drinking became heavier. He now had the added responsibility of taking care of his father. Sick in his old age, but still overbearing, Tim was quite dependent on Pat for his care and support, living at Pat's home during the last years of his life. At about the same time, in the course of a routine physical examination, Pat was found to have a positive Hinton. Knowing that this could not have been due to any misconduct, yet feeling quite guilty and disturbed, Pat kept this information to himself.

Two years later a new supervisor was put in charge of Pat's department. From the start Pat felt resentful, particularly when the usual routine was changed, but he was unable to express his anger. He became depressed, at the same time drinking more heavily. Soon he began to stop for a "shot" and a glass of beer on his way to work, going out again in the early afternoon on some pretext so that he would be able to get another drink. Then there was the long wait until five o'clock when, the day's work finished, he could visit the nearest bar. Always a solitary individual, he was still drinking alone. During this period he had one black-out. Before long he was sent by the company to a private mental hospital, spared from being fired out of deference to the memory of "Big Tim." He stayed at the hospital two months, during which time he had insulin therapy. Though admitted ostensibly for a nervous breakdown, Pat finally learned the chief reason, as far as the company was concerned, had been his alcoholism. Throughout his stay the company continued to pay him his weekly salary.

On his return Pat found he no longer had his old job, but was now reduced to low-level shopwork. Nevertheless, the company continued to pay him his high salary in the hope that he would "snap out of it." Soon Pat began to keep a bottle with him while on the job. A few months later, because of Pat's complaints of weakness and depression, his family doctor began a series of treatments of testosterone and antianemic injections. Pat was now forty-five years of age.

Four years later Pat lost a finger while working at one of the stamping machines. For the ten days he had to remain in the hospital he was without a drink. On his discharge he stopped at a bar on the way home, staying there about an hour. That evening, while at home, he became excited, "seeing" threatening visions. Within a short time he developed the hand tremor characteristic of the alcholic. At work he became less and less efficient, but was able to hold on to his job. Despite the many efforts of his wife over the past few years she was still unable to get Pat to stop his drinking. At one point she got him to go to an A.A. meeting, but feeling himself "above them" Pat did not go a second time.

About a year later Pat was in an accident while driving home late one night. Having spent the evening at a bar he was heavily intoxicated at the time of the collision. Since no one was hurt, he was able through politician friends to get the police to quash the charge of drunken driving. But somehow the company had gotten wind of the mishap. He was told his behavior was a disgrace, and completely unexpected of "Tim's boy." With this he was fired, and deprived of all pension rights. At this point his family doctor persuaded Pat to try City Hospital.

On his first visit to the clinic, one month later, Pat's appearance was described as "passive, obsequious, and hostile in a complaining, obsequious manner." He refused to accept the responsibility for his present difficulties, ascribing all the blame to the company for which he had been working. He was particularly concerned at losing his pension rights, wanting the physician to intercede for him with the company. Except for getting drunk two nights after the accident he had not since had a drink. He was feeling better physically and ready to go back to work. In the meantime he was keeping himself busy with tasks about the house.

On one of his first visits Pat was given a psychological examination. On the Wechsler-Bellevue Intelligence Scales he achieved a full I.Q. score of one hundred twenty-seven, or superior intelligence. His fantasy productions included, among other features, stories in which the hero was beset by perplexity and indecisiveness, an inability to be independent, and problems related to the confounding of sex and hostility. The following examples of his fantasy productions on the Thematic Apperception Test are of especial interest:

1 (TAT # 1)
"Picture of a young boy observing a violin and a bow in front of him. It could be one of two things—the prompting of his parents or—[long pause] he's looking at it with doubt. He hasn't shown whether he's in favor of it or against it. He is just perplexed there. Possibly from here he may or may not continue with the study of the violin."

2 (TAT # 4 MF)
"Appears like a movie scene. The two characters might be sweethearts. They could possibly be married. Now is the climax. He may be endeavoring to leave her to enter some combat not necessarily military. This is along the line of a western story. Or perhaps they reached the climax of an emotional scene where he rejected her and she is pleading either to stay out of conflict or to regain his love. With her personally it is love, but not with him. From the determination in his looks he left her."

3 (TAT #13 MF)
"This photograph presents a picture of a male and female with the male in total despair. This is the climax and prior to it they may have engaged in debauchery although no evidence of liquor bottles is there. From her position and her exposed body this might have been an illicit meeting or party between the two and she might even be dead now. Not necessarily from any physical action like shooting or poisoning her, but because of her position which shows she could possibly be dead. Maybe as a result of their doings. And he at this moment realizes that whatever transpired is all wrong and he shouldn't have engaged in it. He is evidently going to leave the scene and the room and not engage in his previous

actions. I'd say it's a problem more of an illicit love affair carried out to the extreme. He could possibly be a married man."

4 (TAT #18 BM)
"Shows a picture of a young man who seems in great pain. Could be emotional or physical. I'd say he has committed a violent—rather, a violation of criminal law and is being apprehended and taken into custody for his offense. His look is not composed. It could be from the physical restraint or the shock from an auto accident. But I seem to think he might even be an alcoholic and in an alcoholic condition. I'd say he's restrained because of the position of one hand. The thumb is not apparent as if it is used to bring pressure on the neck to restrain him. He cannot support himself. Also there is another hand on his arm in a restraining way. Both come from the rear and are pulling him off balance. From the picture and his reaction, the control of the second person has been accomplished. They took him to the lockup."

Despite his need for help Pat refused to accept any interpretation of the emotional factors in his drinking. He considered alcoholism a physical disease about which he could do nothing. As time went on Pat talked easily of his childhood, and of his lifelong fear of examination situations of any kind long before he had begun to drink. In looking for a job now he was in the habit of letting the person to whom he applied set the wage level. Job seeking in itself was difficult since he had never before had to look for one on his own. Mrs. Quinn had just taken a part-time job in a neighborhood store to earn a few helpful dollars, a disturbing step in view of their previously high social position.

As time went on Pat's situation became worse. He found himself frequently misled by sales managers who promised big commissions in selling their products. But when Pat tried it, he couldn't make a sale. In telling of this Pat became increasingly hostile. Since he was not drinking, what kind of treatment was this? Whenever the therapist tried to point out what might lie behind Pat's drinking, he merely grunted, refusing to accept any of the interpretations. When his underlying resentment was pointed out, Pat accused the therapist of trying to "make me into a belligerent person."

At the end of six months Pat had still not taken a drink, but was still without a regular job. Occasionally he accepted part-time manual labor but only in desperation. He was alternatingly belligerent and depressed as he told of the many jobs he had found but could not get. Each time he had given his former company as a reference his prospective employer quickly learned about the alcoholism. Should he not give any references, they would "suspect the worst."

In the meantime a routine physical had again picked up the positive Hinton, and again Pat was upset. When a diagnosis of congenital syphilis was made, he was sent to another part of the hospital for treatment. But after a few visits he stopped. He also stopped visiting the psychiatrist, feeling nothing was being done for him.

A month later Pat found a job as night maintenance man in a chemical engineering company. He has now been there for six months. Although he is not earning very much money, he sounds quite proud as he tells of getting the job "on my own" and of the many opportunities for advancement. He no longer talks of getting back his old job at American Steel Company. In the meantime Mrs. Quinn is still working to help out. Pat spends his spare time reading and working about the house. At the request of the hospital he recently dropped in for a visit. In the words of the psychiatrist Pat was "as hostile as ever." But Pat's drinking is now under control. Though he occasionally has a drink on special occasions, it has been more than a year since he got drunk. Nor does Pat feel he ever again will have to worry about that.

Mary Fearing

FEMALE OFFENDER

At five-thirty one morning, shortly before Christmas, a young woman was found huddled in a dark corner of a cottage at Women's Prison. A former inmate, she now wanted to return to the institution from which she had been released just two years before. It was difficult to see in this frightened creature the girl whom once a chief of police had called "a dangerous criminal," a psychiatrist had called "a social menace," and her neighbors had called a "friendly, generous girl." Which was the real Mary Fearing?

Mary was the second of six children, four girls and two boys. The family was of low economic circumstances, living most of their lives in the same tenement area of a large midwestern city. Her father, a Catholic, was at first an auto mechanic, then a stockyard worker. His own history since childhood was marked by frequent expressions of violence and other asocial behavior. At the age of thirteen he had been arrested for breaking into a store in an attempted burglary, for which he was given a suspended sentence to the Boys' Training School. Between the ages of thirteen and forty-one he was arrested eleven times, mostly for drunkenness. At the age of twenty-one he married the mother of his three-year-old son. The following year he was arrested for non-support and beating his wife. A year and a half later, when his wife was two months' pregnant with Mary, he was again arrested for beating her while drunk. At this time he was fined and given a suspended sentence to the workhouse. From that time on his arrests were less frequent, with increasing intervals of law-abidingness and hard work. His last two arrests for drunkenness were at age forty-one. Since then he has enjoyed a good reputation in the neighborhood, considered by his neighbors and employers to be a kindly, literate, temperate, and well-meaning person, a marked contrast to the behavior of his younger days. In his relations with his children, however, he was quite strict, hoping through his discipline to keep them from behaving the way in which he himself had behaved in the not-too-distant past.

Mary's mother, a Protestant, was two years older than her husband. Like him, she was literate and of good reputation in the neighborhood. Because of her husband's many difficulties she was forced to make frequent visits to the social agencies from time to time throughout much of her married life in order to secure financial aid for the family. She was a nervous, co-operative woman who took pride in her ability as a housekeeper. She enjoyed good health up to the age of forty, when she had her sixth and last child. At that time she required many transfusions during a long stay in the hospital. From then on she had to make frequent visits to the outpatient clinic. She has always been loyal to Mary in her difficulties with the law, writing and visiting her regularly at each of the places she stayed. From time to time she has expressed the feeling that she might be responsible for some of Mary's difficulties.

Mary's early years were uneventful. A poor student in school, with occasional truancies, she showed no special talents. As she grew older she became a problem in school, noisy, troublesome, and completely indifferent to the demands of her teachers. At times she acted so "irrationally" that the teachers suspected her of being mentally deficient. When spoken to sharply, however, she would improve in her behavior. At home Mary was quite a different child. Mrs. Fearing says she was easy to discipline, capable in housekeeping chores, and talented in decorating the house.

Yet from independent sources it appeared that the mother had little or no control over the daughter.

Between Mary and her father there was a very close relationship. More like a boy than a girl in her early years, Mary would often play baseball and indulge in other physical sports with her father. Of all the children in the family it was Mary who had inherited "her father's temper." When angry with her father she literally stood up to him, fists cocked, something the boys in the family would never have dared to do.

When Mary was just turning fourteen she began to get into trouble. As she herself explained it, she began to associate with a group of boys and girls who had no spending money of their own. She preferred the company of boys, acting as their daredevil leader. On one occasion the mother of a younger boy threatened to report Mary to the police for having taken her son's bike without permission in order to give all the neighborhood children rides on it. At about this time Mary's mother went to the hospital to give birth to her sixth child. While she was there, Mary began to steal in earnest. After first taking, on a boy's dare, a pocketbook laid on a store counter by a woman customer, Mary then continued an intensive few days of stealing. With her gains she took all the children to the movies and amusement parks and gave certain of the neighborhood women gifts of large sums of money. Her mother still feels it all began because "I was sick in the hospital for sometime. She got in trouble with children her own age and older women with familys (*sic*)." But when Mr. Fearing heard of Mary's arrest he was deeply shaken. To explain the money she had of late been carrying Mary had fabricated the story of a part-time job in a downtown store. Each Saturday she had given her father a pocketful of change, telling him she had earned it at her job. Unable to keep this to himself, her father had proudly boasted to the neighbors of what a good girl Mary was to help out the family. When the truth came to light, Mr. Fearing was deeply hurt. Repeatedly he told Mary how disappointed he was in her, and how hard it was not to be able to depend on his daughter at a time when her mother was in the hospital.

At the beginning of this period Mary and one or two boys would visit a number of Chinese laundries on the same day, Mary dipping into the till when the owner's attention had been distracted by the boys. Two days after the birth of her sister Mary and two boys, one twelve, the other fifteen, stole $100 from a local tailoring shop. The three were soon picked up by the police at a nearby beach, spending freely at all the concessions. Mary had $54 left on her, one of the boys another $20. When arraigned in court she was evasive, denying everything. However, after a severe reprimand by the judge she became more truthful, admitting the details of the theft. She was found delinquent, given a suspended sentence to Girls' Training School, and put on probation.

The following month, while still reporting on probation, Mary and a boy took $15 from the desk drawer of a gas station. At the time the police were unaware of her complicity. For the next six months, though she stole from time to time, she continued to report regularly to the probation officer, manifesting a placid reserve throughout the interviews. Her school record, though unsatisfactory, improved somewhat after a sharp warning by the principal. Because it seemed Mary still needed supervision, her parole was now extended for another six months.

Within a month Mary was at police headquarters again, accused of a series of thefts totaling $600. With one or the other of two boys Mary had committed a series of thefts from various commercial establishments. One of the boys confessed that at a local cleaning shop, while he talked with the proprietor, Mary had made a pretext of going to the ladies' room but, once in the back room, had taken some money she saw pinned to a suit. The other boy then described how when he and Mary had gone to a pastry shop to pick up a birthday cake they had both helped themselves to the till. From this store they went to three others, stealing money at each stop.

Despite the boys' confessions to the thefts and their statements that Mary had given money to others, including adults, Mary firmly denied everything. In a quandary the court sent Mary to the local hospital for psychiatric evaluation. When the story appeared in the newspapers, Mrs. Fearing was completely surprised by it all, certain it was all a mistake. Mr. Fearing reacted in an outraged fashion, threatening to "beat up" his daughter if he had her in the house then.

While Mary was awaiting transfer to the Psychiatric Hospital one of the boys excitedly reported to the police that she had shown him a knife, saying: "They will not get me. I have a knife and poison." At Psychiatric Hospital Mary was found to have an I.Q. of eighty-nine. After a few days of observation she was diagnosed as having a conduct disturbance, but was not considered insane or committable. It was also recommended that should Mary continue to show asocial behavior she be sent not to a hospital, but to a correctional institution. When returned to the court, Mary was found delinquent and sent to the Girls' Training School. She was now almost fifteen years of age.

During her stay at Girls' Training School Mary adjusted well. She completed the ninth grade, behaved herself, and shortly after her seventeenth birthday was paroled to her parents. On one occasion she had started to run away from the school but returned because of her "respect for one of the teachers."

Mary's parole behavior for the next two years was good. She got a job as a bench worker in a factory, earning $35 a week with the expectation of a raise. Family life was congenial. Mary was contributing to the family income so that her brother, whom she liked very much, might be able to take piano lessons. Because of her own liking for music, she also paid for singing instruction for her younger sister, at times accompanying her to her classes. She became adept at helping at home, painting and papering the entire apartment by herself. During this period, about a year after she had been paroled, Mary began to go out with Tony, a man twelve years older than herself. Mrs. Fearing took an immediate dislike to Tony because of his jealous stalking of other suitors who might be visiting Mary. About six months later, while the two were out riding one night, Tony broke into a gas station. Though Mary had merely sat in the car, Tony said she was just as guilty as he. Thereafter he persisted in forcing Mary to commit further thefts with him, threatening to tell her parents of this episode should she refuse. In September of that year Mary left her job, having become increasingly moody and dissatisfied. She soon began to make knickknacks at home for Christmas-gift selling. Because her mother during this period was irritable, nervous, and sick most of the time, Mary was doing much of the housework. In December, after an argument with Tony at her home during which he refused to leave, Mary called the police to have him ejected.

Despite their many arguments, during December and the following January Mary and Tony began to break into various large houses in the suburbs, stealing silverware, cameras, clothing, and jewelry. When later questioned about these "breaks," Mary readily admitted her part, saying Tony threatened to tell her family if she didn't continue. At one point in their period of burglarizing they took a trip to Chicago where, Tony later claimed, they had been married but which Mary emphatically denied. What really happened, she said, was that they had taken a room together, where, after having been drinking, Tony unsuccessfully attempted sexual relations. They got into such a noisy argument that they were "thrown out" of the room. Worried lest the police pick them up, they immediately returned home. A physical examination of Mary at the time of her trial revealed no basis for Tony's statement.

After pleading guilty to burglary, Mary was sentenced to Women's Prison for five years. She was not returned to Girls' Training School from which she had been on parole because it was felt she presented too difficult a behavior problem for them to handle. Mary was now just under nineteen years of age.

At Women's Prison Mary had much difficulty in accepting her situation. Quite depressed about the shame she had brought to her family, she now, for the first time, revealed how difficult had been her parole adjustment. Though she had maintained a good front, behaving appropriately, she had found it difficult to face neighbors and friends back home because of the publicity she had earlier received. At this last trial the publicity had been even more extensive, with pictures of her in various poses, including attempts to shield her face. She spoke of the disgrace and humiliation her family must feel, despite her family's acting very friendly and warm toward her and telling her they wanted her back as soon as possible.

A Wechsler-Bellevue Intelligence Test at the time of her commitment to Women's Prison gave her an I.Q. score of one hundred two, Verbal ninety-five, Performance one hundred eight. At that time the prison psychologist wrote:

"Test findings indicate average adult endowment with scatter evident in the performance area especially. Marked impairment was noted in the attention span and memory as well as mental control. Additional tests indicate severe impulsivity and constant repetition of previous errors. No insight was indicated, and the final goal could not be kept in mind. Verbally she was quite inarticulate. It was felt that the impairment in mental control was due to preoccupation. Level of abstract reasoning was not high and comprehension was fair. Although not left-handed she worked for the most part with her left hand during the whole of the performance tests and showed dexterity. She seemingly made herself adapt with great effort. When items were pointed out as difficult, she brightened and approached the task with eagerness. Wholes were not grasped. There was some evidence of grimacing which well may have been due to embarrassment. Natural smile is quite engaging. Although she looked at examiner directly there was tremendous difficulty in self-expression. Days later she returned to talk, of her own will, at which time (there was) marked guilt and emotional upset regarding publicity. Admitted relief when commitment occurred. Inhibited, tension apparent—true feelings caused by what might be interpreted as an indifferent attitude. At times she appeared perplexed. General posture was stooped. Occasionally she appeared furtive and withdrawn. Only real interest expressed was that she like drawing."

An identification photo taken of Mary at this time showed a worried expression, as though she were expecting attack. Prior to her daughter's commitment Mrs. Fearing had written the superintendent assuming the responsibility for Mary's earlier difficulties, but blaming Tony for this latest difficulty. She pointed out how helpful Mary was about the house, particularly at family holiday time: e.g., Thanksgiving, and what a good girl she basically was.

At the prison Mary's first case worker described her as "tall, thin, quiet, pale, and delicate-looking, sweet-mannered and very courteous (but) untruthful and unreliable." The general case conferences at that time provided additional information about

Mary, some of which was consistent, some confusing. Physically Mary was in good health. She had a history of hay fever and evidence of other allergy in atopic dermatitis and slight asthmatic breathing. Her teeth were clean and in repair. She herself was very clean on admission. She had had little or no sexual experience and medically it was doubted that she had ever had intercourse.

Mary told the worker she was glad to be sent to Women's Prison because it was a chance to make something of herself. Though she had feared Tony, she had been unable to confide in any member of her family, all of whom had disapproved of him. Where she had felt her earlier stealing had been "fun," she had all along known the present episodes were wrong.

It was noticed that from the start Mary got along well with the other girls but became expressionless before authority figures. At about this time one of the social agencies that had in the past been helping Mrs. Fearing volunteered some more information. Mary had always been considered a generous, likable girl who put herself out to do favors for her family and friends. Many times she had shown generosity toward some of the poorer families in the neighborhood, seeming to enjoy doing things for them. Like her father, Mary had always been hotheaded, losing her temper easily, but quickly thereafter calming down. The social agencies were hard put to reconcile Mary's episodes of stealing with the general neighborhood description of her as a kindly, generous, and co-operative girl.

Two months after her admission Mary was offered placement in one of the girls' cottages as a step in rehabilitation. She refused the change, saying she didn't feel sure of herself. It meant too much freedom, Mary objected, and she was afraid she might stray. Since her commitment Mary had been reticent, with great difficulty in self-expression. She was full of guilt feelings, particularly because of the disgrace she felt she had brought upon her family. She seldom cried, was apprehensive, and brooded a great deal. Over the next month she grew more listless, apathetic, and withdrawn, resisting attempts by the staff at psychotherapy. Three months after her admission she attempted suicide by drinking turpentine. When seen by the physician on the following day:

"... she was sitting on the side of the bed with her chin propped in her hand, staring off into space. She was very inarticulate, answered questions only in monosyllables, and then only after the questions had been repeated. She [felt] she did not want to live, and, in [her] only emotional outburst . . . said she could not face her family and her uncles and aunts. She denies any auditory or visual hallucinations.

She did say that she did not think the officers here wanted to help her because they knew about her before she came . . ."

On that same day the staff intercepted a long letter, depressed in tone, that Mary wrote to her mother:

Dear Mom

Just a few lines to say hello and to tell you I miss and love you all.

Life up here is getting useless. And I can't take it any more. I know what you're thinking now, you and everyone else think I am a coward and can't take my punishment. But it isn't that. About three and one half months ago I thought I had something to live for, and that is to see little Marge as an opera singer. But I've lost all hope on that. But I do pray she'll end up well.

Mom, I'll never be able to live again. Do you know I just found out that I can't vote when I'm twenty-one cause I have a prison record. Then there is a lot of other things that drive me crazy.

Ma I can't finish this letter. Just remember I love you and I love Dad, and Michael (etc.)

Tell my aunts and uncles I'm sorry for bringing their name down and also that I love them.

Oh mom I wish I could see you all now, I can in my mind, I can see little M . . . all. I do love you and I know you will forgive me. Pray for me.

Good by Mom,
Your Daughter
MARY

On the following day Mary was transferred to State Hospital for a period of observation. During her stay there she remained depressed with intense feelings of guilt and self-accusatory ideas, with no evidence of hallucinations. She made several suicidal attempts. On one occasion she tried to secure by force from one of the employees keys to the medicine closet in order to take an overdose of medication. Frequently she would become disturbed. At the recommendation of the psychiatrist, regular commitment was ordered.

Within a week Mary made the first of seven escapes, being returned by the police after a few days. After her third escape she was given electroshock treatments with consequent improvement in her mood. On her fifth escape she stayed away three months. During this time, using a false name, she married Frank Jennings two days before her twentieth birthday. Though Frank knew of her legal situation, he was not concerned by it. One month after her return she again escaped, this time with what appeared to be outside help. After staying away eleven days she was returned, but escaped again the following week. This time she stayed away seven months, after which both she and her husband were apprehended one day as they were entering their apartment. On this return she was found to be "returned to sanity" and sent back to Women's Prison.

When seen by the prison psychiatrist she presented an entirely different picture from that at the time of her commitment to State Hospital.

> "For the first time she cried, stated she hoped she would not have to do too long in the institution and wanted to be in the community in the right way with her husband and her expected child. . . . She assured . . . she would not attempt a runaway as she knew it did not pay and that she was sure there would be no attempt at suicide because that was all in the past. She was extremely devoted to her husband and wanted to return to him at the earliest possible time. It was felt that her earlier suicidal attempts . . . were more a reaction of temper and showing off than for any real desire to end her life."

A few days later Mary asked to be placed to work in the nursery where she might learn child care and help to provide for her expected child. She still was somewhat depressed, having many fears, particularly in relation to the expected child as well as a fear that she might again become mentally disturbed. Under the physician's guidance she slowly gained in self-confidence and in her trust in the staff. Whenever she felt tense, nervous, or worried, she immediately sought advice, in this way being able to control suicidal thoughts. She responded to kindness readily. The impression she made was of an appealing girl with excellent standards of hygiene. A modest girl, she made friends cautiously, but when she knew one well she was quite friendly. In general, she preferred small groups to large gatherings.

After a difficult confinement Mary gave birth to a son. Though she was still very temperamental she was unusually patient with the baby and breast-fed him for two months. She would come to the nursery early and stay late in case there was anything to be done for him. To all it was evident that Mary sincerely loved her baby.

Mary's husband, Frank, made a good impression when first seen at the time of Mary's return to Women's Prison. A tall young man of medium build, he at first seemed ill at ease, but became more confident as the interview progressed. Though he had signed the visitors' sheet as "Staff Sergeant," he was dressed in civilian clothes. He explained this discrepancy by saying he was now a civilian, having been recently discharged from the air force. Unemployed at present, he planned to live temporarily with the Fearings.

Frank admitted that at the time he married Mary he had known she was a runaway from State Hospital. He had been acquainted with her for two years prior to this, and he had become extremely fond of her. On one of the occasions when Mary was hiding at home with her mother, Frank had married her. Then Mary had told him everything that had happened to her. (It was later found out that Frank had intimated to Mary that he, too, had been in some trouble but he did not talk of it spontaneously, and Mary was reluctant to question him.) The young couple had been extremely happy, according to Frank. Mary had been a good housekeeper, was completely interested in her husband, and had had no periods of depression or discouragement during the time of relative "freedom." However, there was constant fear that she might at any time be found by the authorities and sent back to the hospital. For this reason Frank looked upon her return as beneficial, since it would dispel the shadow under which they had been living. However, Frank wondered aloud about what a prolonged stay in an institution might do to her newly regained mental health.

For the next few months Frank wrote each day, and visited Mary regularly. Following the birth of the baby he was more devoted than ever. In preparation for Mary's return he had painted, papered, and furnished an apartment from his earnings as an electrical repairman.

All seemed favorable until information about Frank's past and present legal difficulties was received by the staff of Women's Prison shortly after the baby was born. Frank had been born in a large far western city, the illegitimate child of a disinterested mother. He had had a poor reputation since childhood, with frequent truancies from school. When Frank was quite young, his mother married. The foster father was a heavy drinker who never accepted Frank as his son. When Frank was in his early teens, the family came here to C——. On finishing the tenth grade he worked as a busboy, pin boy, truck driver, and at many other jobs. Soon after Frank left school, his parents separated. His mother remarried, then left the boy, in whom she had never shown any interest. Her present whereabouts were unknown.

At eighteen Frank was arrested for the first time, when he got drunk and stole an automobile. This was the first of many arrests during the next two years, but he was not imprisoned. In the Army he made an unsatisfactory adjustment with many incidents of AWOL. His rebellion at this time seemed to be a continuation of his earlier rebelling against authority, his foster father, by running away. A short time later he stole an automobile while on escape from the guardhouse. For this he received a six-year sentence to the military penitentiary. Here he showed real progress and increasing maturity. He readily picked up electrical skills, expressing a marked ability in this area. At the end of two and a half years he was paroled to a job as gas-station attendant in a military auto pool. Four months later he was arrested for stealing $90, given a dishonorable discharge, and sent to jail for one year. About one year after his release he fraudulently applied for re-enlistment in the air force, changing some of his papers to read "Staff Sergeant" and denying any previous criminal record. It was shortly after his prior record had caught up with him, forcing dismissal from the service, that he married Mary. He was given a suspended sentence in federal court two months after Mary had been returned to Women's Prison. Three weeks later, shortly after the baby was born, he was again arrested, for trying to steal a camera. Because of his employer's strongly favorable recommendation, Frank was freed and given a suspended sentence.

It is at this point that we again take up Mary's story. After the birth of her son she seemed to improve in her relations with herself and with others. She spent most of her time in the nursery, caring for her child and learning a great deal from Mrs. Grey, the nurse in charge. As time went on Mary began to develop a relationship with her that was stronger than any she had previously enjoyed within the institution. It was to her she would go for advice and support. And it was to Mrs. Grey, as we shall see, she later returned when problems at home began to overwhelm her.

Seven months after her return to prison Mary was again seen by the psychiatrist. He now felt her to be ready for parole consideration, despite her history of occasional mood swings. Indeed, he strongly recommended parole as soon as possible lest she lose her positive frame of mind and realistic future plans. Two days later Mary left her room at ten-thirty at night to go to the nursery to see her baby. She paid no attention to an officer's order that it was too late, continuing to the nursery, where she changed the baby's diaper. Later she came down to the officer's office. Shaking her finger in the officer's face, Mary shouted:

"There is no officer or any person, you included, that is ever going to tell me what I am to do.

"When I want to see my baby I'll go over to the nursery any hour of the day or night, even if I have to smash every slat in my door or break other doors to get to him."

On the following day Mary was visited by her husband and father. During the visit Mr. Fearing got into a loud argument with the officer because the baby was not left with them for the full visiting hour, and also because he was not allowed to whisper to his daughter.

Two months later, in time for Thanksgiving, Mary was released on parole to her husband.

On parole

The first few months back with her husband were full of happiness for Mary. The apartment had been completely furnished with new furniture before her release. Mary at once began to busy herself with making a good home. Frank soon opened his own electrical repair shop, making calls all day while Mary answered the telephone. The baby stayed during the day with Mary's mother nearby. On her regular visits the parole officer sensed increasing stability in Mary with no signs of depression. Mary's happiness was also apparent in the frequent letters she sent to Mrs. Grey, beginning immediately upon her return. In them she eagerly asked for news of the activities of the other girls whose babies were in the institutional nursery. Particularly glowing was Mary's account of the first Christmas together with her husband and baby. ". . . Just being here was the best gift of all." Frank had visited Women's Prison the week before to give his services freely to an electrical problem. At that time he had left a few dollars for one of Mary's friends, one of the young mothers Mary had left behind. All was going well.

But a few months later circumstances began to change for the young couple. The parole officer was the first to learn of it, since Mary wrote to Mrs. Grey only of her happiness, and of what a good job she was doing caring for her child. At that time Frank had driven out of the state to a promised lucrative job, but on arrival had found he was to be a strike breaker. He was beaten severely, his car was wrecked, and Mary had to borrow enough from a loan agency to help him return home. Now they were being dunned by the loan agency. On investigation it was found that Frank still owed much money to the same agency for his earlier expenses in getting the apartment ready for Mary's arrival. With the help of the parole agent this matter was soon straightened out, and life again went on smoothly for a while.

Later that spring Mary, Frank, and the baby were invited by Mrs. Grey to attend a picnic at Women's Prison, where they all had a pleasant day. Mary was expecting another child in a couple of months, they had moved to a larger apartment, and once again it seemed that the skies were untroubled. But Mary did not tell Mrs. Grey that a few days prior to this she had become angry at her husband for coming home drunk and boisterous from a late evening "with the boys." So annoyed had she been that she had called the police to have him arrested. The day of the picnic Frank was "on probation" in so far as Mary was concerned.

In August of that year a second son was born to Frank and Mary Jennings. Frank was doing well in his shop, to the extent of looking for a partner to help with the work. In October Mary asked her parole officer for permission for Mrs. Grey to visit, saying the baby was not feeling well. When Mrs. Grey arrived, it became apparent Mary had really wanted to talk about herself, using the baby's health as a means for circumventing the authority of the parole agent. Mary told Mrs. Grey of feeling lonesome and a little blue despite her pride in the physical aspects of her home. Specifically she felt neglected by her husband, who was working long hours at his shop. At Mrs. Grey's suggestion the prison chaplain visited the young couple. In his sensitive way Reverend Millet was able to help them, at least temporarily, and another minor tempest was over. The following Christmas was again a very happy time. Mary sent a Christmas card to Mrs. Grey, then a letter thanking her for the gift she had sent the baby. Though Mary now seemed again completely engrossed and happy in repapering and painting the rooms in her apartment, Mrs. Grey was becoming increasingly worried about her. Sure enough, during the next year—a year marked also by many jurisdictional conflicts between the parole agency and Women's Prison—obstacles piled up for Mary.

In January Mrs. Grey invited Mary and Frank to visit, using as an excuse some electrical repairs Frank might take care of at one of the cottages. To Mrs. Grey at this time they both seemed to be happy and fond of each other. But in March the parole officer saw an entirely different picture. Frank had been drinking rather heavily, paying less and less attention to his business. One night after their return from an evening out together, Frank offered to drive the baby sitter home. When he did not return until the following morning Mary went to the police. On her complaint Frank was arrested on suspicion of "molesting a female child." Because of the girl's denial that anything wrong had taken place, the case was filed. But Mary now refused to let Frank come back home. Though Frank had been giving her plenty of money to live on, she hoped by keeping him out of the home for a while to straighten him out. One week later Mr. Fearing talked Frank into returning home, where he was welcomed with open arms. Once again all was calm. The next visit by the parole officer found Frank attending to business and Mary again busy painting and papering.

In the latter part of June the Jennings family rented a summer cottage at Lakeville, in northern Ohio. Two weeks later Mary appeared at Women's Prison looking for Mrs. Grey, only to find she was away on vacation. The following week the family was back in the city. Frank had just been arrested for driving a car without license plates or license, and the cottage money now had to be used to hire a lawyer. Two weeks later the parole officer received an emergency call from Women's Prison saying Mary had appeared there that morning asking to be committed. When it had been explained that she had done nothing that would warrant her commitment, Mary said she had been drinking the night before, in violation of parole regulations.

During the ride back home Mary told the officer of the dreadful state of her marriage. Despite Frank's generosity they had been having many squabbles. Frank was drinking again. The loan agencies were again bothering them. She was "fed up" with it all. Last night Mary had gone to a movie where she met a former inmate of Women's Prison. After leaving the girl that night, Mary had decided to stay out all night to spite her husband. As she drove aimlessly but ever nearer Women's Prison, she tried to get arrested. She went the wrong way on one-way streets and speeded, but each time she was stopped, despite a lack of a driver's license, she was told only to be more careful next time. In the morning she found herself at Women's Prison.

After they got to the apartment, Frank went for a walk with the officer to tell her a somewhat different version. Mary, he complained, had became an awful "headache" to him. Though occasionally he went to a bar with some friends, Mary was out until 2 or 3 A.M. practically every night, visiting girls who used to be in Women's Prison with her. To the parole officer at this time Frank seemed congenial but irresponsible.

When Mrs. Grey returned from her vacation, at the beginning of August, Mary called to tell her that everything at home was satisfactory, but did not tell Mrs. Grey of having asked the parole officer for aid in getting a legal separation. In the middle of August Frank was drunk over an entire weekend. On the next visit of the parole officer, Mary told her she was now so sick of married life that she would like to place her children and get away. As Mary continued to talk, the officer got the impression that she wished the court would send Frank to prison when his case came up next month. In this way she could get financial aid from the state, and she would no longer be dependent on Frank.

Two weeks later, one evening early in September, Mary telephoned Mrs. Grey to say that she was so discouraged she felt like "turning the gas on" to do away with herself and the two children, at the same time admitting to having had a few drinks. The entire conversation was reported to the parole officer, who went to see Mary the following morning. The drinking was laughingly denied by Mary, but she admitted things were going badly again. Frank was working as many as sixteen hours a day, leaving Mary alone for long periods. This Mary resented. In addition, though he liked to have something to drink when he came home at night, Mary objected to his bringing beer or whisky into their home. As a result many nights on his way home he stopped to visit at a bar. By closing time he was drunk, which was quite obvious to Mary when he finally arrived home about 2 or 3 A.M.

At about this time the parole officer began to feel that Mary was playing Mrs. Grey and herself off against each other, and insisted that Mary be referred to her should she again try to reach Mrs. Grey.

In October, when Frank's trial came up, he was sentenced to two years in prison. In trying to carry on his business without him Mary hired an electrical repairman. A few weeks later he disappeared, taking with him many of the tools.

On Thanksgiving night Mary telephoned Mrs. Grey at the prison. Left alone with the children and the business, Mary was now desperate and unable to work things out. She had been drinking all that evening to get up enough courage to call to tell her troubles. There seemed to be nothing to live for. Again Mary was told to call her parole officer for help.

At five o'clock one morning in mid-December Mrs. Grey was awakened by the ringing of the telephone on the second floor of her quarters. It was Mary, whispering into the telephone on the first floor, where she was now sitting in the dark. For the next hour and a half, as Mary and Mrs. Grey sat together, Mary went over and over her desperate situation. She didn't know where to turn or what to do. She apologized for disturbing Mrs. Grey, but had remembered she always arose at 5:30 A.M. After promising to get in touch with the parole officer, Mary left to go home.

On the following day the officer found Mary and her brother sitting in the cold of the closed electrical shop. Among other problems she found a new trial for Frank would cost $200, there was no coal to heat the home, and Mary was herself now beginning to drink. From time to time, to get food, Mary had been forced to sell some of the electrical supplies. That evening Mary was arrested for having ignored two court summonses about nonpayment of debts. As soon as she was released from jail the next morning, Mary again called Mrs. Grey, telling her how upset she was and how much she needed help. Mrs. Grey could only tell her to call the parole officer. Later that day Mary sent a telegram to Mrs. Grey, saying she would visit her that night. On hearing of this the parole officer instructed Mrs. Grey to have Mary call the parole officer. The officer then saw Mary's mother, who had been unaware of all that was going on. She immediately offered to have Mary and the children spend the rest of the winter with her.

When Mary appeared at Mrs. Grey's that night she had with her an expensive-looking camera that she wanted to donate to the girls in the prison. (Though it was accepted at the time, there was much concern that it might have been stolen earlier by her husband.) This, she said, was the sole purpose of her visit that night. Again Mary promised to go to her parole officer.

Two days later, on the morning of the twenty-first, Mary broke her appointment with the parole officer. Her mother noted at the time how depressed she was. Early that afternoon Mary again called Mrs. Grey. She had just been in a minor automobile accident not far from Women's Prison, and asked if Mrs. Grey would come down to get her. Again Mary was told to get in touch with her parole officer immediately. Despite this advice, later that afternoon Mary appeared at the prison office. When spoken to she was unreasonable, giving the impression of being out of contact with reality. She cried that she was considered only a piece of furniture that could be moved anywhere. After a while she calmed down, agreeing to go home immediately and visit the parole officer in the morning.

Later that same evening, however, Mary again called Mrs. Grey from a café in a neighboring town. She seemed more disturbed than ever, making frequent suicidal threats. At one point she claimed to have "seen" the superintendent of Women's Prison, who had told her she should go to State Hospital. Late that night, in locking her quarters, Mrs. Grey found Mary huddled in a corner in the dark. On the following day, December twenty-second, Mary's parole was revoked.

Mary's mother was not surprised at the turn of events. Everything had just piled up on Mary, she said: Her husband's being away, leaving her alone with many debts, and the children had been more than her daughter could take. Mrs. Fearing was now going to keep her grandchildren with her until Mary's release.

Back in Prison

Though the prison photograph this time showed a smiling young woman quite different from the frightened girl of four years before, Mary had a hard time accepting her return. On her second day back, the day before Christmas, Mary asked to be put into solitary confinement. On Christmas afternoon she was calmer and ready to join the other girls.

In early January Mrs. Grey received the following letter from Mary:

> "Apologies are always difficult, especially mine, as I am always truly sorry.
>
> "I can't forgive myself for the numerous amount of times I've pestered you (and at such ungodly hours too).
>
> "You know I don't have much use for a fool and a boor. So to find myself in the position of being both is rather hard to take.

"I offer no excuse for myself as I really can't see any. But I do hope that you will forgive me."

One month later the parole board formally voted an indefinite postponement of her parole. Late that night, after being told the news, Mary had to be given a sedative to help her sleep. She was upset at not being able to get out right away, worrying about the many bills she owed. At noon of the following day Mary climbed a ladder to get up to the attic, where she proceeded to barricade herself. Soon the sound of breaking glass could be heard by those below. When Miss Otto, Mary's case worker, called to her, she came down the ladder, blood gushing from her right arm.

After having her arm sutured at the hospital Mary was put into solitary. The next morning Mrs. Fearing telephoned that not only had she obtained money with which to pay the rent on the house and the shop, but also was going to put the furniture in storage. She would keep at home with her the special items, including Frank's tool kit, about which Mary had worried. When this news was relayed to Mary, it seemed to have a quieting effect on her. Somewhat bitterly she said: "So they really are going to do something for me, after all." That afternoon she was much quieter, asking later for some medication to help her sleep.

But the calm was short-lived. About three days later Mary began a series of disturbances and suicidal attempts that ended in her again being sent to State Hospital. Among other incidents she had been acting queerly one evening, repeating her desire first to see her husband, then to attend to his business. When she felt someone might be watching her, she became noisy and loud. Later that night she set fire to her mattress, which she had put into a corner of her room, then stretched out on her bed as the smoke rose near her. On being led out of her room she tried to reach the overhead bulb to crush it in her hands. A few hours later, during the night, she again created a disturbance, shouting as she sat on the floor and tore her blanket to shreds. On the following day Mary was sent to State Hospital for four weeks of observation.

For the first three weeks of her stay at State Hospital Mary was very pleasant and co-operative, helping out on the ward. Neither in her examinations nor in her ward behavior was there any evidence of disturbance. However, during the fourth week, as time for her staff conference approached, Mary's behavior underwent a marked change. She began to act in a disturbed fashion, breaking windows and cutting her wrist on a piece of the glass, all the while making numerous suicidal threats. Despite this behavior, at the end of the fourth week Mary was returned to Women's Prison as non-committable. The State Hospital staff had felt her behavior to have been more psychopathic than psychotic. She was accused by their psychiatrist of choosing "in cold-blooded fashion to dodge responsibilities, acting out every impulse, and trying to outwit anyone who picks up the challenge of her provocative behavior."

On her return to Women's Prison Mary still seemed suspicious and upset. Again she committed acts of violence and made unsuccessful attempts at suicide. Two weeks later, on March the second, Mary slashed her wrist severely enough to require sixteen stitches. On the fourth of March she was returned to State Hospital. On the twenty-sixth she was sent back to Women's Prison, her behavior again diagnosed as an anti-social reaction for which she was non-committable. Special emphasis was placed on her

> ". . . hair-trigger type of temper which quickly flares up with minor frustrations. She keenly resents the implication of being psychotic and has claimed persistently that she knows what she is doing and that there is nothing wrong with her mind."

This time Mary seemed much quieter and more relaxed on her return to Women's Prison. She said she was finished with trying to injure herself, wanting to go home to pick up her own responsibilities, including the care of her two boys. She was now able to sit quietly as she discussed her affairs. As a special favor she asked for hard physical work about the grounds to use up her energy so that she might be able to sleep at night. As time went on she became less and less subject to moods, although on weekends or at night she would frequently become tense and preoccupied, sitting quietly by herself for minutes at a time. On one of these nights she was reported by another inmate as being nervous and needing help. When the officer went to her room, she found Mary extremely nervous, wringing her hands and looking into space. However, on being given medication Mary expressed gratitude and soon was fast asleep.

Where Mary was ambivalent toward Frank at the time her parole was revoked, loving him one moment and hating him the next, she now was looking forward to re-establishing a home with him and the children. She wrote long letters to him, asking his advice and discussing their future plans. Though she realized his instability, she said, she knew how much she needed him. Frank, in turn, soon began to blame himself as the cause of her difficulties. In May Mary was paroled to her mother, to await there Frank's future release from prison. To have kept her any longer at Women's Prison, it was felt, would serve no useful purpose.

Mary has been home now two years. About a year ago she got into an argument with Frank when visiting him one day. Two days later Frank escaped from prison to try to see Mary, but was caught a short distance away. Because of this Frank is now serving an additional sentence. In the meantime Mary has become "disgusted" with Frank, accusing him of having escaped "just to spite me."

In talking about Women's Prison Mary is quite bitter, accusing them of having done nothing for her, or even of having had any interest in her. "Why should they? I'm a phony. Nobody knows what I'm really like. I've been a phony all my life, in everything I've done. Even when I told my father I was working, all the time I was out stealing—just a phony." Unhappy because of Frank's plight, cynical in her attitude toward parole boards ("If I had a thousand dollars I could get him out in a week"), and worried about the welfare of her children, Mary sees no hope in the future.

Throughout all this Mary's family have remained loyal, helping out with encouragement and occasionally gifts of money. Even her younger sister, who used to be so "jealous because my mother wrote to me every day in prison," helps out when she can. As Mary tells it, apparently her sister has realized "my mother would have done the same for her." The one unspoken thought in the minds of the Fearings is what will happen to Mary when her period of parole supervision is ended.

In Mary's speech at present there is again evident much of the blocking she had at the time of her commitment to State Hospital. From time to time she will pause in the middle of a sentence, shake her head as if to clear it, then ask: "What was I talking about?" Occasionally the cigarette she is holding will drop from her fingers as though there is lack of motor co-ordination. Her mood is labile, at one moment quite depressed, tears flowing, at the next moment she is joking and gay.

Callie Kakes

MENTAL DEFICIENCY: I, MENTAL DEFECTIVE WITH SEVERE PERSONALITY DISTURBANCE

CALLIE'S PROBLEMS began long before she was born. A by-product of sexual promiscuity, her history is so intimately enmeshed with that of her mother that one must begin with the story of Mrs. Kakes and the family from which she came.

Callie's mother was born in 1885 in Arkansas, one of four siblings. Her parents and paternal grandparents had all been alcoholics. In addition, both parents had suffered from tuberculosis, the father dying of it at the age of forty-six. As a young child, Mrs. Kakes herself had been physically well but subject to temper tantrums. She was obstinate, hard to manage, and when with other children extremely quarrelsome. She began school at six, staying out frequently because of family difficulties. In school she was considered less bright than the average. At thirteen she contracted scarlet fever, diphtheria, and rheumatic fever. At fifteen she left school, having reached the sixth grade. At about this same age her hitherto-persistent enuresis ceased. For the next few years she worked at odd jobs, all at an unskilled level. By the time she reached her twentieth birthday she had become sexually promiscuous, sometimes for gain, sometimes not. Before long she began to drink to excess. When she was twenty-three she married an itinerant laborer who had been discharged from the Army for alcoholism. Before long she left her husband to go to Florida, where she got a job at a hotel. While there she was intimate with a plumber, resulting in the birth of Callie. The year was 1911.

When Callie was six weeks old her mother placed her in a foster home, paying each week for her care. Shortly thereafter the mother again became illegitimately pregnant. Because of the difficulties associated with her previous abortions she did not dare attempt another. When this child was born, Mrs. Kakes gave him away for adoption.

In 1913, when one and a half years old, Callie first came to the attention of the state authorities. The woman with whom she had been left notified them that since she had not heard from the mother in seven weeks, the child was probably abandoned. When Mrs. Kakes was ultimately located by the authorities she denied having intended to abandon Callie; she had just been "looking for work." When contacted by the authorities, Mrs. Kakes's brother refused to help out because he considered his sister unbalanced. Eventually, however, at the age of three, Callie was discharged by the state to her mother.

Callie was always a sickly child, traceable perhaps as far back as her premature birth at seven and a half months. She was late in beginning to walk as well as in developing in other directions. Later, frequent illnesses combined with her mother's migratory inclinations to keep her out of school for long periods or forced her to move from one school to another. When Callie was five her mother remarried, this time to the owner of a small fishing boat in New Orleans. At about this same time Callie was operated on for a congenital torticollis. That same year she began her schooling in a small country school. At six she had severe whooping cough, following which she stayed in a tuberculosis camp for six months. The family shortly after moved to Missouri, where Callie was placed ahead into the third grade because of her age. When Callie was fourteen her stepfather died, following a cerebral accident. At this relatively late age she was just entering the fifth grade. At the end of the year her mother took her out of school, placing her in a doctor's home where Callie did household chores and answered the telephone in return for her keep. Mrs. Kakes, in the meantime, returned to Arkansas where she obtained work as a cleaning woman. At the end of two years she went back to Missouri to get Callie.

For the next year or so Callie shared a room with her mother in various rooming houses. From time to time they would move, following the work wherever it might be. Callie had no friends her own age, but this was not new for her; she had never in the past been able to make friends with the other children, partly because she and her mother had moved so frequently, and partly because, being not so quick as the other children, Callie easily became the butt of many of their jokes. She soon began to worry about her physical condition, complaining of many ills. Before long she became openly antagonistic toward her mother, one cause of which was her unhappiness in staying in her room during the day. At night when her mother came home Callie would give vent to violent temper tantrums. She also threatened her mother and at times even stole from her. After a while she began to spend most of her time hanging around outside of the local police station.

In the meantime Mrs. Kakes's health was failing. She was tired and sick. Occasionally she would have periods of excitement followed by periods of depression. More and more she worried about what would happen to Callie if she were not there to care for her.

At about this same time Callie spent a week in the County Hospital because of a pelvic inflammation. Because of her inability to respond appropriately to any questions she was given an intelligence test there, achieving at the time an I.Q. score of forty-six. Two weeks after her discharge Callie returned to the County Hospital, complaining of a recurrence of the same pains. Physical and neurological examinations were negative, but when a second intelligence test at this time had resulted in an I.Q. score of sixty-five Callie was recommended for commitment as feeble-minded. Partly because of this, but also because she herself was about to enter the hospital for surgery, Mrs. Kakes appealed to the state authorities for help in making sure Callie would be cared for. One month later Callie entered the County Home for Girls.

At the home Callie was well behaved, willing, and industrious, but worried constantly about her health. She exaggerated her ailments to such a degree that the matrons felt she was only looking for sympathy and attention. She was emotionally unstable, suggestible, and described as overaffectionate. At times she would become depressed, keeping to herself. Though tidy in her behavior, she was careless in her personal appearance, having to be spoken to about it from time to time. At one point she caused a stir by saying her menstrual period was overdue and wishing aloud she could have a baby. On examination this proved to be a false alarm. Much time and care were taken with Callie's general physical condition in the hope that with physical improvement she might also measure higher mentally. But Callie's physical misfortunes continued despite the care. During her third month at the home Callie was sent to the County Hospital for an appendectomy. Four days after her return she had a fall, ruptured the sutures, and again want to the hospital, this time to be operated on for intestinal adhesions.

In the meantime Callie's mother, Mrs. Kakes, was having problems of her own. During her convalescence from the gynecologic surgery she had become unco-operative on the ward, finally developing paranoid symptoms. After a period of observation, she was committed to State Hospital. There she was resistive and disturbed, refusing to get out of bed. She became profane and abusive toward the personnel. After a week she got up, dressed herself, but showed a staggering gait and inability to walk. She fell several times but did not hurt herself. No neurological basis could be found for this defect. As the weeks went by she became more disturbed, tearing her clothes and demanding to go home. Two months later she was still irritable, from time to time attacking other patients. At this time she showed no interest whatsoever in Callie whenever the name of her daughter was mentioned to her by the social worker.

Due to the mother's complete breakdown making it unlikely she would soon be home and her own emotional difficulties, Callie was finally committed to the Training School for the Feeble-minded. She was just seventeen at the time. When first examined at the Training School prior to her admission Callie had achieved an I.Q. of sixty-seven, but due to visual and emotional difficulties this was not felt to be representative of her true ability. However, from her history and general reactions the examining staff were certain she was feeble-minded, though not typical of the average mental defective usually seen. Complicating the whole picture was the suggestion of an incipient psychosis.

Physically Callie presented a picture of inferiority. She was five feet, three inches, weighing one hundred six pounds, and in general looked malnourished. Her thyroid gland was palpable and visible. Her head was microcephalic, five cm. smaller than average. Her face was asymmetrical. Her ears were of a simple pattern with adherent lobules. Her upper jaw projected, leading to poor occlusion. The palate was of a high-arch type. Her eyes were small and deep-set. Her hairline was low on her forehead. Her hands were moist and clammy, with evidence of nail-biting over a long period. As she talked there was an obvious lisp.

Immediately upon her admission to the school Callie continued to indulge in her disruptive behavior but to a far greater degree. She complained of being very weak, blaming it on being out of bed only two days. An examination at the time revealed no physical basis for her feelings of weakness. Three days later she complained of pain in her stomach and abdomen, saying she felt a "pulling" around the incision from her recent appendectomy. She vomited and was constipated. From time to time she cried hysterically, refusing food or medication from the matron, but accepting it when given personally by the physician. Because of the disturbing effect of this behavior on the other girls, as well as the tendency for some of the girls to excite Callie, she was sent to the school hospital. There she remained one week. During this time she seemed much more quiet, except when talking of ailments, at which time she would become excited. Despite urging she was quite reluctant to get out of bed during the daytime.

On her return from the hospital she again became excited, crying for long periods at a time without apparent cause. On one such occasion she screamed for hours, complaining of a bellyache. However, when the matron talked with her, she quieted down, said she had no pain, and soon dropped off to sleep. From time to time, in her chronically mournful voice, Callie would repeat her complaint of pain around her abdominal scar, insisting that the surgeon had left a sponge inside. She was not at all concerned with personal cleanliness, having to be coaxed to bathe or change her clothes. Many times she would make statements, usually complaints, that were purely imaginary in basis, but then deny having said such things should she later be questioned about them.

Callie continued in this fashion for the first year of her commitment, manifesting the willfulness and insecurities of a young child in a strange atmosphere. As in the past she did not get along with the other girls of her own age. In retaliation for being the butt of their jokes she frequently "squealed" on them, truthfully or otherwise, a practice that only furthered her estrangement. When Callie was asked about her mother she spoke of her at times as being dead; at other times she seemed to realize that Mrs. Kakes was in State Hospital.

At one point about halfway through that first year Callie became quite negativistic, refusing to speak to anyone or do as she was told. Instead, she cried loudly as she pushed furniture over. When she thought someone wanted the doors open, Callie would close them. She kicked out at anyone who came near to find out what was wrong. In desperation the matrons put her to bed for the afternoon, but it did not quiet her. She refused her meals, screaming she wanted something for her constipation. Yet when given a laxative she continued to scream and yell on into the night and the next day. This episode of excitement lasted for about a week, then subsided. At the end of that week she was taken off her regular kitchen duties to help care for the little children on the ward. This new duty was followed by a great change in her behavior. She became more co-operative, carrying out orders as they were given. She enjoyed playing with the younger children, occasionally vieing with them for attention from the matron, and, like them, was subject to quick changes of mood. In turn the matrons were becoming more adept at handling these tantrums. For example, early one evening Callie began to cry, holding her hands over her abdomen and complaining of pain. Soon the matron appeared on her way back from supper. Taking from her pocket a piece of candy she had saved from supper, she offered to share it with Callie. As she ate Callie became more friendly, forgot her pain, and made no further complaints.

During the second year of Callie's stay she began to have visits from her mother who had recently been paroled from State Hospital. Perhaps at this point we should temporarily leave Callie's story, going back to pick up the trail of Mrs. Kakes. As you will remember we had left her shortly after Callie's commitment to the Training School. At that time Mrs. Kakes was in State Hospital, acutely psychotic and not at all interested in her daughter. After about five months of violent behavior alternating with quiet periods during which she manifested difficulty in walking, Mrs. Kakes began to show improvement. She quickly put on weight, gaining twenty pounds in a few weeks. Finally she became agreeable and friendly enough to be put to work as a waitress in the patients' dining room. Three months later she escaped from the hospital by walking off the grounds, but was picked up a few hours later wandering around in a daze through downtown Little Rock. Three weeks later she again attempted to escape, climbing down a rope made of bedsheets. Halfway to the ground the "rope" broke, resulting in painful back injuries and an aggravated mental state. Two months later she became negativistic, refusing to eat. After some tube feedings she became more cooperative, but again developed a "paralysis" of the legs similar to that of a few months previous. From this state she again gradually improved so that one year later she was considered to be well enough to be paroled in the care of her brother. It is at this point that we found her beginning to visit Callie at the Training School.

At the time Mrs. Kakes began to visit the Training School Callie was behaving in a much more adjusted fashion. Though still somewhat "peculiar," she was not quite so prone to outbursts as she had been at first. Along with this change in her behavior was a more favorable attitude on the part of the matrons toward her. Which came first cannot at this point be determined, though the two were definitely related. The one area in which Callie had not improved was in her relations with the other girls. She frequently said disagreeable things to them or about them, yet at the same time couldn't understand why they should dislike her. Many times, when all the girls were supposed to be quiet, Callie would break out in uncontrollable giggling. She made it her business to be around whenever anyone entered her dormitory, trying to find out as much as she could about the person. Yet the conduct reports about her from school and physical-training classes were now almost uniformly good. However, while working as a waitress in the staff dining room she was at times reported for being noisy and boisterous. Her hypochondriacal complaints diminished greatly, although she frequently complained that she needed an operation on her nose because of a sinus condition.

During the next year, however, Mrs. Kakes continually agitated for permission for Callie to be allowed to come home for a visit with her. Just as consistently these requests were turned down by the school because of Mrs. Kakes's poor moral reputation. Still a good-looking, quite youthful-appearing woman, albeit of limited intelligence, Mrs. Kakes traveled around from hotel to hotel, working as a chambermaid by day and being promiscuous by night. From time to time she would send Callie little gifts.

Whether due to the pressure from her mother or in a passing moment of pique, Callie had a short-lived tantrum while helping with the decorations at Christmastime. For no apparent reason she threw herself on the floor, kicking and screaming. On the whole, though, she was now a very good worker at whatever job she was given. Whether she was cleaning rooms or washing dishes she was conscientious about her work. The more work she had, the happier she seemed to be. Her only difficulties occurred over assignment changes, at which times she would refuse to do the job, complaining of fatigue. Once on the job, however, whatever it might be, she soon became interested, quickly losing her fatigue.

Despite the school's insistence that Callie would not be able to adjust on the outside, Mrs. Kakes did not give up her attempts to get Callie back with her. Advised by a lawyer to propose a responsible person as Callie's guardian, she began to work on her brother. At her insistence he applied for Callie's discharge in his care. The request was turned down, not only on the basis of Callie's need for the protective environment of the institution but because investigation revealed the uncle to be in precarious economic straits, living in a congested, low-income area with three children of his own. Again Mrs. Kakes pleaded with her brother, until finally, against the advice of the school, he was willing to assume all legal responsibility for Callie. One week later, exactly three years after her commitment to the school, Callie was paroled to her uncle.

Four months later, in June, Callie's uncle reported he would no longer be responsible for her welfare. Shortly after going to live with his family she had found a job as a waitress, but after two days her uncle had asked her not to continue because the hours were long, the duties too strenuous. Since then she had had no job. Despite her being twenty years of age, her behavior was more like that of a child. She began to tell the neighbors her uncle and in fact all of her relatives were very wealthy despite his attempts to persuade her otherwise. Whenever he gave her some pocket money she would immediately spend it, then report that she had lost it. She also began to tell the neighbors that the distant relative who owned the house in which the uncle lived was destitute and had nothing to eat, his true circumstances, however, being quite the contrary. As time went on Mrs. Kakes began to visit her daughter, interfering with her care and resulting in Callie's becoming resistant to the demands of her uncle. Finally, Mrs. Kakes took her daughter away with her, telling the uncle they were going to work at a resort hotel in the southern part of the state. With all this interference the uncle felt it would be impossible for him to do anything with Callie.

Immediately the Training School social worker began to hunt for Callie and her mother, but to no avail. In September mother and daughter returned to the city, where they rented the basement of a decrepit tenement building. A few weeks later Mrs. Kakes again became ill, shortly thereafter having to enter County Hospital for abdominal surgery. Just before going to the hospital she and Callie again moved, this time to a boardinghouse, where Mrs. Kakes left Callie. Here the uncle finally was able to catch up with them. Horrified by the neighborhood and the evidence of drinking all about Callie, he begged the Training School to take her back. No longer able to care for her, he admitted he was wrong to have taken her out in the first place.

In the meantime, just before her uncle found her, Callie

had been going to the welfare agency, where she demanded to be taken care of. She began to have dizzy spells and feelings of weakness that she blamed on lack of food. In the course of many such visits to the agency Callie would faint in the social worker's office. Finally, because of her many physical complaints which had been fast increasing, Callie was sent to County Hospital. There she told the doctors of being left alone in the house with no food when Mrs. Kakes went to the hospital and of having fallen many times in the street because of the resultant weakness. Even when her mother had been with her Callie had always been hungry, chewing bread all day long. Yet, she boasted, weak as she was, she still kept the room clean and neat. Many tests were done on Callie at the hospital, but as each test proved negative, she would complain of pain in some other part of her body. At the end of the third week Mrs. Kakes reappeared on the scene, having herself recently come out of the hospital. With her was the social worker from the Training School who was ready to take Callie back with her. However, Callie refused to go with them, saying she was unable to walk. She still blamed this weakness in her legs on having been without food three weeks before.

Feeling sure Callie's difficulties were purely mental, the doctor had her transferred to the Psychiatric Institute for observation. There she appeared well oriented but of poor judgment. When taken to the lab, she had to be supported because of her continued difficulty in walking and fear of falling. Many times during the tests she burst into tears, sobbing she didn't want to go back to the Training School. For the first few days on the ward Callie was very noisy, refusing to be interviewed. After the third day she got out of bed and walked, although there were occasional days after that when she would refuse to walk at all. When something was said or done that displeased her, she reacted with periods of crying and prolonged periods of hyperpnea. Some days, when displeased, she refused to talk or eat, occasionally going through contortions in imitation of a convulsion but not typical of any. She was frequently noisy, calling out at any time of day or night. As before, she was markedly untidy and unconcerned with her personal cleanliness. Though the results of psychological tests at this time (I.Q. sixty-three) indicated borderline intelligence they were felt not to be representative because of suspected resistance on Callie's part. Instead, she was thought to be merely retarded. Neurological examinations were negative.

At this point a general staff meeting was held comprised of representatives of the Training School and hospitals involved. It was decided that Callie should be committed directly to State Hospital rather than returned to the Training School. Despite this decision the actual diagnosis was not so easily agreed upon. However, a diagnosis was necessary in order officially to close Callie's record at the Training School. After much discussion the decision was reached to have two diagnoses: one, held firmly by the superintendent, was that of "psychoneurosis, hysterical type"; the other, held by the rest of the staff, "psychosis with mental deficiency (moron)." Two weeks later, just before her twenty-first birthday, Callie was transferred to State Hospital.

In order to facilitate her removal to State Hospital Callie had been heavily sedated with paraldehyde, which resulted in her having to be carried into the ward. She slept the rest of that day and through the night. The following morning she awoke, confused and delirious, still under the influence of the paraldehyde. Shortly after she had what resembled an epileptic seizure. During this episode, which lasted only a minute or two, she shook all over, frothed at the mouth, and bit herself. She then complained of feeling the bed go up and down and tip from side to side. At one point she thought she was lying on the floor, the light coming from the floor rather than the ceiling. After this she was actively hallucinated during which she heard her mother's voice on the ward, then saw a physician giving "a white medicine" to the mother and two other women patients that caused them to fall dead.

On the following day she was quieter and clearer mentally. She had forgotten the hallucination, but was now sulking. During the next month Callie was much clearer, denying any hallucinations or delusions. However, she again began to show difficulty in walking, complaining of pain and limitation of movement, but the absence of fever raised official doubt as to the organicity of the symptoms. After a while her leg began to look cyanotic. When she attempted to walk she limped considerably, yet when she kicked at a chair in a moment of pique one day there was no apparent limitation of movement. For a brief period there was evident a slight swelling of the leg posteriorly but this quickly disappeared. When her leg complaints subsided, Callie began to have episodes of tantrum behavior.

Toward the end of the month Callie was moved to another building. Immediately she began to object loudly. She became very excited, breaking a chair and pounding on the window guard. She then threw herself down on the bed and went into what appeared to be a convulsive state. Her head and neck became rigid, and with her mouth wide open she uttered peculiar animal noises like "ah-ah-ah." She continued in this way for a half-hour. At times her eyeballs seemed to turn a little to the left, but both pupils were equal. Her left arm began to appear a little cyanotic. Then a peculiar tremor was noticed in that arm, beginning first in the thumb, then spreading to the whole hand, then gradually increasing to a more generalized jerking motion that lasted for half an hour. There seemed to be a little more coldness in the left hand than in the right. When a wet cloth was laid on her forehead, both pupils were equally dilated. When the cloth was removed, the pupils began to contract. Because of a distended abdomen she was given a high enema, the results of which showed her to have been quite constipated. After the enema she quieted down, becoming quite peaceful.

Following this episode Callie again complained of stiffness in her left leg and pain when she tried to walk. However, there was no evidence of swelling or heat from the affected limb. She continued to limp for the next two months. Besides her chronically sullen behavior she would occasionally have episodes of excitement during which she screamed and rolled on the floor. During such episodes she apparently had very good use of her affected leg. Nevertheless, X-rays were done, again with negative results. In addition Callie had special treatments and massage because of the cyanotic appearance of the leg. Gradually she showed some mental improvement from these treatments, at times talking a little more easily. In her movements she was still clumsy, frequently bumping her leg against various objects but not with enough force to hurt herself. Throughout all of this Callie gave the impression of craving sympathy and attention.

For the next six months, despite frequent complaints and occasional periods of excitement, Callie was for the most part adjusting fairly well. A psychological test at this time again gave her an intelligence rating of borderline intelligence (sixty-five). At a staff conference she answered questions willingly and well. When asked about her previously disruptive behavior she attributed it to being locked up, saying that as a child she was in panic when alone, frightened of any shadows she might see. In May Callie had her first menstrual period since her admission seven months before. Ever since the onset of menses at thirteen she had suffered from frequent menstrual disturbances, either dysmenorrhea or complete absence.

In August, because of her teasing some of the elderly woman patients on the ward, Callie was moved to another building. Again she became excited, angrily breaking a window on her first night there. Gradually, though, Callie was becoming easier to care for, doing her work as required. Her mother was away, working at a resort hotel but corresponding regularly. Each time a letter arrived Callie's spirits were markedly improved.

For the next six months Callie continued her previous adjustment, working as required but continually complaining of poor circulation in her extremities. Occasionally she indulged in a tantrum, particularly when moved through a change in job assignment or in residence. As winter came on Mrs. Kakes again began to demand that Callie be allowed to go with her on visit. Finally, the following February, Callie went home to her mother against the advice of the hospital. The plan was for Callie to visit with friends during the day while her mother was at work, then go home at night to sleep.

Five days later, at the height of a snowstorm, Callie showed up at Psychiatric Institute. She had started out for State Hospital but had lost her way. Conditions at home were not as the mother had represented them. Mrs. Kakes had been out of work for some time, borrowing money from friends in order to live. To avoid paying rent she had moved frequently from one neighborhood to another. Instead of allowing Callie to visit friends as planned, Mrs. Kakes had kept her locked in a room while she went off each day. After an initial period of confusion on her return to State Hospital Callie became co-operative and helpful on the ward. Worried at first about what she had done, her mind was much relieved when her mother came to visit her.

For the next nine months Callie presented no major problems. In view of her mother's financial condition she felt much better about being in the hospital. During the summer Mrs. Kakes again went out of town without first telling Callie. When her mother didn't appear on visiting days, Callie again became emotionally upset, but a letter from her mother explaining where she had gone quickly relieved her mind. In the fall, on her return to town, Mrs. Kakes again began agitating for Callie's being allowed out on visit. And so, once again, in November, two years after her commitment, Callie went home to her mother. This time, however, Mrs. Kakes was explicitly warned that should the police have to bring Callie back, she would not again be allowed out to her mother.

Three days later Callie voluntarily entered County Hospital for dysmenorrhea. After five days she returned home, then one month later again entered County Hospital with the same complaint. She was discharged four days later when no gynecologic pathology could be found. However, on the third day after this discharge she again entered County Hospital with the same complaint. All lab tests showed no pathology. At no time did she have a fever. So long as she was allowed to rest in bed undisturbed, Callie created no excitement, but whenever an attempt was made to get her out of bed she immediately went into a paroxysm of screaming and moaning. On one such occasion she threw herself on the floor; at another time she threatened to jump out the window. When the use of a bedpan was discontinued she withheld urination for twenty-four hours, making it necessary to catheterize her. By then the County Hospital was ready to ask for her commitment, not knowing Callie was at the time a patient out on visit from State Hospital. Mrs. Kakes wanted to take Callie home with her, but Callie insisted on staying in the hospital. Finally, at the end of her sixth week there, the hospital was able to persuade Callie to go home with her mother.

Two days later Callie got herself admitted to a hospital in the next county. Again physical examinations, including X rays and lumbar puncture, were negative. She complained constantly of leg pains and headaches, which the staff soon found could be relieved with the injection of a sterile hypodermic. At times she became so excited that restraint was necessary. However, when at the end of three weeks she was told she would be committed, Callie left against advice, quietly, and walking normally. Two days later she was in another hospital, the State Infirmary for the Poor. In three days she was transferred to the psychiatric observation ward because of emotionalism and a tendency to expose herself. While on the medical ward she had been noisy, crying, and talking loudly, then wandering through the corridors where she exposed herself. It had become necessary to use drugs to calm her.

During all of this Mrs. Kakes was busy trying to dissuade the hospital from keeping Callie. She pointed out how much her daughter enjoyed being in a hospital, so much that on previous occasions Callie would either herself or with the aid of a neighbor call for an ambulance "just to surprise me when I got home and find she's in the hospital." When Callie's difficulty in walking was mentioned, Mrs. Kakes angrily exclaimed: "She walks as good as I do. I don't believe there's anything really wrong with her."

Despite the mother's pleas Callie was kept on the observation ward. She continued to expose herself, was assaultive when the nurses tried to take her temperature, and had a typical hysterical episode with convulsions, muscular contractions, and noisiness. Attacks of excitement followed her being crossed in the slightest or when minor changes in treatment were made. Physical and neurological examinations were again negative. Though she had no hallucinations or delusions, she was difficult to care for because of her excitement, wandering at night, noisiness, resistiveness, and use of foul language.

One morning about a month later Callie suddenly began to cry for no apparent reason. She tore off her clothes, throwing them about the ward. Climbing on a window sill, she pounded on the guard screen, shouting loudly all the while. She refused all food, and was finally put in a cold pack. She continued to shout and roll from one side of the bed to the other, at times hanging her head over the bed, at times pounding her head against the bed. When taken from the cold pack she groaned and pounded her head hard against the wall. She refused all medications. That night she again was noisy, shouted, pounded the window, and exposed herself. The next day she refused to get up to have her bed made, had to be lifted into a chair, and refused to wash. Physical examination revealed the onset of menstrual flow.

One week later Callie was transferred to Fairview State Hospital for a month's observation. Though her first three days there were marked by agitated depressive periods she responded well to wet packs and sedatives, gradually becoming quiet, reasonable, and co-operative. For the remainder of the month her behavior was above reproach, though she was again walking with a limp and favoring her right side. No psychotic symptoms were manifested. Despite her being closely confined on a ward of relatively deteriorated patients, Callie kept herself under good control. At the staff conference Callie admitted that her previous behavior had been used chiefly to gain attention, claiming she had been perfectly conscious of her acts and able to control them. Now she wanted to be released to her mother. But this was impossible since by now Mrs. Kakes had again taken off for parts unknown. As Callie was considered to be not committable at this time, she was returned to the State Infirmary.

No sooner had she reached the infirmary than her previous bizarre behavior reasserted itself. On the first night she loudly and forcefully refused to sleep. The next night she screamed and yelled so loudly that she frightened the other patients, keeping them awake a good part of the night. When the staff had just about decided it was impossible to care for Callie at the infirmary, information finally came to light about her still being officially a patient at State Hospital. When confronted with this and threatened with prosecution Callie blamed it all on her mother. It was her mother, she said, who had told her not to say anything about her old commitment. With a sigh of relief the staff sent her back to State Hospital, despite Callie's objections.

In the car that was taking her to State Hospital Callie was obstreperous and resistive, threatening to escape. After her admission she was crying but co-operative. Though she made many vague threats she said she would not be noisy if only the hospital could make her happy. On the ward she was resistive and quick to irritation, with many somatic complaints. She blamed her tantrums at the infirmary on having been nervous and frightened whenever her door was locked. Her mood was quite depressed, due in part to not knowing where her mother might be and in part to feeling that her return when not quite twenty-four years of age meant there was not much hope for her.

For the next four months Callie's behavior on the ward was above reproach. There was no evidence of mental confusion but she remained quiet and depressed, with occasional periods of crying. Repeatedly she wrote to friends on the outside for news of her mother's whereabouts, but to no avail. Finally, in October, Mrs. Kakes showed up to visit her daughter. Almost immediately Callie was in better humor. Soon she began playfully to tease other patients. But in November, for no apparent reason, Callie suddenly became quite depressed and restless again. She complained about not eating well. At night she was noisy and unable to sleep. Despite heavy sedation her depressed mood persisted. For the next two months Callie had many vague bodily complaints. She again began to complain of numbness and pains in her right leg and once again X-ray results were negative. In February her leg complaints stopped, but in their place came markedly disturbed behavior. She cried loudly and from time to time pounded her head against the wall. Soon it became necessary to put her in restraint for her own protection. In two weeks her behavior improved almost as suddenly as it had come on. She got out of bed one day, dressed herself, and on the whole was quieter and more cheerful. Soon she began to go out walking with her mother on visiting days, returning to the ward each time in good spirits. And once again Mrs. Kakes began to ask about taking Callie home on a visit. Because of Callie's being underweight as well as emotionally unstable the hospital advised against the request. For the next two months Callie showed gradual physical improvement but had frequent sudden changes in mood. From being cheerful she would quickly change to crying, complaining about never being able to go home again.

In the latter part of May, disregarding advice of the staff, Mrs. Kakes took her daughter home on a visit. One week later she brought her back. On leaving the hospital Callie had gone to stay with a cousin but soon complained of not feeling well, and had asked to be taken back to the hospital. Now Mrs. Kakes felt it might be better to take Callie out for a few hours at a time rather than for any extended visit. Though Callie had complained of being sick when she came into the hospital that day she was unable to describe any symptoms. That same evening she became quite disturbed, pounding her head against the wall. Again restraint became necessary. After a couple of days in wet packs she got over her excitement, but within two days again became agitated and had to be returned to the wet packs. A few days later she was again calm.

Early one evening in July Callie impulsively slapped another patient. When one of the other patients came to the defense of this girl, Callie ridiculed and taunted her about her mental condition. Whereupon she struck Callie in the back, severely enough to require attention.

For the rest of that year Callie continued in this fashion. At times she would lie on the floor in a childlike tantrum. On three occasions she was attacked by other patients. She increased her physical complaints, whining as she asked the physician for medication. Should he not give her medication when she asked for it, she went to sleep on the floor or climbed up on the guard rail of the porch. She accumulated a number of bumps on her head from hitting it against the door or throwing herself on the floor. During her menstrual periods she suffered from dysmenorrhea, complaining frequently. Her only happy moods came when her mother occasionally took her out for the afternoon.

During the next two years Callie was still complaining. Because of her antagonizing the other patients by pulling their hair or slapping their faces, she was from time to time attacked by them. On one occasion she was thrown across a bed and kicked in the abdomen by a disturbed patient. During her own agitated periods Callie would be abusive and self-mutilative, with occasional threats of suicide. When treated for a physical illness or being X-rayed she was invariably unco-operative. Because of her whining and morale-disturbing behavior Callie was frequently moved from one building to another, each move being followed by agitation and banging her head against the bed or wall.

In 1940, after a period of poor eating, weight loss, and fever of undetermined origin, Callie was found to have tuberculosis. For six months she remained in the tuberculosis building, her mood predominantly depressed. When she was transferred out of it on recovery, she again had a short period of agitation. But during the next five years Callie began to improve. With much coddling she worked fairly well at a variety of jobs, though she continued actively to seek sympathy. She particularly enjoyed the authority that came with some of her jobs. Fewer and fewer times did she fall or close a window on her hand. And as Callie improved so did the attitude of the matrons toward her.

In 1948 she was making a good adjustment at work but not on the ward. Almost every night she would become disturbed during which time she broke glasses and windows. She was forever complaining. She felt that certain persons "have it in for me and are after me." She carried tales back and forth. Often she would come to the physician's office with tears in her eyes but a bit of pampering soon made them disappear. She referred to herself as a little girl. On one occasion she was offered transfer to the parole ward, usually a preparatory stage to leaving, but she refused because "I might commit suicide."

Toward the end of 1949 Callie again began to lose weight, becoming at the same time somewhat excitable. Though she refused to eat the regular hospital fare, it was noticed that she never refused to eat ice cream, cookies, or cake. She continued in this way for the next five months, eating very little. In frequent periods of mild excitement she called the staff by bad names, complaining of not getting enough attention. Whereupon she would sob like a child. Physical, laboratory, and X-ray examinations at this time were uniformly negative.

In the middle of 1950 a new pathologist came to the lab, a motherly, understanding woman who quickly became interested in Callie as a person. Gradually Callie's spirits began to improve. Her job in the lab became more and more important to her. In an effort to make herself indispensable she began to hide gloves, towels, and other equipment so that the technicians would have to come to her to find them. In the morning, neatly dressed and clean, she would be at the lab long before the others arrived. Throughout all this, however, Callie had not given up her somatic complaints, resulting in many X-rays and other studies all of which proved negative. Despite her normal E.E.G. of four years ago, and another at this time with similar findings, Callie now began to insist she had epilepsy. She demanded and received dilantin, but was observed throwing it into a wastebasket when she thought no one was looking. She bumped her head at times to show evidence of a seizure, then began to make facial grimaces she hoped would be interpreted as a nervous tic. Yet none of this behavior took place in the lab, being reserved for when she was back in the dormitory each night. At the lab she tried hard to be considered a member of the staff, but seemed to resent the fact that she was the only unpaid worker. From time to time she would not go to lunch in the patients' cafeteria, openly expecting the technicians to share their lunches with her. Though they were frequently irritated by Callie, Dr. Lasker, the pathologist, each time calmed the troubled waters.

In May 1951, as part of an attempt to wean Callie away from the hospital with a view to outside placement, she was transferred to another dormitory, and relieved of her laboratory job. Immediately Callie was in a furor. She resisted the transfer so strongly that it took four men to carry her into her new quarters. During her first day there she received a total of twenty-eight grains of sodium amytal, but it seemed to have no effect at all. Throughout the day she had many hysterical seizures during which she could feel no pain but was able to control the rate and intensity of the seizures and all bodily movements. Though she feigned unconsciousness during the seizures, it was obvious that she could hear and understand the physician as he repeatedly told her she would have to adjust to the new building. For the next two days she continued to be excited, frequently requiring bed restraint during the day and sedation at night. She smashed a total of six windows, in the process of which she cut both wrists. She refused to eat but soon changed her mind when threatened with tube feedings. On the fourth day Callie ended her disturbed behavior as suddenly as she had begun. Her request now for ground privileges was granted, but only after she had agreed to work wherever she might be placed.

In July of that same year Callie was allowed home on a visit with her mother. That evening she reappeared at the hospital, saying she was not satisfied with her mother's apartment and demanding to be taken back. In August the hospital arranged for Callie again to go out on a visit, this time to a family in a nearby suburb with whom she was to live as a domestic. But on the following day she came back complaining that the woman had not only worked her too hard but had not given her enough to eat. Besides, she complained, "I was lonely." In October the same thing occurred. Callie again returned on the day after being placed with another family. Her reasons were the same as before. She had been lonesome and had not been given enough to eat.

Toward the end of the year Callie again became depressed and excited, this time quite severely. Over a period of five weeks she was given six electro-shock treatments, at the end of which her depression was markedly relieved. She became much quieter, more co-operative, and soon went back to work. During the following spring she made three overnight visits to her mother, with no difficulties on any of these occasions. She soon returned to her old job in the lab, where she again appeared happy. She was neat, friendly, and co-operative. Her mood remained cheerful, her somatic and other complaints dwindling. When asked about her future plans she bluntly stated that she preferred to stay in the hospital.

Two years later Callie was called in for a psychometric examination. She was apprehensive from the start about being tested, stating immediately in a worried fashion: "I hope this doesn't mean that I'm going to be sent somewhere. I don't want to be out of here." During the examination she responded rapidly to questions, talking readily and at length in her test answers and on her own initiative. She reacted somewhat impulsively to the test problems, working hard but tending to give up most readily on problems with which she had difficulty. She wrote and read adequately, spelled poorly, and performed simple additions and subtractions by counting on her fingers. Her speech and actions were appropriate throughout. Despite the examiner's attempts at reassurance, she remained apprehensive and ill at ease. At the end of the examination she made a final tearful plea that the test not be used to "send me anywhere." Test results on the Wechsler-Bellevue Intelligence Scales were Verbal I.Q., seventy-five, Performance I.Q., ninety, Full Scale I.Q., eighty, placing her between borderline and dull normal intelligence.

Callie is now a graying woman of forty-four, "tomboyish" in dress, manner, and physique. She is still working in the lab, assuming responsibility for seeing that it is orderly and clean. She still hides equipment so that the others will have to come to her with their needs. She considers the autopsy room her domain, allowing no one else to clean it up. It is Dr. Lasker's boast that she now has the cleanest, most orderly autopsy room in the state of Arkansas.

The relationship between Callie and Dr. Lasker is strong, with Callie jealously seeing to it that no one else is able to get close to her supervisor. At times her habit of eavesdropping or spying when Dr. Lasker has visitors becomes annoying, but if reprimanded Callie will sulk all day. Any expression of approval or appreciation by Dr. Lasker will make Callie beam. Aware of this need on Callie's part, Dr. Lasker is lavish with praise. Occasionally, when an autopsy is unexpectedly required on a Sunday, Callie will let Dr. Lasker sleep late, then call to tell her to come to the autopsy room. There Dr. Lasker will find all preparations made, the instruments laid out and the cadaver on the table.

Callie's relations with the lab technicians are not so smooth as with Dr. Lasker, partly due to her tendency to try to boss them. She continues to sit in the lab during the lunch period, making the other girls uncomfortable because they hadn't planned to share their lunch with her. When the salary checks are given out each payday, Callie will jokingly ask: "Where is my check?" Yet the other girls respect her for her hard work and the long hours she voluntarily puts in. When other physicians call the lab for information it is Callie, out of all the girls, who usually is able to tell them what they want to know. It is now a standing joke with some of them to tell Dr. Lasker: "Whenever I want to know anything I call your feeble-minded assistant." And at Christmastime and other holiday occasions it is Callie who is the "life of the party," joking and clowning before the other girls.

Callie has achieved a peculiar role within the hospital. She shares an "apartment" on the grounds with another girl, which makes her much happier than when she lived in a dormitory. Whenever any administrative move is contemplated concerning other patients, Callie somehow finds out about it. Though Dr. Lasker doesn't ordinarily attend the regular staff conferences, Callie soon tells her what has transpired. "How she does this I don't know," says Dr. Lasker in wonderment. And when another patient has been attacked, or when the police suspect that an attack on the outside was committed by a patient from the hospital, Callie will in each case tell Dr. Lasker who she thinks the culprit was. A couple of months later investigations confirm Callie's statements. Occasionally Callie becomes a little too bossy in the lab, or gets into an argument with one of the other girls. A remark from Dr. Lasker that maybe Callie ought to work elsewhere will immediately bring peace and quiet.

On weekends Callie visits relatives in nearby suburbs. Many of these trips require frequent streetcar and subway changes, but Callie seems to have no difficulty with them. "The way she dresses and behaves when she goes out each weekend you'd never guess she was a patient," marvels Dr. Lasker.

But should any member of the hospital staff mention the possibility of Callie's someday leaving the hospital for good, she quickly becomes sulky, upset, and withdrawn, "just another patient."

Fanny Staggles

MENTAL DEFICIENCY: II, MENTAL DEFECTIVE INSTITUTIONALIZED

THE CONSTITUTIONAL ODDS were against Fanny from the moment of her conception. Hers was a premature birth at six months, the last of seven pregnancies. Of Mrs. Staggles's first four pregnancies, two had ended in miscarriages, one in a still birth, one in an infant who lived only a few hours. At the time of Fanny's birth her father was forty-four, her mother thirty-eight and seriously ill with pneumonia. Fanny spent the first three months of her life in an incubator, being fed by medicine dropper. When she was six months old she became quite ill with pneumonia, and for a while was not expected to survive. About a year later she developed whooping cough.

By the time Fanny was two years old the family had noticed her backwardness in all phases of development. Her first teeth had begun to appear when she was a year old. She began to walk between the ages of two and three, and did not talk until she was almost four. After the first grade Fanny spent the rest of her school years in special classes. When tested at the age of eight years, eight months, Fanny was found to have a mental age of six years, two months, giving her an I.Q. score of seventy-one (Binet). She learned very slowly though she was able to make some progress in the domestic skills taught her. Finally, at sixteen, Fanny was legally able to stop her schooling. By this time she had become interested in cooking, and was even able to prepare a meal though she required supervision while doing it. At home she did much of the housework while Mrs. Staggles was away working, although her carelessness frequently made it necessary for her mother to do the cleaning all over again when she came back from work.

There was very little opportunity for Fanny to make social contacts with others of her own age, since she spent most of her time at home with her family. Her only girl friend had been another member of the special class at school, whom Fanny no longer saw after leaving school. With younger children Fanny felt more comfortable, though she was apt to become impatient with them and slap them. When she was teased by the older children, Fanny was ready to fight it out with her fists. She was a very sensitive girl, ever conscious of the differences between herself and her two older, normal sisters. Perhaps because of this she was subject to wide mood swings, now quiet and calm, now nervous, irritable, and crying about being picked on. Yet when shown friendliness and kindness by an adult, Fanny was quick to respond.

When Fanny was eighteen and a half her mother again took her to the school clinic for evaluation. At this time she achieved a mental age of nine years and an I.Q. score of fifty-six (Binet). One month later, at the request of Mrs. Staggles, Fanny was admitted to the State Training School. In marked contrast to her mother, who was a well-dressed, poised woman, Fanny presented a picture of inferiority. Her face was asymmetrical, with a nose that deviated to the left, a broad, high forehead, large, simple-patterned ears with no lobules, prominent frontal bossae, and spaced incisor teeth. She had a high, narrow palate and a tongue that protruded in the midline. Her hands were moist and hypotonic with long, slender fingers. Physical examination revealed a soft systolic murmur at the apex of the heart.

Two weeks after her admission Fanny told her matron she had had her last menstrual period four months before. Because of Fanny's difficulty in handling time relationships, the matron paid no attention to her statement. Two days later a letter was received from one of her sisters asking whether Fanny might be pregnant. When asked about this she said she "got in trouble" with a boy while working in a neighbor's home at the time. On another occasion, Fanny went on, while she and her family were in another town, "I got in trouble with another one," the brother of a girl Fanny was later to meet as a fellow resident of the State School. Somewhat concerned about her missed periods, Fanny had written her brother-in-law about it, asking for his advice. He had apparently told Fanny's sister, which prompted the letter to the school. When questioned further, Fanny became uncertain as to just when she had had her last period, but whether this was due to her general lack of conception of time or her unwillingness to tell could not be determined.

On the following day Mrs. Staggles appeared in response to the news, very much upset, but uncertain as to what to do. Two days later she returned, this time indignant over what she was sure was a mistaken diagnosis. She knew for a fact that Fanny had had her periods. At the hospital's suggestion Mrs. Staggles took Fanny out for the day in order to seek an independent diagnosis, but when they returned late that afternoon it was found that Mrs. Staggles had had something else in mind. Instead of taking Fanny to a physician, she had taken her to confront the boy involved, and succeeded in getting from him a confession of his responsibility. Despite this, Mrs. Staggles refused to demand that they be married.

Five months later a girl was born to Fanny Staggles at the Community Hospital. When the time came for Fanny to return to the school she sobbed out her unhappiness. Repeatedly she asked would she be able to see the child, could she write the nurses in charge of the child, and what should she say to the other girls at the school. Patiently it was explained to Fanny that she would not be able to see the child but might make inquiries about her welfare through Mrs. Staggles. This procedure, they explained, not only was what the law demanded, but also in the long run would be better for both Fanny and the child. As far as the girls at the school were concerned, Fanny was to say absolutely nothing to them of the whole affair.

For the next two years Fanny worked at various jobs around the school, at none of which was she especially satisfactory. Nor had her general mood improved. She was particularly abusive to Mrs. Staggles when the two were out for the afternoon, returning to the school each time in an agitated state. Following one such occasion, when Fanny had been especially disturbed, using foul language and accusing her mother of keeping her locked up, Mrs. Staggles herself became upset. Marching into the director's office, she demanded to know the condition of Fanny's mind and the reason why her daughter was so irritable. Questioning of the mother, however, revealed that on these monthly outings with her daughter she would first take Fanny home, then to see the baby where she was being boarded. It was then explained to Mrs. Staggles how unwise this was, and why it was so disturbing to Fanny. Furthermore, should Mrs. Staggles continue to do this she would no longer be permitted to take her daughter out for the day.

At about this time Fanny was given another psychological examination, in which she achieved a mental age score of ten years, two months, and an I.Q. of sixty-four (Binet). As she sat there, her expression dull, she seemed to be paying attention to all the questions but was slow to think and to respond. The quality of her performance was variable, seeming "very stupid" in spots. On concrete items she was poor, and though fair on verbal abstractions, did not in her performance seem as relatively bright as her score would indicate. She was pleasant and untroubled by obvious errors. Because of the marginal quality of her responses her work at times was difficult to score.

During the next two years Fanny continued in her indolent way at the institution, going out once a month with her mother. Each summer Mrs. Staggles arranged her own vacation so that Fanny was able to leave the school to be with her for the entire period. Despite the constant attention and encouragement Mrs. Staggles gave her daughter, Fanny continued to upset her mother whenever the two were together. It was only on the extended summer visits that Fanny seemed to be somewhat happier. During the rest of the year Mrs. Staggles had a very unhappy time whenever she visited her daughter. Fanny would be depressed, crying all during the visit. At one time Mrs. Staggles became so frustrated that she walked out on her, saying she wouldn't stay if

Fanny was going to cry all the time. Mrs. Staggles continued to feel guilty about Fanny's being at the school, wondering aloud to the social worker if Fanny was getting worse instead of better and even whether she had done wrong in not letting Fanny marry the boy four years ago. Of course, she mused, these moods were not entirely new though they now seemed more severe, for Fanny had always been an "introvert." When she used to take her for a ride Fanny never saw the beauties of nature, and when she occasionally pointed out to her a pretty flower Fanny would just glance at it and say nothing.

On one extended visit home, not "liking her looks" at the time, Mrs. Staggles had forced food on Fanny to "build her up." Fanny must work pretty hard at the school, she thought. But her attempt to fatten her up was unsuccessful, for on her return Fanny was found to have lost a pound. Just before leaving home to return Fanny upset her family by saying the father of her child had been to see her with an offer of marriage. Mrs. Staggles was up in arms about his being allowed to visit, but on complaining to the director found it all to have been a hoax, a figment of Fanny's imagination.

During the next year Fanny contracted the measles, then later chicken pox. Occasionally she stayed in bed for a few days at a time complaining of a cough or other symptom, but with no rise in temperature. On each of these occasions she was suspected of using her complaint as an excuse for not going to work. A staff evaluation at the end of her fifth year at the school described her as neat and attractive, getting along fairly well. She was shy, inclined to be lazy and quarrelsome, and required constant supervision. If corrected for her poor work performance she was more likely than not to go to bed for a few days. Her speech was still markedly defective, her mood predominantly depressed. Though she complained frequently of being too tired or sick to work, she never missed any of the regular amusements at the school.

During the next five years Fanny continued in the same careless, lazy manner. Occasionally she spent her spare time reading or doing embroidery work. Except for frequent colds and aches in her legs during menstrual periods, her health was generally good. At one point, due to Fanny's insistence, Mrs. Staggles tried to get her released from the school. But when it was found that both parents were working and could give Fanny none of the required supervision, the request was turned down. And Mrs. Staggles again had the unhappy job of trying to explain to Fanny why she had to remain despite her being a grown woman of twenty-six.

The following year Fanny was again tested, and again she was vague and inexact in her thinking. Completely lacking in initiative, her successes were consistently on those items commonly found easy by retarded individuals. Her score was a mental age of ten years, seven months, and an I.Q. of sixty-six (Binet). The only change was a hint of graciousness in her bearing that had not been there on prior occasions.

When Fanny was twenty-eight she was given her first chance at an outside work placement. She was now a very slim, fairly well-developed brunette woman, in good health, and fairly attractive. During the interview in which she was told of her possible parole her ordinarily listless, unenthusiastic attitude gave way to eagerness. With tears in her eyes she said she wanted more than anything else to go out. "I promise to do my best." Three days later, as a temporary placement, Fanny was paroled to a job in a private guesthouse to replace another parolee who was on her summer vacation. For the first few days her employer was quite discouraged with Fanny, who just couldn't seem to do anything well, making it necessary for the woman to do it over. The social worker tried to explain to the employer that in addition to Fanny's being naturally slow she was so tense and apprehensive lest she not succeed at her first job that she just wasn't able to function well. Another disturbing factor was the confusion of transients coming and going over the weekends. Within three weeks, however, Fanny began to improve as she became less apprehensive, showing for the first time some initiative. However, when the other girl came back, Fanny had to return to the school, the plans for her permanent placement in the meantime having fallen through.

The following month Fanny was placed with a private family to whom she immediately felt attracted. Though still apprehensive about succeeding, she worked hard and willingly. To add to her joys she now had a room and bath all to herself. For the next two years she stayed with the same family, gradually losing her apprehensiveness. Outside of frequent visits to her mother she felt no need for making further social contacts. On her day off she would shop or go to the movies alone. Once in a while the social worker brought with her one of Fanny's friends from the school. While the social worker and the employer talked on the terrace the two "girls" chatted constantly over a picnic lunch under a tree.

One problem that recurred was Fanny's lack of judgment regarding the handling of money. Since most of her salary was deposited for her by her employer, Fanny occasionally used her mother's charge account to buy gifts for the family with whom she was living. At one Christmas she spent more for gifts than she made in a month's work, realizing it only after the charge slips came a month later. Despite her employer's attempt to teach her, Fanny just couldn't understand the value of money.

At the beginning of her second summer on parole Fanny was transferred to another family for the next three months. In the fall she was to rejoin the first family on their return from a long trip. In her new job Fanny was to help out at a private rest home while the wife and children of the owner vacationed at the seashore. Within a few weeks there Fanny ran into difficulties. In a call to the hospital demanding Fanny's immediate removal, the wife accused her of making advances to her husband who had been left behind to run the resthouse. The social worker made a hurried visit to the home. There the woman's mother made the same serious accusations, adding that Fanny had followed her son-in-law about to the point of annoying him. She was especially apprehensive lest Fanny say anything to the neighbors. "Such a girl could make statements that would hurt a man's character!" When the social worker asked why the man had not reprimanded Fanny and sent her back to her job in the kitchen, his mother-in-law quickly became irritated and demanded to know if she were inferring that he had behaved in an improper way. When Fanny was called into the room, she was dazed with fright. As if about to faint, she turned pale and had to sit down on the bed. At first she seemed unable to move when the social worker suggested she pack her things, but after this suggestion was repeated she moved about as if her mind were elsewhere. On the way back to the school Fanny sat quietly in the car, showing no emotion as she refused to answer any questions.

When called to the office the next day, Fanny seemed more like herself. She was less frightened and looked rested. Much patient questioning revealed that Fanny had found the man attractive, and had spent much time talking to him when he was in the house. Reluctantly, as if not wanting to blame him, she finally admitted he had made some advance to her. Though she admitted having once kissed him when they had met in the kitchen, she denied any more serious behavior between them.

On the basis of Fanny's story it was decided to keep her at the school for the rest of the summer and also to remove the other parolee who was working at the rest home. A few days later the husband and wife came to the school to protest the action. Though the social worker attempted diplomatically to blame Fanny's familiarity with the husband on the wife's being away from the home, the husband said he was to blame for letting Fanny feel she could overstep her position and take advantage of his friendliness. At this point the social worker made it clear that though Fanny was to be blamed, in the case of retarded individuals more of the responsibility rested with the employers.

In the fall Fanny was paroled back to the same family for whom she had previously worked for such a long time. She was overjoyed about going out again, particularly to the people with whom she had been so happy in the past. She immediately fell in love with their new home in the country, and at Christmastime didn't even want to visit her mother lest she miss the old-fashioned country Christmas at her new home. But this lasted only a year, for the next fall the family decided that since the children were now grown there was no longer need for extra help. After a parting marked by tears on the part of both Fanny and the woman for whom she had worked, Fanny was taken back to the school.

Fanny is now a woman of thirty-five, though psychologically much younger. She has just gone to another placement, this time to work at a summer resort. Though happy to be going to the seashore to work, she is particularly overjoyed—"like a little girl"—because two other parolees from the school will be working next door. What will happen in the fall seems to be the school's problem at this point, not Fanny's.

Clarence O'Rourke

MENTAL DEFICIENCY: III, MENTAL DEFECTIVE RETURNED TO THE COMMUNITY

When Mrs. O'Rourke was returned to Women's Prison for continued neglect of her family, the state authorities took the four youngest children out of the home. Clarence, aged thirteen, and his three younger siblings were sent to foster homes. Before very long it was noticed that though Clarence was trustworthy and helpful in the foster home, he was not able to keep up with children his own age when it came to learning new tasks. When examined at one of the traveling school clinics he was found to have an I.Q. of sixty-nine (Binet). He had gone as far as the sixth grade in school but hadn't been able to do the work there. A sensitive boy, on one occasion he had become ill when chastised by the teacher for not being able to do his lessons. Application was now made for Clarence to enter the State Training School. Two years later, just after he had turned fifteen, Clarence was able to enter the school, filling the first vacancy that had occurred.

Clarence's family had been a problem to the local agencies for many years. Three years before the birth of Clarence Mr. O'Rourke made his first visit to the State Children's Bureau. Because of poor health he had had to take a job working out of doors in another state. On his return he had found his wife had run off with his brother, taking with her their year-old baby. From the other children he had learned that their uncle had lived at the house during his absence and "had slept in the same room with their mother." When the mother had been located she agreed to return home, since Mr. O'Rourke was quite willing to take her back. His brother, however, remained behind to pay up the bills he and Mrs. O'Rourke had contracted.

The family stayed together, albeit with much bickering, for the next eleven years. When Clarence was eight years old Mrs. O'Rourke was brought to court for neglect of her children. In an attempt to keep the family together the judge at that time placed her on probation. Eight months later she again deserted her family. After being located she was this time sent to Women's Prison. A few months later she was paroled, due in great part to Mr. O'Rourke's pleas for her. Two and a half years later she again disappeared. After a period of heavy drinking and promiscuity with many of the town's undesirables she was finally located in an apartment she was sharing with two men. She was then returned to Women's Prison to serve out her prior sentence.

Throughout all this Mr. O'Rourke had tried to keep the home together. A quiet, meek man, he had over the years been chronically upset and nervous over his wife's behavior. Of limited mental ability and initiative, Mr. O'Rourke was overwhelmed by his domestic difficulties. Nevertheless, each time his wife deserted him he did his best, with the help of the older daughters, to manage the house and the young children. The family had been able in this way to get along fairly well each time until Mrs. O'Rourke's return. Following one of her returns, Mr. O'Rourke had become depressed to the point where he took an overdose of barbiturates. After a month in the State Hospital he was able to return home. Unlike his wife, Mr. O'Rourke did not drink. But instead of its being a helpful factor it served only to upset Mrs. O'Rourke. She constantly quarreled with him, blaming her frequent departures on her not being able to stand his "sanctimonious" air.

Six months after his wife had been sent back to Women's Prison Mr. O'Rourke was badly injured in a serious accident while working on a construction job. For the rest of the year he remained in the hospital. At first the social agencies were going to remove the children from the home, but postponed any action when, at Mr. O'Rourke's request, the two older girls, ages nineteen and fifteen, agreed to keep the home together. At the same time Mr. O'Rourke extracted from the younger children their solemn promise "to behave."

Just to make sure things went along all right the social agency and the local chief of police planned to maintain close contact with the family. Within a week the older girl began to quarrel with the other children, stayed out late each night, and finally left to stay with some relatives in another state. The fifteen-year-old girl didn't feel like staying home either. For a while she worked in a local grocery to help get food for the other children. As the situation became worse, Mr. O'Rourke again asked for his wife's release that she might care for the children. Within a month Mrs. O'Rourke was home, full of determination to do a good job. But her good intentions did not last very long. She soon began to drink at home with two women friends. Needing drinking money, she cashed the Soldiers' Relief checks to which her husband, as a World War I veteran, was entitled. The proceeds she spent on herself rather than on food for her children. Instead of remaining at home with her children she spent more and more time, day and night, with disreputable companions of both sexes. Three months later she again disappeared. When the children were this time brought before the court as "neglected," the four youngest were turned over to the state. It was at this point that we had begun this tale, when Clarence was thirteen.

Clarence had been the eighth of eleven pregnancies, with one miscarriage. Of these some were illegitimate, but because of the father's official acceptance of all his children one could not be sure just which ones they were. Two children were now dead, one of a fatal illness at ten, shortly before Mrs. O'Rourke's first "disappearance"; the other had been a World War II casualty. The rest of the O'Rourke children, however, merely added to the difficulties the community had been having with the parents. One brother drank heavily, was quarrelsome and unstable. At one point he had been in State Hospital, diagnosed as catatonia. A few years later he had married a "peculiar" girl from another disreputable family in town. The older sister mentioned earlier was described by the police as "boy crazy" and a poor influence on the younger children in the family. Another brother had been before the court three times on delinquency charges. The fifteen-year-old girl mentioned earlier had been fairly well balanced but couldn't get along with Mr. O'Rourke. Unlike the others, however, Clarence and his younger siblings had all made favorable impressions on the neighbors, almost as though they had been cut of different cloth. Nevertheless, of these latter, two besides Clarence were mentally retarded.

At the State School

Physical examination of Clarence on his arrival at the school revealed a fairly well developed, thin youth of fifteen, with facial acne, adherent ear lobes, and mottling of the extremities. There was evidence of an active rheumatic heart disease that he had had since his early teens. Otherwise his physical history was negative, except for the usual childhood diseases.

Clarence was placed in an advanced class for boys. A psychological examination at this time gave him an I.Q. of seventy-six (Binet). Throughout the examination he was rather nervous, but followed directions quite well. There was marked carelessness in his work as he constantly corrected and recorrected himself. In the classroom Clarence made good academic progress, his achievement ranging from low fifth-grade geography to high sixth-grade spelling. This would at first glance seem to be a high level of accomplishment for a retarded individual, but analysis of Clarence's work showed it to be based on rote learning. When asked to solve problems or deal with tasks based on reasoning he became nervous and incapable of continuing. In his relations with other boys he was self-conscious and lacking in confidence. Ordinarily he was polite and co-operative but could show a bad temper when aroused or thwarted.

About four months after Clarence's arrival at the school Mr. O'Rourke wrote to request his son's return home for the summer. Mrs. O'Rourke was now home on parole again after having spent another short period in Women's Prison. Both Mr.

and Mrs. O'Rourke felt Clarence would be able to get a summer farm job and so help out his family. Before answering Mr. O'Rourke the school asked a number of persons and agencies, including the local chief of police, to make another evaluation of the family situation. On the basis of these reports, some consisting merely of an emphatic "no!" Clarence was not allowed to go home.

According to the chief of police Mr. O'Rourke was still unable to work, hobbling around on crutches as a result of his accident. The only source of income was the weekly check from Soldiers' Relief. Mr. and Mrs. O'Rourke were still bickering, often late at night. On many such occasions the neighbors complained to the police, hoping to get the O'Rourkes evicted. Mr. O'Rourke was still having his problems with his wife's behavior and the companions she was likely to bring home with her. On occasion, unable to put up with this any longer, Mr. O'Rourke made a surreptitious phone call to the police, asking them to break up a drunken spree. The chief of police was now adamant that neither Clarence nor his younger siblings should be allowed back into the home. Not only were the parents a poor influence, he felt, but the older children were also behaving in ways that might be harmful to Clarence and the others.

Just to make sure that the chief had not been prejudiced in his report, the local child welfare agent made an unannounced visit to the O'Rourke home, a barren, poorly furnished tenement in a frame house. There at the time she found Mr. and Mrs. O'Rourke, the two older girls, and the daughter-in-law. Mrs. O'Rourke looked pale and "washed out," her face showing the ravages of prolonged dissipation. Though she immediately took the initiative in answering the social worker's questions, there was little force or spirit to Mrs. O'Rourke's conversation, except to denounce the chief of police whenever his name came up. Unlike his wife, Mr. O'Rourke remained quiet and reserved throughout the interview. The daughter-in-law, sitting dejectedly in a corner, impressed the worker as being herself of subnormal mentality.

Mrs. O'Rourke was adamant about Clarence's returning for the summer, the most cogent reason being her certainty that he would be able to find work and earn some money. When told she would first have to get permission from the chief of police, Mrs. O'Rourke became highly incensed. "I don't see why he should have anything to do with it. It isn't his affair." Mr. O'Rourke said nothing at all, except to express some satisfaction when told Clarence would be given vocational training while at the school.

For the rest of that year Clarence continued to do well at the school. He joined in the athletic games, soon taking part quite efficiently. He was still somewhat nervous, but adapted well and quite co-operatively to all training. His health remained quite good. In school his level of achievement was as good as his mental age level on most tasks, and even higher in reading, spelling, and writing. Despite the good impression he made on his teachers, causing them to consider him of borderline intelligence rather than feeble-minded, psychological testing at this time only confirmed the earlier findings. In the opinion of the psychologist it was felt that though his I.Q. rating might in the future rise from his present seventy-two (Binet), "it would only be a statistical variation, not a real improvement in capacity."

Six months later Clarence was again tested. On the Wechsler-Bellevue Scales he achieved the following scores: Full Scale I.Q., eighty-two, Verbal I.Q., eighty-six, Performance I.Q., eighty. Throughout the test he worked seriously, trying his best. His reaction time was extremely long because of his habit of pausing to ponder over each problem. In contrast to the usual test behavior of the feeble-minded, Clarence did somewhat better on the verbal scale. He seemed almost lacking in the abstract approach, as evidenced by his very poor performance on the block design subtest and other tasks requiring this ability. There was also evident a marked lack of awareness of detail. His only significantly good performance was on the Object Assembly, in which he quickly grasped the task, then assembled the parts rapidly and accurately. From the findings this time the psychologist was now inclined to change the diagnosis from "feeble-minded" to "borderline intelligence."

During the following year Clarence's next older sister was married. Almost immediately thereafter she asked for Clarence to be allowed to visit her, since she now had a home of her own. When investigations showed conditions there were quite good, Clarence was given permission to visit. Before long Clarence was making fairly frequent weekend visits there. The opportunity to visit with members of his family made a great difference in his outlook. Though the school staff had in the past tried to explain it wasn't their intention to cut him off from his family, that it was better for him to live at the school where he would obtain training with which he might someday support himself and even his younger brothers and sister, it was not until these visits began that for the first time he seemed completely happy. Not only was he now able to visit his older sister, but on occasion, through the arrangements of the social worker, Clarence was even able to have his two younger brothers out to the school for the afternoon.

In his activities at the school Clarence was steadily showing improvement. He was now working in the dining room of his dormitory in addition to his school classes. Somewhat taller and heavier than when he had first arrived at the school, he was now in excellent physical condition, with no sign of the heart murmur that had previously been detected. In his spare time Clarence enjoyed the movies and dances at the school, but was still too bashful to ask a girl for a dance. Occasionally Clarence was moody and homesick, but responded quickly to a few words of encouragement. Before long Clarence was transferred to the barbershop, then to the storeroom. On each of these jobs he did good work, learning the skills without difficulty. Throughout he was pleasant and agreeable toward all with whom he had to work.

In late spring of the following year Mr. O'Rourke again requested Clarence's return for the summer, and again the agencies concerned refused the request. Despite attempts this time by Mr. O'Rourke to use "influence," the school remained firm in its stand. The situation at home, it was found, had not changed in the past two years. A gang of young men came to the house at night to hang around until the wee hours. Though Mr. O'Rourke was well meaning he could not exert sufficient discipline. It was felt that despite Clarence's good conduct at the school he would not for long be able to resist the influence of the drinking and loose living at home. Nevertheless, because of his own personal interest in Clarence, the chief of police suggested that Clarence might be allowed home for a few days at a time, and that he would "drop in on Clarence" during his visits. He also suggested that these visits begin on a Sunday rather than at the beginning of a weekend in order to avoid the periods of heaviest drinking in the home. During the next year, following this suggestion, Clarence made two or three visits to his home. He semed to derive much pleasure from being with his family on those occasions, but was quite happy each time to return to the school.

In the meantime the social worker had been working especially hard trying to locate an outside work placement for him. However, it was not until the following year, just four years after Clarence had first come to the school, that she was successful in finding what seemed to be a suitable job, that of kitchen helper in a small private institution. When told of this Clarence was quite enthusiastic, losing for the moment his usual shyness.

How much getting the job meant to him was strikingly evident a few days later when he was seeing the psychologist. It was obvious how concerned he was about his performance; he flushed often, his hands trembled, and occasionally he stuttered. Even more than on previous occasions he was disturbed by obvious failures, reluctant to admit he didn't know the answer to a question. For what seemed an interminable period he pondered over each question. Despite all this, however, he now achieved an I.Q. of eighty-four (Wechsler-Bellevue).

One month later Clarence was paroled to the job. A nice-looking, pleasant lad of nineteen, he made an immediately favorable impression on his supervisors. He was to live at his place of work, sharing a room with two other boys who were also on parole from the school. Clarence was happier now than he had ever been.

Over the next year Clarence made excellent progress. He was polite, willing, and industrious—qualities that endeared him to his supervisors. However, at Christmastime an incident occurred that served to remind one that Clarence was still somewhat limited intellectually. He had gone to visit at his sister's, the whole family then going to visit at a brother's home in another city. As a consequence Clarence got to work at noon on the following day, instead of early in the morning, as he was supposed to. For a long time his supervisor tried to make Clarence see the importance of returning on time, of fulfilling his responsibility. Finally Clarence said he would make up the time, obviously missing the point of the entire discussion which had to do with his understanding of what "responsibility" meant.

One of the potential problems as far as the visiting social worker was concerned was the presence of young high-school girls working part-time in the kitchen. When it was reported to her that Clarence was paying much attention to one of these girls, the social worker immediately took it up with him, reminding him of the parole rules forbidding dates, etc. Quickly Clarence said he had not seen the girl away from work, nor would he, since the chance to be on parole meant too much to him. On that same day the social worker helped him open a savings account with part of his salary check, the book to be kept for him by his employers.

During the next year Clarence continued to merit "excellent" ratings from his supervisors. On one occasion, when one of the other boys was ill, Clarence willingly covered both jobs. Gradually he accepted more and more responsibility. When the social worker wanted to transfer him to another job to diversify his training, her efforts were stoutly and successfully resisted by Clarence's supervisors.

In his interpersonal relations Clarence was becoming less shy, engaging in bantering conversation with the girls in the kitchen. At small employees' parties he would occasionally help out with the entertainment. The first time he asked the social worker for permission to go to a high-school dance with some of his co-workers, she pointed out the dangers of becoming involved with girls when he was not supposed to make dates. Only after Clarence had promised not to make any dates after the dance was he given the permission. From then on Clarence went to many dances and parties at the high school, but never twice with the same girl. That he was well liked by the other employees, from high-school girls to elderly women, was attested by the surprise party given by them on his twenty-first birthday.

Occasionally Clarence was irked by the restrictions that were part of his parole situation. For example, when he had to spend an entire evening figuring out what he had done with his money, so that the bookkeeper could send an accounting back to the school, Clarence couldn't understand why he might not do as he liked with his own money. Nevertheless, after much struggling with pencil and paper, he was able to make his figures balance.

Clarence has now been at his job five years, adding limited responsibilities to it as time goes on. Two years ago he was discharged from parole as being "capable of self-support." In his interpersonal relations one might say he has also been successful, recently marrying one of the girls who used to work with him. As for the rest of the O'Rourkes, Clarence has had less and less to do with them.

Bill Glanvin

BRAIN SYNDROME: I, CEREBRAL ACCIDENT

At thirty-five Bill Glanvin was a success by any standard. In his job as chief copy writer of a large New York advertising agency he had won the respect of his superiors as well as the admiration of the many other up-and-coming young advertising men along Madison Avenue. His organizational ability as well as the ease with which he could turn a neat phrase marked him as one who was destined for great things. In his family life Bill was also a success. Happily married and the father of two children, he now owned his own home in a fashionable Connecticut suburb, was a member of the local country club, and had a host of friends with whom he and his wife exchanged frequent visits.

All of this was quite different from the circumstances in which Bill, the child, had found himself. Orphaned early through an unfortunate accident, Bill had grown up in the home of a paternal aunt, being accepted by her and her family as though he were one of her own children. In school Bill had been a good student, popular with his classmates and active in school affairs. Not one to be idle, Bill had managed to engage successfully in athletics, class politics, and the school paper, all the while he was earning a scholastic record of A's and B's. On his graduation from high school at seventeen Bill took his first job with the Black and Lewis Advertising Agency, that of file clerk. For the next six years Bill worked there, learning whatever he could from observation and attending evening classes at a large urban university. By the time the war came along Bill had been made a copy writer, one of the many in the agency. After four years of honorable but uneventful service in the Navy Bill was discharged with the rank of lieutenant, junior grade. He returned to his old job with Black and Lewis, married, and started to raise a family. Over the next seven years Bill had frequent promotions until, at thirty-five, he was put in charge of the other writers.

Bill had always been able to adjust well to any demands, physical or mental. Should he have a pain anywhere he would be more likely than not to shrug it off and keep right on working. And so when on this particular Sunday Bill had a severe frontal headache shortly after dinner he ascribed it to having eaten too much and lay down for a few minutes. About an hour later Mrs. Glanvin noticed that Bill seemed to be acting as though he were confused. He complained of having an upset stomach and walked about as though he were intoxicated. In a few moments he began to vomit, at the same time complaining of having chills. Late that afternoon he suddenly seemed to become very lethargic and stuporous, then went into a semi-comatose state. He was rushed to the local hospital, and on arrival was noted to have a paralysis of the right half of his body. A lumbar puncture at the time revealed grossly bloody spinal fluid. During the next twenty-four hours Bill had a few more episodes of vomiting but his vital signs remained essentially stable. He continued to remain in a restless and stuporous state. His right hemiparesis seemed to improve in the next week but did not disappear.

A few days later Bill was transferred to a large general hospital in New York City. At the time of his admission he appeared quite drowsy and at times restless. The hemiparesis was still present. He was put on conservative bed rest therapy and after the first two weeks his condition started to show gradual improvement. There also seemed to be improvement neurologically. The hemiparesis on the right side lessened, and the definite signs of motor aphasia seemed for a short time to improve, then remained static.

A week later a left cerebral arteriogram revealed a space-occupying lesion in the left temporal parietal region. Lumbar punctures done a week apart indicated a progressive increase in intracranial pressure. From time to time Bill complained of left-sided headaches. However, he gradually improved to the extent of being able to walk around the ward although he showed some instability while doing so. Examination of his eye grounds revealed developing papilledema and marked hemorrhage formation. During this time there was noted a complete homonymous hemianopsia on the right. There were also signs of parietal lobe insufficiency in his right upper extremity. An E.E.G. during sleep revealed a slow-wave focus in the left intermediate fronto-parietal region. A left temporal craniotomy at this time revealed an intracerebral hematoma in the left parietal lobe, and this was then evacuated. Following the operation the surgical wound healed well. Although the general clinical condition and neurological signs had not changed much there was a slightly more pronounced motor aphasia in addition to right hemiparesis. He seemed to have lost all language functions, being able neither to say what he wanted to say nor to understand what was said to him. There was no question of any hearing loss. Two days after the operation Bill was up and around on the ward. He now no longer complained of the severe headaches he had had before the operation. Because Bill would now need help in overcoming the severe aphasic aspects of his condition, he was transferred to the aphasia service of the hospital. The official transfer diagnosis at the time was "Left temporo-parietal lobe intracerebral hematoma, etiology unknown."

Shortly after his arrival on the aphasia service Bill was seen by the psychologist for evaluation of his intellectual and expressive deficit. He appeared interested and eager to participate. Despite his many failures on test items, to which he reacted with dismayed surprise, he continued to maintain his high level of interest. He showed gratitude to the tester and enthusiasm for any test procedure suggested to him. He had good insight into the nature of his handicap and was alert to what went on about him.

Because of his obvious language difficulty he was not given the verbal scale of the Wechsler-Bellevue Intelligence Test. On the performance scale he scored an I.Q. of eighty-six, indicating below-average efficiency with perceptual motor tasks. The weighted subscores were as follows:

Picture Arrangement	8	*Object Assembly*	5
Picture Completion	6	*Digit Symbol*	4
Block Design	8		

There was evident in his performance great difficulty in noting significant details when they were imbedded in a larger familiar configuration. This specific deficiency in combination with impaired insight into spatial relationships was felt by the psychologist to have depressed Bill's score out of proportion to the small degree of deterioration apparent in other situations.

After some confusion in grasping the instructions, he was able to present the two alternative solutions to the Color Form test, revealing good retention of ability in abstract reasoning.

The psychological report then went on to say:

> "His difficulty with perceptual motor tasks was emphasized in his copying of the Bender Gestalt drawings. He sometimes lost details in trying to account for the main outline; at other times he lost track of the whole while attending to the parts. In all of his performances he was self-critical, making exclamations of disappointment at his inaccuracies which he could not quite identify. On the Draw-a-Person test he expended energy which he could not direct to a co-ordinated and accurate performance by spreading out over several pieces of paper."

When Bill was asked about this he said he had drawn it large because he hadn't understood he was supposed to draw an entire body. He drew the profile with confidence, then seemed to be baffled by the rest of the body, and said he had never drawn "lower than the neck." In his drawing of the body he tried to account for each major detail, including the representation of kneecaps.

The Rorschach performance was difficult to evaluate because of Bill's severely paraphasic speech which made it necessary for the examiner to supply many words for him. For example:

"In attempting to give the association 'sunset' he perseverated with the word 'fire' which he had previously used and said: 'It could be in the distance, reflected, disappearing at six or seven o'clock in the afternoon, as it disappears. . . . [pause] . . . fire. Get only one thing in my head—fire! fire! fire!'"

Despite Bill's expressive difficulty there was still evident in his performance his drive, intelligence, and conscientiousness. The effects of his brain injury were seen in the reduced number of associations, perseveration of ideas, lability when confronted with emotional stimuli, and inability to differentiate definite portions out of the gross configurations of the blots. Further analysis of his Rorschach brought forth evidence of aggressive impulses, anxiety, and creative energy not ordinarily found in a record so dominated by the effects of brain injury. In the judgment of the psychologist the Rorschach performance indicated of Bill that

"through his ingratiating and pleasing personality he has been able to repress the powerful hostile feelings engendered in his interpersonal relations. The hostility may be the source of both the anxiety and the constructive drive he showed. Although consciously hampered by the stickiness of his associations and a sluggish flow of ideas he displayed a varied range of interests and the ability to introspect and inhibit action during the times when his feelings overwhelmed him."

The aphasia test battery indicated a moderate predominantly sensory aphasia with nearly complete agraphia and severe dyslexia. Bill's speech appeared normal in rate, inflection, and articulation. The grammatical automatisms were not affected but there was evident a severe amnesic word-finding difficulty and difficulty in formulating replies to specific questions. His speech efforts were marked by frequent paraphasic word substitutions and paragrammatic sentences. That he was relatively fluent in free conversation and aware of the nature of his difficulty were illustrated by his spontaneous comment: "I don't know what I am saying. I can talk and not know what I am talking about half the time." He seemed more able to name numbers, letters of the alphabet, and colors than to name pictured objects.

Tests of speech comprehension revealed frequent confusion among names of parts of the body and letters of the alphabet but good perception of most other isolated words. He appeared to understand simple directions well but was severely confused by a change of subject or by questions that required him to discriminate between alternative words of the same general capacity; e.g., he would be confused by questions concerning one of several named days of the week or one of several mentioned relatives. He was able to perform simple commands, but as they became more complex he required them to be repeated and had to have time to think them through before he could carry them out.

On the tests of reading comprehension Bill was able to grasp many individual words and read some aloud. When confronted with simple paragraphs at the primer level he was able to complete only the two simplest items composed of three- to five-word sentences. Though he was able to understand simple words in a situation that called for them he did very poorly in writing to dictation. He was able to work written arithmetic problems providing they did not involve carrying numbers from one column to the next. Some of his scores on the Stanford Achievement Test were:

Word Meaning—below second grade
Arithmetical Computation—above the third grade
Spelling—below the second grade

Bill was then put into the hands of the speech therapist, who saw him daily for almost a year. Since the greatest deficit was primarily in the receptive area, therapy consisted of using auditory, visual, and kinesthetic cues in helping him to recognize and name objects, then from simple words going to sentences and finally paragraphs. For example, a pencil would be held up and the word "pencil" spoken, then he was shown the word "pencil" as it might be written and finally he would use the pencil in writing the word "pencil," saying it aloud as he did so.

At first Bill's speech, though well articulated, was made up of many automatic phrases coupled with words that made little sense in context. There were many paraphasic substitutions and perseverations as well as a lack of awareness of his own speech. He found it difficult to answer specific questions no matter how simple. He could not speak on intention even to answering questions about the day of the week or the work he had done. Of great concern to him was his inability to give the names of his immediate family when asked.

After a month of speech therapy Bill learned to say the alphabet in normal sequence and could with some difficulty identify various letters shown him out of sequence. However, he couldn't identify letters from auditory presentations. Though able to name days of the week and months of the year and to count, he was never certain he was giving the correct series. His gross word-finding difficulty was still apparent. At times he would be able to tell the purpose for which an object was used but was unable to recall its name. Through imitation he was able to "get" the name of an object but only after having it spoken many times by himself and the therapist. He had spent much time working on the names of objects with which he had worked in the past, names of his family, and of parts of the body, and though showing some gain in the auditory and written recognition of the words he had been drilled on, he still seemed somewhat confused.

In his attempts at reading, during the first month of therapy Bill could occasionally match a word with an object or picture. When he failed, he blamed it on his double vision. Later he overcame this to some extent by breaking the line of vision of one eye with his hand.

When he first began therapy Bill was able to write his name and a few other words on intention though frequently he couldn't read back the words he had already written accurately from dictation. At the end of the first month, through daily practice, he was able to write his name and complete address with accuracy. Throughout this period Bill showed surprise each time he was not able to perform some language function when requested to do so, but didn't allow himself to become discouraged.

In the group sessions, made up of men suffering from similar language deficit, Bill had difficulty in understanding conversations. He soon learned to cover up this difficulty by responding correctly with automatisms after having gathered from the speaker's expression or gestures the general idea of what was being said. As time went on Bill was able to follow conversation with one person by watching his lips and interpreting his gestures and expression. However, a change of topic or conversation in a group situation was confusing. (His seeking out cues also explained his better ability to understand whole paragraphs read orally in sentences or phrases since he could pick up more key words.) Throughout all this Bill was unaware that his own conversation was not understandable to others. Because his thoughts were clear to him he felt his expression of them was equally clear to others.

For the next few months therapy went along slowly but steadily. Though there was some improvement in his capacity to understand he still had great difficulty in understanding spoken words and writing. During the fifth month, on his return from a weekend pass he complained of having had moderately severe profuse headaches during his last day at home. A spinal tap revealed clear colorless fluid with an initial pressure of one hundred fifty. After a few days of bed rest his headaches cleared up.

At the end of six months Bill was still making gains, although of a limited nature. He often would get a general impression of the meaning of a sentence from a few key words but was unable to be specific as to detail. When asked to repeat a sentence after the therapist, he frequently would have to have it repeated three times before he could recite it completely. He depended chiefly on visual imagery rather than auditory impressions. Many times he would have to write a word with his finger before he could grasp it, though he had said it and spelled it correctly orally.

The psychological test battery was repeated six months after the first administration. There was marked improvement in his intellectual functioning as measured by the Wechsler-Bellevue, although there was still discrepancy between his verbal and performance scores (V 101, P 121). The weighted subtest scores were as follows:

VERBAL		PERFORMANCE	
Information	11	*Picture Arrangement*	14
Comprehension	13	*Picture Completion*	12
Digit Span	3	*Block Design*	12
Arithmetic	6	*Object Assembly*	12
Similarities	11	*Digit Symbol*	10
(*Vocabulary*)	(12)		

It was felt that the performance score was an approximate indication of Bill's premorbid intellectual functioning though depressed to some extent by his impaired eyesight. The depressing of the verbal score seemed to be primarily the result of a restricted attention span for meaningless or neutral material such as digits and arithmetic problems. To a lesser extent it was a function of some residual confusion and delay in understanding instructions and his poor ability with verbal abstractions. Memory deficit was particularly evident when there was exclusive dependence on auditory perception. When other sensory avenues were utilized, as on the Bender drawings and Digit Symbol, there was an improved performance. Further evidence of the facilitative effect of other sensory modalities on memory came from Bill's occasional device of writing out a word in an attempt to recognize it and recall it. Likewise where concept formation was solely dependent on verbal abstraction ability it was severely impaired, but on non-verbal measures of abstractive ability (e.g., Color-Form Test) there was little of this conceptual deficit.

The Rorschach record showed considerable over-all improvement in comparison to his previous performance. The brain injury per se now seemed to be playing a minimal role in Bill's performance, with the personality features being less disguised by organic interference. There now seemed to be a more realistic appraisal by Bill of his deficit, with admission of and sensitivity to the dependency conflicts that the injury had created or reactivated. This awareness in turn seemed to have fostered much turmoil with some depressive elements. However, Bill now seemed better able to cope with the problem. Where the previous record had been characterized by the use of denial, distance, and a number of directly aggressive images, this record manifested more of an acceptance of the present handicapped state and the regression it involved, as well as a more controlled, more socially acceptable use of aggressive images. The blind fury in the previous record was replaced by more open expression of inadequacies and limitations and an attempt to deal more constructively with them. Despite this over-all increase in insight into the problems of readjustment and in effectively dealing with them, there were still signs of intellectual deficit. The record still lacked some of the elaboration and structural differentiation that might have been anticipated from one of his intellectual caliber; e.g., 50 per cent W, 50 per cent D.

On the Draw-a-Person and Bender Gestalt Tests there was considerable improvement, primarily due to increased visual motor co-ordination. On the former Bill was able to complete each drawing on one sheet of paper. Though he still drew profile views, with hand outstretched, arm bent at the elbow, and with the head drawn slightly downward, there was not so much concern with details as before. He was able to draw more freely and to articulate much better. Content-wise, however, there was increasing concern with the problems of independence and dependence in relation to his self-image.

Tests of language showed marked improvement since the previous administration. He had now to a great extent recovered from his nearly complete agraphia, though there was still a moderately severe dyslexia. In free conversation Bill was found to be fluent and articulate, with a minimal amnesic word-finding difficulty. He seemed to have insight into those aspects of language functioning that had shown relatively less improvement: comprehension of complex commands, recognition of absurdities, and a more pervasive difficulty in remembering neutral material for any length of time. Indicative of this latter was the little improvement in reading comprehension as measured by the Stanford Test. On the same test in other areas he had made marked progress: Arithmetic Computation was now above the fifth-grade level, and Spelling near the seventh-grade level. His receptive difficulties for a particular test item necessitated frequent repetition by himself and by the examiner before Bill could understand it. In this way a question or item would often become clearer to him and he would be able to respond adequately.

After the first six months Bill's work in the therapy sessions seemed to improve at a faster rate. He began to read current magazine articles orally with good comprehension of both the general significance and the details. His reading had good inflection, but the general rhythm was sometimes halting, due perhaps to his double vision. Pronunciation of some words was difficult because of his accenting the wrong syllables. At times he could correct himself, but often he required help.

Bill continued to make gains in all areas until his discharge one year from the time of his cerebral accident. When he left he was able to write letters, original articles, and summaries of articles read from current magazines. The most common error in his written work was an occasional misuse of prepositions. His sentence structure was varied and fully expressed complex thoughts. By the time of his discharge Bill had complete return of speech.

Comprehension of speech had greatly improved but still remained Bill's chief difficulty. He did much better in maintaining a conversation if he could watch the other person speaking. He began to read newspapers and magazine articles with increasing speed and of greater length without tiring.

Though Bill felt he could read to his own satisfaction, his reading speed was much slower than before his illness and not fast enough for his old job.

Bill was seen again a year after his discharge. Examination revealed he still had an incomplete right homonymous hemianopsia. He also complained of some hyperesthesia of the right lower extremity. There was no demonstrable motor deficit.

The originally severe aphasia had disappeared except for some residual auditory aphasas. He was now again working full time in the same advertising agency but as messenger and mechanical assistant.

Frank Brown

BRAIN SYNDROME: II, BRAIN INJURY

FRANK BROWN'S CHILDHOOD was uneventful. One of three children in a middle-class family, his early development was not much different from that of the other children in the small town where his father was a clerk in the local bank. In school his grades were average, on a par with his interest in most of the subjects. He was a fairly quiet individual who occasionally took part in sports, but preferred fishing above all else. Following his graduation from high school Frank went to work in a local store and attended evening classes in mechanical engineering. After a year of this Frank decided to look elsewhere for his opportunity. He moved to another city where he lived with an uncle for the next two years. In all that time, however, he was unable to get work because of a general lack of employment in the area.

At twenty-one Frank was drafted into the Army. Because of his earlier interest and training in things mechanical he was put in charge of teaching other soldiers the rudiments of vehicle maintenance. Within a year he reached the rank of staff sergeant. While in the Army Frank married "the girl next door," and a year later became the father of twins. Shortly after the birth of his children Frank was sent overseas to the Pacific theater. For the next year he saw much combat, during which he was wounded on four separate occasions. The last wound he suffered, when he was hit in the chest by shrapnel, was so severe that he was flown back to the United States. A few months later Frank was given a medical discharge.

On his return home Frank was very nervous. He was easily startled by sudden noises and frequently had difficulty sleeping because of nightmares. He tried assembly work in an electronics plant but soon found he was too nervous to endure the monotony of the job. Finally, after three years of trying out many jobs, he got a job as a trainee in the traffic division of a large industrial plant. Before long he was enthusiastic about his job, particularly enjoying the many trips he would have to take in expediting shipments.

Throughout this period of adjustment Frank's family was a source of strength to him. The constant devotion of his wife and children had helped hasten his recovery from the effects of his war experiences. Mrs. Brown had been particularly patient and understanding, reassuring him repeatedly of her faith in his ability to do well. The deep love they felt for each other helped them rise above the repeated daily disappointments.

Frank had been working a year when he suffered the injury that was to change his whole life. One day as he was walking out of a store there was a loud crash as two speeding automobiles collided. Just as Frank turned in the direction of the noise, a flying metal fragment from one of the cars pierced his skull. He was immediately rushed to the hospital where he was operated on. For about a week his condition was considered hopeless. He remained in a comatose condition and had to be tube fed. After two weeks his swallowing reflex began to improve and he started to take water by mouth, though he still had to be tube fed. A month and a half after his operation he could see hand motion with both eyes. Soon he began to eat, then to talk, and a week later was discharged to the care of his wife.

Back home Frank was in a semi-dazed condition with fleeting periods of amnesia. Three months later he was briefly rehospitalized for the insertion of a plate in his skull. Before long Mrs. Brown became worried because Frank's mental condition was not clearing up. Occasionally when walking along the street he became lost and had to be directed home. Where he used to be congenial to friends, he now became indifferent to them. For the next six months Mrs. Brown tried patiently to care for her husband but gradually became disappointed that he was not making better progress. Although Frank could feed and dress himself he was now a problem because of his untidy appearance, his general indifference to social standards, and his chronic irritability. On occasion when irritated he would hurt his wife by grabbing her with all his strength. A few times while the family was having dinner Frank urinated at the table. In his relations with his wife and children he was unpredictable. At times he was oversolicitous of their welfare, yet when there was some emergency, like the rushing of one of the little girls to the hospital for an emergency appendectomy, Frank acted as though he were completely indifferent to it all. When Mrs. Brown could stand no more of this, she took the advice of her family physician and had Frank admitted to the hospital for possible rehabilitation.

On admission Frank was in good contact and co-operative, complaining chiefly of his severe memory defect. He said if he told his wife something in the morning by the time evening had come around he no longer could remember what it was. He also complained of some stiffness in his legs after any prolonged period of sitting. If only he could get a change of jobs, Frank felt, everything would be all right. Yet he had not worked since his accident because he couldn't remember enough details to do his job efficiently. During the interview he had no delusions or tendency to confabulate and was well oriented in all spheres.

Physical examination at this time revealed a lemon-shaped skull defect of the right fronto-temporal region, approximately three inches by two inches, external strabismus of the right eye, and loss of lateral vision of the left eye and nystagmus. During the neurological examination Frank was somewhat euphoric and showed some retentive difficulty. The examination proper revealed residuals of cerebral trauma, consisting of third and sixth nerve involvement on the right, and optic atrophy, bilateral, as well as slight pyramidal signs on the left.

On the ward Frank presented no management problems, being able to care for his personal needs. He was soon given ground privileges and sent to woodworking classes. Before long he was telling the doctor his memory was improving, that he not only knew the day of the week but was aware of recent events. However, he admitted counting the stairs when he walked up or down lest he fall, and that his fear of falling made him walk slowly at all times.

As part of the planning, Frank was seen by the psychologist for evaluation of the extent of the intellectual impairment as part of the planning toward a vocational goal. During the examination he seemed to be unconcerned with his appearance. His pants were unbuttoned, he did not bother to wipe his dripping nose, and in general was unkempt. At one point he accused the aides of having beaten him up at dinner the night before because he had dawdled over his coffee. Questioning by the psychologist revealed that Frank had ignored the request to finish his coffee, remaining in the dining room after all the other patients had left. The "beating" had consisted merely of the aides' taking him by the arm and marching him back to his ward.

Despite his reference to this manhandling Frank maintained throughout a relaxed, jocular, somewhat flippant attitude. Even his occasional references to his skull injury were flip and jocose. Many times now, he said, he often guessed when he didn't know something: "Since I got hit in the head I have nothing to lose; if by a millionth of a chance I'm right, swell!"

On the Wechsler-Bellevue Form I Frank achieved a Verbal I.Q. score of one hundred twelve, a Performance I.Q. of eighty, and a full I.Q. score of ninety-seven. The subtest weighted scores were as follows:

VERBAL		PERFORMANCE	
Information	12	*Picture Arrangement*	6
Comprehension	10	*Picture Completion*	9
Digit Span	10	*Block Design*	5
Arithmetic	10	*Object Assembly*	4
Similarities	11	*Digit Symbol*	2
(*Vocabulary*)	(14)		

On the Wechsler Memory Scale Form I Frank scored a memory quotient of ninety-four. Analysis of the subtests revealed low scores to have occurred on Digits Backward, Visual Reproduction, and Associative Learning. On the Goldstein-Scheerer Cube Test he was unable to analyze the elements contributing to the total stimulus pattern unless he was presented with the large lined design or an actual model. He also found it difficult to fit all the blocks together. At one point, when presented a pattern constituted of blue and yellow blocks, he commented: "It looks like a blueberry pie, but I've never seen yellow crust on a pie."

A factor contributing to his low-performance scores was what seemed to be his complete obliviousness to time. On both timed and untimed tests he did not hurry, was distractible, occasionally stopped in the middle of his performance to blow his nose, and frequently initiated extraneous conversation. As he went on to new problems he seemed to work somewhat faster and more efficiently, though still not adequately. For example, on the Minnesota Form Board Frank's time on trial A was twenty minutes, on trial B ten minutes, yet even this was poorer than 90 per cent of the population.

For the next few months Frank attended woodworking classes and visited the vocational counselor for aid in finding a suitable job goal. But at the staff conference six months after his admission, evidence of Frank's defect continued to increase. Neurologically there was no difference from the results of Frank's earlier examination. The optic atrophy was quite striking and considered severe enough to account for the restricted visual fields of which Frank had been complaining. As far as Frank's general performance went, all who had come in contact with him had found him unreliable and his memory spotty and generally poor.

In his woodworking classes Frank was described as speaking slowly but reasonably intelligently. Occasionally he would complain of having sore knees and a general difficulty in walking manifested by slowness and unsteadiness. He seemed to have some trouble getting in and out of a chair. In his movements Frank was slow and deliberate because of his difficulty with control. Partly because of this he gave the impression of laziness. He would take three or four hours to do a job that ordinarily should have taken only ten minutes. Even with this deliberateness Frank's work was consistently of very poor quality. One day, when trying to make a picture frame, he made two cuts correctly, then tried to put the molding upside down in the miter box for the next cut. Yet the molding wouldn't even fit in the box when upside down. Frequently he complained of his eyesight though he would sit and read sometimes for an hour at a time. His general comprehension of responsibilities was very poor.

In his visits to the vocational counselor, just as in his visits to woodworking, Frank was unpunctual and unreliable. On several occasions he didn't show up at all, later explaining that he had forgotten the appointments. On one occasion he appeared the day after his scheduled appointment. Several times he lost his direction en route to the counselor's office. Once, after having visited the counselor a few times, he came to the pavement between the counselor's office and another office, but couldn't figure out in which direction to turn.

In his conversations with the counselor Frank tended at times to minimize his defects, yet when laboriously copying onto a piece of paper the date of the next appointment he would admit his memory loss. On one occasion he admitted having been sideswiped by a car he hadn't seen coming, yet deprecated his visual impairment. Frequently he talked of being ready to go home and back to work, yet couldn't develop any planning for this. One of his problems was his wish for his wife not to have to work, but he couldn't figure out how he might himself find work and make this unnecessary. He described how it upset him when home on a visit because his wife babied him and accompanied him on the street lest he get hit by a car, yet he was unable to do anything to change the situation. Repeatedly he talked about being "the breadwinner again when I go home," but would then quickly act as though he were indifferent to it all.

Frank has now been in the hospital one year. Recently he was transferred to another, smaller ward where he would get more personal attention. He is allowed to rest whenever he feels like it, and is helped and encouraged in his efforts to follow a simple routine. In the meantime Mrs. Brown has become increasingly resistant to his returning home in his present condition. She complains that he is not the same man she was married to and that she can't possibly care for him as he now is. An attractive, well-dressed woman, she is beginning to develop other interests outside the home and is even ready to return to the career she gave up at the time of her marriage.

Tony Rolando

BRAIN SYNDROME: III, ALCOHOLIC DETERIORATION

TONY WAS A GOOD BOY, well behaved, and his mother's favorite. The family was a close one, large and happy, and still carrying on many of the Old World customs. Tony's father, Mr. Rolando, was a laborer, a hard-working man who had brought his family to America from Italy shortly after the turn of the century and then had immediately gone to work as a ditch-digger. Through Mrs. Rolando's careful watching of the finances the small income served adequately to clothe and feed the family. Occasionally Mr. Rolando got drunk on a Saturday night, but so did the other men of the neighborhood.

Tony left grade school at sixteen, shortly after the accidental death of his father. Being the oldest of the children, it was Tony's responsibility to take care of his mother. He got a job in a textile mill and before long was spending his evenings at the local saloon. Always a shy, somewhat seclusive person, Tony had few friends other than his drinking companions. He never went out with girls, saying he wasn't interested in them. For this he was praised as a "good boy" by his mother. He was a steady worker, turning his money over to his mother each payday. Since his early years he had drunk wine and beer as part of the general pattern in the neighborhood. He was a moody person who preferred to be by himself. He had no interest in sports or in going out with a group of boys his own age. Instead, he enjoyed going to the movies or sitting at home listening to the radio.

Tony served in both wars. He received a regular discharge after World War I and a medical discharge because of low back pain after a year and a half of service in World War II. In between he had continued to work seasonally in the mill, spending his spare time as before in drink or listening to the radio with his mother. At the age of forty Tony's sisters and brothers began to worry about a sudden change in his behavior. To them he seemed to be "acting queer." Always one to prefer solitude, he now actively avoided groups or crowds. When company came to the house Tony would immediately leave, returning late at night. Shortly after World War II, when Tony was forty-five, his mother died. He and his younger brother, both of whom had stayed at home to care for their widowed mother, now went to live in a rooming house. Both began to drink heavily, Tony more than his brother. For the next five years Tony consumed a quart of wine each day. For the most part he was unemployed, joining his brother in an occasional hunt for odd jobs. He became a well-known character in town, but since he was causing no trouble he was tolerated. At infrequent intervals he was arrested for drunkenness but was released the next morning when sober.

When Tony was fifty he was taken to the hospital following a heart attack. While there it was noticed that Tony had difficulty in remembering things and was acting childishly. Because he couldn't remember he began to confabulate, making up stories about his past that were either untrue or confused in sequence. A month later Tony was transferred to one of the state hospitals. On arrival there he was disoriented, slow in responding, and confabulating. He was actively hallucinated for a few days, "seeing" threatening monsters that were after him. These visions cleared up and Tony was able to shrug them off as imaginary and due to his drinking.

For the next six years Tony remained in the hospital. At one period he spent three months with his brother on a trial visit but drank so heavily he had to be returned. At the hospital he worked very little, complaining of fatigue most of the time. Despite the precautions taken by the hospital Tony was somehow able to obtain liquor, frequently staggering as he entered the dining room.

One year ago Tony was transferred to another hospital for possible rehabilitation. On admission he showed both emotional and intellectual flattening. Despite a fairly alert expression, he appeared to be apathetic. Outstanding in his difficulties was his impaired memory and partial disorientation. He was quite inconsistent regarding dates, changing them each time he repeated the same topics. When asked to give the present date his answer was wrong as to day, month, and year. Although he realized that his memory was impaired he did not seem at all concerned by it, nor did he seem to be worried about his drinking. Though the name of his new hospital was repeated to him several times, a few minutes later he couldn't recall it nor could he recall its location. He tried to explain away his difficulty by saying he had "so much" on his mind that he couldn't remember. When asked what his plans for the future were, Tony could give none. Instead, he constantly repeated that he felt fine and just wanted his family to take him out. He also spoke of applying for an increase in the veterans' compensation he was getting so he could live "like I used to."

When Tony visited the psychologist he was mentally depressed, with little interest in the procedures, and at one point refused to co-operate because he didn't think "it would do any good." He said he didn't work because he easily got physically rundown; nor did he socialize with the other patients, he said, because "they are all mixed up." He showed little concern about his mental condition, nor did he think his heavy consumption of alcohol had in any way hurt him.

On the Wechsler-Bellevue Form I Tony got a full scale I.Q. score of ninety-four, Verbal ninety-eight, Performance ninety. The following are his weighted subtest scores, with the exception of Object Assembly, which he refused to do.

VERBAL		PERFORMANCE	
Information	8	*Picture Arrangement*	4
Comprehension	11	*Picture Completion*	7
Digit Span	10	*Block Design*	6
Arithmetic	3	*Digit Symbol*	3
Similarities	8		
(*Vocabulary*)	(8)		

On the Information test he couldn't remember the name of the previous president. There were constant references to himself and the frequent intrusion of idiosyncratic material. On Comprehension he said one should mail a letter found in the street "unless you're inquisitive." On Block Designs he couldn't visualize the components of the design, beginning his attempts with the middle block and trying to work outward.

On the Wechsler Memory Scale he scored a memory quotient of 69 per cent. General impairment was shown on this test. There were gaps in information, orientation, and intellectual control. He was very poor on memory for designs, and was unable to do the simplest tasks in associative learning, a higher order level of functioning. When asked to repeat the memory passages he was unable to do so correctly, but instead of admitting this he confabulated details that fitted into the context but were not correct. This was different from the irrelevant confabulations of the actively psychotic individual, and suggested an attempt to compensate.

On the Draw-a-Person Test Tony started to draw the outline of what with generosity might be called a head, then refused to continue. He mentioned a man he knew "who can really draw." As a substitute he offered to write, and very large, with many flourishes and curlicues, he wrote the names of two cities in which he had been.

Noticeable throughout the interview was Tony's inability to concentrate, to sustain a mental set, and to be motivated to the task. Once or twice he mentioned that he was being held in the hospital against his will and wanted to get out.

Three days after ground privileges were granted Tony disappeared from the hospital. Two days later, looking much the worse for having been drinking heavily, he was returned by the police of a town near his home. One month later he again disappeared, and again was brought back drunk. Over the next year he made frequent "elopements," alone or with another patient, getting drunk each time. On the last occasion he and another patient stole out for the afternoon. At six o'clock, heavily intoxicated, they drove up in a taxi. When they got out of the cab, Tony revealed he had no money to pay the fare but with a grand gesture told the driver he could be paid from their account at the hospital.

Carol Bottomley

SEVERE CHARACTER DISORDER IN A MALE WITH DEPRESSIVE AND HOMOSEXUAL FEATURES

CAROL WAS AN ILLEGITIMATE CHILD, the product of a short-lived but poignant affair between Margaret Bottomley and Bill Murray. Margaret was a student dietician in her last year at Mercy Hospital, a strapping, buxom girl, Bill a young physician on the visiting staff. By the time Margaret discovered she was pregnant, Bill had had a change of heart, and married a girl whom he had known for years. Margaret vowed never again to fall in love. Fortunately the baby was not expected before her graduation, making it possible for her to finish her studies. In the meantime she explained her predicament to her mother, who immediately took over control of the situation, just as she had in the past whenever any family problems arose. Margaret was to have her child, then give it into her mother's keeping to be brought up as though it were her own. And so it was. Following her graduation Margaret went home to await the birth of her child. Two months later, in the family home in a quiet Vermont town, she gave birth to a normal, healthy seven-and-a-half pound boy whom she christened Carol, giving him her own family name but putting on the birth certificate the name of the true father. After a short convalescence Margaret went to work in a nearby town, "giving" Carol to her mother to be brought up as her own. Both Margaret and her younger sister were to be known only as his "sisters," the uncle as his "brother."

The family into which Carol was born was highly religious and moral, proud of their English ancestry but in reduced economic circumstances. Margaret's father was a hard-working mill hand, aloof and antagonistic in his attitude toward all with whom he came into contact. Though he drank steadily and heavily, at no time did it interfere with his work, for through drink and hard work he was able to forget his family problems. Despite his going along with the fabrication regarding Carol's parentage he was unable to conceal his especial antagonism toward the boy who was responsible for the family shame. His frequent ridiculing and name calling served only to build up a strong hatred in Carol toward him that lasted until his death a few years later. In marked contrast to the father, Margaret's mother was a calm, highly competent woman to whom many of the neighbors came for advice. Though so easily able to solve the neighbors' problems, it was harder for her to make peace in her own family in the many quarrels that arose between the sisters or between the sisters and their brother, who was subject to alternating periods of irritability and depression.

Carol began his schooling at four and a half years, soon demonstrating ability to learn quickly. Though he was an "A" student from the beginning, his emotional development was not so favorable. Happy at first, his witnessing of frequent quarrels and jealousies at home soon helped to turn him into a shy, moody youngster who played by himself. Dutifully he went to Sunday school three times a week. Each weekend, on her visit home, he heard Margaret argue with her mother about not being strict enough in his upbringing. Gradually Carol began to feel "picked on" for every little mistake. He became more and more tense, biting his nails from an early age. Soon he became unhappy with his own progress, disgusted with himself for falling short, just as Margaret in her own earlier days had felt disappointed in herself and so inferior to her mother.

Though Margaret's attitude was partly due to the high, rigid standards she had learned as a child and never questioned, it was reinforced by the close relationship between Carol and his grandmother. He loved his grandmother dearly, respecting and trusting her judgment. "She was a guide to me, but not domineering." On many occasions he would lie in bed with her, "quite palsy-walsy," the two of them discussing what he would become when he grew up, and how she would use her savings to send him to college. It was this "petting and pampering" to which Margaret objected. She wanted her son to be independent and self-sufficient, not, as she frequently complained, "always demanding attention." Priding herself on her achievements at school and at work, Margaret was especially disturbed to see weakness in her son.

When Carol was thirteen his grandmother became bedridden. Carol began to carry her about the house, putting her to bed in the evening. He spent his Sundays sitting by her bed in case she needed anything. Soon his schoolwork began to suffer because of his worrying about his grandmother. The savings with which she had planned to send Carol to college had to be used for the medical care that she was to need until her death seven years later.

Because of her mother's complete incapacity Margaret gave up her job to take over the household responsibilities. Family tension increased as she tried to imitate her mother's competence. Though she prided herself on being the "strong one" of the family, she had difficulties in getting the others to do as she wished. Carol began to spend more time sitting at the bedside of his grandmother. In the past he had not been able to ask his friends to the house because there was no predicting the mood of his uncle; now, with Margaret "bossing everybody," his grandmother was his only source of comfort.

About a year later, when Carol was fourteen, he suddenly learned the truth about himself. While he was out playing in the yard one day, Margaret and her younger sister got into a violent argument. At its height the young girl suddenly felt unable any longer to contain her anger at her sister and her jealousy of the attention Carol was getting from her mother. Running outdoors, she shouted at Carol: "You're a bastard! Nobody ever wanted you!" Once the words were out she regretted having said them, but it was too late. Margaret was quite disturbed by the incident, but soon recovered when she found no apparent change in Carol's attitude toward her. If anything, he became more respectful toward her. However, he continued to call her by her first name, reserving the term "Mother" for his grandmother. Many times Margaret tried to "put backbone in him," as she called it, but never felt she had succeeded.

In school Carol's grades took a sharp drop after he had learned of his illegitimate birth. Despite this he was able to finish high school at seventeen with no difficulty. Because of the many expenses associated with his grandmother's illness and the country-wide economic depression at the time of his graduation Carol had to take any odd jobs he could get. He resented having to accept any menial jobs, preferring office work or any other employment in which he would not have to get dirty or which he felt was not beneath him. In order to improve himself he went to secretarial school at night. The following year he attended night college, studying stenography, bookkeeping, and Spanish. In his spare time he continued his long-standing interests in religion and esthetics, with never a thought of sports.

When Carol was twenty his grandmother passed away. Though he had been quite close to his grandmother, becoming increasingly upset as he watched her waste away, he showed no unusual behavior at the time of her death. In the eyes of the rest of the family he seemed to have accepted the fact quietly. He continued his attempts to comply with Margaret's demands, albeit with unexpressed resentment.

Carol had very little to do with girls, being uncomfortable in their presence, yet at the same time interested in them. From the time of puberty he had masturbated frequently, experiencing strong feelings of guilt on each occasion. At eighteen he began to have fears that he had developed a venereal disease because of his masturbating activities, but felt too guilty to mention it to anyone. One year later he was approached by a homosexual ex-college athlete of thirty-two. "There was a strong paternal feeling and a sense of quiet security—no sex, no liquor." Within the next few years he had two other encounters with homosexuals, in both of which Carol was the passive partner. The first of these he described as being with a "borderline homosexual," slight of stature, quiet, refined, and reticent. The emotion was "ethereal. I had a strong desire to kiss the person and hold him closely, but there was no sex involved." The other incident consisted of his being approached by a "true homosexual, not too refined, and an exhibitionist. I felt a teasing torment and a desire to scratch his face and almost make him bleed." As in the other encounters, there were no abnormal sexual relations, merely an attraction to these men and a feeling of security in their closeness. "At no time during these four years did I have a desire for abnormal relations with a strong man." He began to drink during this period, frequenting the bars visited by homosexuals.

Even as an adult, Carol's relations with women were not typical of other young men. "In my early twenties being with women of my own age was a frightening emotion. There was never any sex involved. But with women twice my age I felt a great companionship. I would take them to the theater and feel a sense of protection while sitting with them."

Carol was twenty-five, working as a clerk, when World War II began. When he had to register for the draft he ran into difficulty because of not knowing how to ask for his birth certificate at the town hall. Unable to find the certificate at home, he called Margaret at work, and she told him the name under which it was listed. And for the first time he heard of "Dr. William Murray." Strangely enough he did not question Margaret about Dr. Murray, seeming to be completely disinterested at the time. Nor did Margaret feel inclined to bring up the matter herself.

When Carol got his draft number he became visibly upset and anxious. For some time he debated with himself the advisability of enlisting. Though he constantly asked his mother for advice on this problem, she refused to give any. Much as his indecisiveness disturbed her, she repeatedly pointed out that this was his own decision to make, hoping thereby to "put iron into his soul." Feeling the pressure of her attitude, and hoping to have more choice in his military placement than if he waited to be drafted, Carol volunteered a few months later for immediate service. On the day before he was to leave he overturned a car he was driving, but suffered no injuries. On the following day, when he was to leave for the Army, he refused to have Margaret see him off, fearing that somehow the use of her maiden name might reveal his illegitimacy. However, his going off alone was felt by Margaret to have been a "maturing experience."

From his letters and occasional visits home Margaret felt that Carol was continuing in the Army his earlier craving for attention and affection. (In telling of this years later Margaret's tone was hard and scornful.) For the first half year following induction Carol was assigned to guard duty, but was so easily fatigued that he was finally made a clerk. He seemed quite happy with the change, especially after being told that now he probably would not be sent overseas. All in all, the Army, it seemed, was not such a bad life after all. During this period Carol's uncle was admitted as a mental patient to the Green River State Hospital. Though his uncle had always been moody and unpredictable, he had frequently been the only one, since the grandmother's death, who had been kind and considerate to Carol. Because of this Carol from time to time made the long trip to the hospital to visit with him.

Suddenly, out of a clear sky, Carol was told that he was to be assigned overseas. The shock was profound. He again began to suffer from chronic fatigue. His letters to Margaret changed in tone from contentment to panic. "What shall I do, Margaret?" After he got overseas his letters diminished in frequency, but those he did write were full of despair and hopelessness. He even wrote of his unhappiness to his former commanding officer back in the United States, an understanding person who had been protective of Carol because of "his sensitive nature." He became actively interested in religion, surprising his mother when he wrote of his wish to enter a monastery after the war. Thinking this was just a passing fancy that could be dealt with when he got home, Margaret raised no objections at the time.

Perhaps related to his decision to enter a monastery was the increasing difficulty Carol was having with his sexual problems. Duty overseas in isolated areas in the Pacific gave him much time in which to think about himself.

> "Being cooped up in the camp on the islands I had the constant thought I was a homo. As a result I would not bother with the true homosexuals in the outfit. The constant associa-

tion with strong men gave me a desire to do something abnormal. We had sailors in our outfit. Their strong bodies in tight uniform made me go out on pass. I thought if I am a homo I might as well do something abnormal! Under severe liquor I picked out the strongest character and for the first time I did something abnormal. If I could have bragged about the women I had been with, like the other fellows, I know I would have been all right."

A few months after V-J Day Carol arrived back in the United States. On the day following his arrival, while on pass to town, he was struck down by an automobile as he crossed the street. He spent that night in the station hospital, but next morning was flown to a separation center near his home. On his arrival there, he complained of a sore arm, and asked to be admitted to the hospital. Later that same day he slipped on the ice, hurting his shoulder in the fall. He then returned to the hospital, again demanding to be admitted. This time he was successful. After a few days' stay, during which time X-rays revealed no fracture, he was released. He remained at the separation center until his discharge four months later.

When he returned to his home town Carol found, to his dismay, that Margaret had shortly before been forced to give up the family home. It was a "shock" to Carol, who had looked forward eagerly to returning to the only home he had known throughout his life. He felt resentful toward his mother, but there was little he could do about the situation. Since Margaret herself was living in a furnished room, working every day at her job, she suggested to Carol that he live at the "Y." But he refused to fall in with her suggestion. He found himself wanting to rebel against her domineering manner, particularly after having been away for four years. "As soon as I got home she, as always, hurried me. She brought me down to the draft board as though I were a child." Later that day, somewhat blue and lonely, Carol went to a monastery in a nearby town and asked to be allowed to live and work there while he studied religion. Frequently, while living there, he would visit his mother, but on each occasion they would argue about what he was to do. About a week later, while he and his mother were having dinner together, he again felt upset because it seemed she was trying to domineer over him. After a heated argument he went to a tavern where he immediately began to drink quite heavily. A few hours later, after many drinks, he made a homosexual approach to a stranger outside the tavern. The response was violent and quick, the stranger hitting him so hard that Carol fell, and struck his head on the curb. Somewhat confused, his speech garbled, Carol took a taxi to the monastery, where he was put to bed. Three days later, when he had become delirious, Carol was taken to the hospital where he was operated on for the removal of an intracranial clot. At the time of his discharge a week later Carol felt he had brought enough trouble to the monastery fathers and that he should leave them. While he was at the monastery packing his things the incision began to bleed. Unable to pay for medical attention, he went to the local hospital clinic. When examined there he seemed confused and depressed, and spoke vaguely of suicide. For his own safety, and at his own request, he was sent to Green River State Hospital as a psychiatric patient, the same hospital where he visited his uncle.

Despite his behavior at the hospital clinic, when Carol was admitted to Green River he was well oriented and clear in his thinking. In the initial interview, throughout which he was cooperative and courteous, he admitted having been suicidal, even while in the Army, but with no real intent. "I just haven't got the guts." He still complained of occasional ringing in the ears and dizziness accompanied by blurring vision. His memory was intact with some amnesia for the events immediately prior to his skull fracture, although it was later felt that this might have been reticence rather than true amnesia. He complained of being depressed and of not having been able to sleep "for years."

Physical examination was essentially negative. He was described at the time of admission as "a well-nourished male of medium build with a female type of fat distribution on the breasts and hips." There was also a marked facial acne rosacea of long duration that in the past had seemed worse whenever he was emotionally upset.

At the time of Carol's admission the staff of the Green River Hospital was just recovering from the suicide of one of the patients. When Carol began to mention the possibility of taking his own life the staff became quite upset, watching him closely and trying in every way to keep from frustrating him beyond his limits. This oversensitive attitude on the part of the hospital, however, seemed only to encourage such expressions on Carol's part. By the time the hospital was ready to try another approach, more than a year later, Carol had played a number of pranks, such as leaving some of his clothes in the woods and disappearing for a couple of days while the staff worried about what had happened to him. As we shall see, for the next seven years at Green River Carol continued to manifest the same patterns over and over again that he had enacted in the Army and at the time of his admission.

Two months after his admission, in August, Carol again became quite depressed. At the same time his acne got worse. He repeated that he would be better off dead but killing himself was not "Godlike, not Christianlike. I wouldn't have the guts." He would then blame himself for not being strong enough to commit suicide. After a few weeks his depression lifted, but in October he again became despondent, verbalizing suicidal thoughts. He told of having had suicidal ideas ever since he had first learned of his illegitimacy, at fourteen, but had never had the courage to carry them out.

> "I have no guts. I used to say I will do anything to whip it. Now I just can't seem to get started. Every time I start to do anything I stop, there is a tight feeling in my stomach. It is fear. It's something. I don't know what it is. I'll never do anything. I'm in too much trouble as it is without worrying about the hereafter—I have a fear of everything. I'm all mixed up."

After watching him closely for the first six months at Green River, during which period he spoke many times of suicide, the staff finally decided he probably would not carry out his threats. In the past he had had too many opportunities, particularly overseas while armed, of which he had not taken advantage. Along with these suicidal impulses, and usually immediately preceding them, were his many homosexual impulses while on the ward: "But I have too much decency to do anything about it." He spoke quite freely of his homosexual background to anyone who was interested, patient or staff member. The result was the gradual development of his reputation in the hospital as "a character."

At Christmastime Carol was permitted to visit the monastery for a week, but on Christmas Day he asked the fathers to take him back to the hospital. While at the monastery he had acted somewhat confused, feeling insecure and unsure of himself. He told the physician he had been afraid of doing something to himself that would only get the monastery into trouble. (In recalling this incident a year later he referred to the fathers as "all a bunch of homosexuals.") On his return from the monastery Carol was depressed, becoming increasingly so as he ruminated about the hopelessness of his situation and the worthlessness of his life. On the following day, while in the lab for a test, he managed to steal some powder he thought was poison. After swallowing it he told the attendant, who immediately called the physician. Investigation disclosed that he would have no ill effects, not only because the powder was not particularly potent but also because the amount he had taken had been so small that it could not have hurt him.

Following this episode Carol became more cheerful. He began to work in the hospital, seeming, on the whole, to have lost all ideas of suicide. He was in good spirits and paid much attention to his dress and personal neatness. He deprecated the suicidal attempt in which he'd swallowed the powder as being not real but "a dramatic effort to attract attention."

However, three months later Carol disappeared from the hospital one morning, returning voluntarily late that night. In consequence he was transferred to a ward where he would have less freedom. Immediately he became irritable, restless, and depressed. A few days later the following letter to Margaret was intercepted in the routine censoring of patient mail:

I haven't slept since 1941 at home

Friday

Dear Margaret: Please take me out

I want you to read this letter very carefully. Margaret, I am desparate. I fooled them in saying I was a little better and am in Ward A. Margaret, please come up very soon.

Margaret, please, you can take me out on a visit . . .

I'm suffocating all nite long from no air. All the windows are closed and hot blankets. I don't sleep all nite long—didn't in the Army and can't here. I have no money and can't buy things. I'm here for the rest of my life. Margaret if you had any love for me you'd take me out for a few days, please, please, please please. Why let me suffer. I don't have peace of mind one minute during the twenty-four hours—no sleep all night and radios going all day long and hollering. All attendants everywhere you go.

I'm here on a serious charge and I'm afraid during later life when these nice times blow over I'll be beaten. Please promise me you'll take me out for a few days. You laugh and say "Let the state take care of him." It's better to be dead, Margaret. I mean it. I'm boing [sic] try to keep my spirit good a few more days in Ward A. You can go against all the medical doctors' advice here.

Margaret I'm trapped and if anything please take a week off and take me *out*. Please, please, please, please, please, please, please, please.

I did 4½ years honorable service.

They treat me like a dog here. I can't go on 30 more years here without sleep.

Please promise you'll come up here very soon and take me out for a few days airing. Please, please, please.

Margaret, please come up. Please come up here. I'm scared.

CAROL

You can demand to take me out for a few days. Margaret you've got to before they put me on Ward X for life. I can't see, I can't sleep. Please come up.

When seen by the physician Carol was in a severe depression, expressing many self-destructive ideas. He complained that his head was of "solid concrete." A few days later he was intercepted attempting to swallow a bedspring. He kept repeating: "I want to be dead. I haven't slept in years. I'll be here for the rest of my life and my heart will keep beating." He repeatedly requested the doctors to "take my body and experiment with it."

Sometime later he made another abortive attempt at suicide, this time by tying sheets about his neck in noose fashion. To the physician he explained that he had tried to do away with himself because "I'm sorry for my mother, that she has to put up for all my foolishness. I wish I was out of the way for her sake. She's been too good to me and I'll never be well enough to do anything for her. I'll never get out of this place."

Feeling Carol was undergoing a psychotic reaction the staff decided to have him permanently committed, rather than maintain his original status as a voluntary patient. At the same time they felt electro-shock therapy was now indicated. Two weeks later, as Carol was being studied for any physical contraindication to convulsive therapy, a routine X ray disclosed the presence of foreign bodies in his abdomen. Surgical exploration revealed fragments of a plastic mechanical pencil he had broken up and swallowed. These were removed.

To the psychiatrist Carol revealed that he had swallowed the insides of the pencil three weeks before, just after having written the long letter to his mother. "I was depressed because I felt that I would never get well or ever leave this hospital." He hadn't told anyone of his act because "I didn't want anybody to know how foolish I was. I kept doing a lot of foolish things. I've been doing foolish things all my life." He then told the psychiatrist that only yesterday, when Margaret had visited him, he had begged her to give him "cyanide." Now he asked the psychiatrist to "write my mother and tell her never to come up and see me again." Throughout all this Carol's affect was dull and depressed. Suicidal thoughts were quite active.

One week later electro-shock therapy was begun. After the third treatment there was a decided change in Carol. His attitude became more co-operative, his speech was more relevant. The suicidal expressions ceased, giving place to a concern with living and a general pessimism about his own abilities. At the end of two months he had had thirty-one electro-shock treatments in all. His condition was considered improved. However, one day, about a month later, he again was depressed and talking of suicide, but was able by himself to change his mood by reading his mother's letters over and over. Carol blamed this setback on the heat and "not being visited by my mother."

At about this time Carol's case was taken over by another therapist, Dr. Peters. Before long Carol looked upon him as a "kind of father to me." Though he had by now become quite sophisticated in applying psychiatric jargon to himself, Carol was gradually able to establish a relationship with Dr. Peters. He began to talk of his early family life and the difficulties he had had. He again became depressed, castigating himself because he hated his mother, yet at the same time loved her. Crying, and threatening suicide, he told of how his family life had always been full of hatred, of how his mother and uncle, who was at the time still a patient at the same hospital, hated each other so they would never eat together at the table, of how even his mother didn't understand Carol, often speaking to him in a very discourteous and disparaging fashion.

Despite Carol's suicidal threats and the letters in which he told Margaret he could still fool the doctors about his real condition, that he still felt depressed and hopeless, Dr. Peters told him suicide was his, Carol's, responsibility and prerogative, and that it was entirely up to him whether he was going to get well. He, Dr. Peters, was going to concern himself with Carol's problems, not his suicidal threats. From this point on Carol's attitude changed. He began to feel that Dr. Peters was "the best psychiatrist in the hospital." Within a month Carol was trying to "psychoanalyze" his fellow patients. Instead of being appreciative they began to resent his attitude, leading to many squabbles. Just as in the past he had always felt he was somehow better than or at least different from others, Carol felt he was at least one notch above the rest of the patients. He paraded before them not only his higher intelligence but also his homosexual experiences. He began to feel that in interest and ability he had more in common with the staff than with the other patients.

One of the allied factors complicating his hospital treatment at this time, as well as later, was his ability to ingratiate himself with older women, uniformly working in them a strong desire to mother him. This was particularly true in his relations with the social workers at Green River, resulting in some difficult periods for Carol when the relationship threatened to get too close. The first of such incidents involved a social work trainee, a Miss Drake, a woman about five years his senior. Miss Drake first met Carol a year and a half after his admission to Green River, when Dr. Peters felt the time had come to get Carol a job in some nearby community as a first step in planning for his ultimate discharge. Miss Drake immediately became interested in Carol's case, particularly after hearing him tell of his past. Because of her own strongly religious background in the same church as Carol she felt a strong affinity toward him. Strikingly unattractive and without male companions, she at first threw herself wholeheartedly into the task of trying to get Carol a pension for his mental disability. But, like other social workers before her, she was unsuccessful. Gradually she began to spend more and more time with Carol during the evenings, when she would discuss with him religious problems and his own attitudes. As she became more and more involved with Carol, the inevitable gossip began. But, as Dr. Peters was well aware, the suspicions were groundless. It was Carol himself who abruptly stopped spending time with Miss Drake, after telling Dr. Peters how uncomfortable she made him feel "wanting to hold my hand and look at the moon." Soon Miss Drake left for another job, easing the minds of Carol and the staff, but for different reasons.

At the time of Carol's contact with Miss Drake he was also seen by the vocational counselor as part of job planning. From the beginning of the interview Carol talked of his self-doubts, saying he felt confused and unable to keep his mind on working. Reassuring him, the counselor asked what sort of work he thought he might do. But Carol found it difficult to express any preferences, saying he was very anxious to "get started at something" and would do anything the counselor suggested. As the counselor continued to discuss employment possibilities Carol began to perspire profusely. Before long he was visibly so upset that the interview was terminated, but he was told they would later again discuss plans for getting him a job.

About ten days later Carol disappeared from the hospital in the afternoon, but returned the following morning. He told Dr. Peters that he had felt discouraged, and not knowing what to do about it had merely walked off the grounds. He had wandered about the town for a while, had a couple of beers, then spent the night in a waiting room of the railroad station. Early in the morning he had asked the policeman on duty to return him to the hospital, but was told to hitchhike back. This he did. On his return he complained of still feeling discouraged, and hoped he wouldn't be punished for what he had done. He explained it all as a passing mood, that once again his mother had upset him on her visit the previous day by telling him of her financial difficulties. To Dr. Peters, however, the behavior seemed rather to be motivated by a wish for restrictions because of Carol's anxiety about possibly being discharged from the hospital. For this reason, in place of punishment, an attempt was made to reassure Carol.

Two months later, in March, a job was found that seemed to be appropriate for Carol. It was a simple laboring job, not too strenuous in demands, under an employer who was quite sympathetic to Carol's needs. The hospital impressed upon the employer the need to keep Carol busy so he would not ruminate. Within a short time his employer had found a room for Carol in the home of a widow and her son. This made it possible for Carol to live away from the hospital, returning once a week for interviews with Dr. Peters. For a few days all went well. His landlady was immediately taken with Carol's politeness and gentlemanly manners. Carol was seemingly making a good adjustment, performing his duties satisfactorily. But on the morning after his second night away from the hospital Carol went to a small store near-by where he bought a package of razor blades. After walking a short distance away, he came back into the store, went into a back room, and there used one of the blades to make a superficial cut over his left wrist. Immediately after he shouted to the storekeeper what he had done, and asked him to call the police to take him back to the hospital. Just before leaving with the police he handed his room key to the storekeeper, asking him to return it to the widow "with my regrets."

Back at the hospital he was depressed and agitated but in good contact. When he saw Dr. Peters he told him how discouraged he had become, because of the feeling he was not doing well on his job. At the same time "I got very lonesome living by myself." The night before the incident he had been particularly discouraged about going to his lonely room. He had become nervous with many "thoughts of the past" to plague him. "I had no money, hadn't been paid yet, and couldn't go anywhere, so I got depressed . . . I can't be alone. I get very lonesome." He had also been upset because he didn't have any clean clothes. He complained that his landlady had seemed difficult to please: "the sort of person who wouldn't like to have a cake of soap out of place in the washroom." Despite his having funds at the hospital and his employer's frequent questioning of him as to whether he needed any money, Carol complained also of having been without funds so that he had not eaten for the two days he lived away from the hospital. Nor had Carol complied with Dr. Peters's request that he call to tell him about the job. When questioned about the suicidal attempt Carol treated the whole affair deprecatingly, saying he knew he couldn't have carried it off successfully. Again it was decided that Carol was not quite ready to leave the hospital.

One month later another attempt was made to get Carol out of Green River. This time a job was secured for him as an attendant in a county hospital, but after two weeks he again showed up at Green River.

For the next few months Carol stayed in the hospital. His depressed mood had cleared a few days after his return. However, though Carol was feeling happy, his behavior on the ward was becoming a problem to the staff. With new patients he had gradually been assuming the role of an older brother who knew all the ropes, interfering with the work of the staff. Despite his explanation that he was really trying to help the new patients, the actual effect of Carol's "advice" was most upsetting to them.

Another source of difficulty was the friction that had arisen between Carol and another patient who also had a problem of homosexuality. Despite his tendency to talk freely of his homosexual escapades, Carol resented anyone's ridicule or rebuffs even though he himself had brought up the topic. At one point in his visits with Dr. Peters he brought forth a "document" in which he had listed all of his homosexual experiences, as well as his thoughts about this and other problems while in the hospital. He described most vividly his conflict between homosexual impulses and a desire to act and be like other men:

> "Now while working during the day I see a very masculine patient and I have the desire to get liquored up and do

something abnormal. But I wont. In my bed before going to sleep I imagine that particular person with whom I was working in bed—and me doing something! Either that, or I change over and wish and visualize him having intercourse on top of me (me as a woman). Complete remorse the next day. A new day, but futility, with my thoughts constantly about (1) my grandmother, (2) Dick, the college athlete, (3) the girl I met at a dance, (4) Dr. Peters. Then a deep sense of guilt as my grandmother would have liked me to be something. When my mother comes to visit I have a strong dislike for her positiveness. When she leaves, a dream that I wish that she had married a nice man which would have softened her and made her sweet.

"Then seeing young patients, some wise guys who had done everything, some in service for three months, six months, etc., who go out and make good! Then I think of the fracture—looking backward saying Gee, with my mother and father, a good background—why couldn't I get somewhere? Then the dance with the girl that I really like—wishing I hadn't got into this trouble. Seeing a home for her and for me. Perhaps taking foster children from the state—getting a store—and being a *man*, but all the time *thinking she is stronger*. Then each day more futility, no one seeming to have much use for me, only Peters. Rebuffs by my uncle here and mother. Then a feeling I might *go on*. Good appearance gone. No occupation."

A few months later, after a marked improvement in his spirits, Carol again became depressed following a visit from his mother at a time when he felt he didn't want to see her. Suddenly feeling he just had to leave the hospital, he again walked off the grounds. This time he stayed away for a week, again returning voluntarily. He had spent the time living by himself and visiting relatives out of the state. He would not talk of anything else he might have done, but after his return expressed disgust with himself for his "homosexual tendencies." He said he just "couldn't take it any longer" by himself. Now that he was back in the hospital he felt better. After some reassurance by the staff and the attention he needed so much of, Carol again became cheerful.

At about this time another social worker became interested in Carol. Between Carol and this much older woman there developed a relationship similar to that between him and Miss Drake sometime before. Like Miss Drake, she was much impressed by Carol's sincerity, feeling he had been wronged by not having been given a pension for his illness. And like Miss Drake she also was unsuccessful in trying to get him one. She wrote many letters for him and spent hours with him in an attempt to give him the understanding she felt sure the staff could not give him. Despite Dr. Peters's warnings, she soon became so deeply involved in the situation that it was finally necessary to transfer her to another hospital.

Efforts were intensified to get Carol out on a job, primarily for his own ultimate welfare but also to relieve the hospital of some of the strains he had been causing. Within a month another job as hospital attendant was found for him. For the first time he seemed to be happy on a job. Once a week he returned for an interview with Dr. Peters. During these sessions he now began to express feelings of hostility and guilt about them in reference to both his mother and Dr. Peters. He talked of his mother's lack of feeling ("just like a man") and her unsympathetic attitude. Though he seemed to have insight into the forces leading to his present condition, he could not change his attitude about them. During this same period Carol sent Dr. Peters two tickets to the opera for him and Mrs. Peters. In the following interview he readily accepted the interpretation that they were really meant for himself and Dr. Peters, that he wanted to be the wife. In the next interview Carol asked Dr. Peters to go to the opera with him. After a lengthy discussion Dr. Peters agreed to go with him but only if each paid for his own ticket. From his observation of Carol during the performance, Dr. Peters felt his accompanying Carol had, as intended, been an effective expression of reassurance.

Before very long Carol began to have mixed feelings about his job. For one thing, he found himself constantly tired from the hard work. For another, the bleak atmosphere over the

Christmas holiday depressed him. At the end of the second month on the job Carol was shaken by the death of an elderly patient whom he had attended. His anxiety was soon increased when he had to prepare the body for the morgue. Immediately thereafter Carol left his job, going to live with a former patient from Green River who now had an apartment of his own. During this time he also visited his mother. At the end of two weeks, his money all gone, Carol returned to Green River, asking to be taken in again. On the whole, though, he said he felt pretty good, and would probably be ready to leave the hospital in a few weeks.

For some time Dr. Peters had been feeling that Carol was taking up too much of his time, and perhaps should be transferred to another building and another physician when in the next interview Carol told Dr. Peters that he wasn't going to leave the hospital "and be a feather in your cap." Dr. Peters put through the transfer.

For a month Carol worked in the clothing room, marking patients' garments. Then one morning he received some underwear from the women's building for marking. Instead of putting small letters inside the waistband, as he was supposed to do, Carol stamped large letters across the seat. When upbraided for this he seemed at first indifferent, then suddenly stopped working, and stomped out of the room. The following day he disappeared from the hospital, making his way to where his mother lived. He tried to talk her into letting him stay, but she felt she had no room nor could she get a larger place. Angry at her refusal, he sat up all night, refusing to go to sleep in an effort to annoy her. In the morning he returned to Green River. When interviewed he said he was discouraged but not depressed, and that he now realized his mother could not accept him because he had been an illegitimate child. His reason for leaving the hospital, Carol said, had been to gain attention. He told how much he missed talking to Dr. Peters, who, he was sure, no longer wanted him. Nobody at Green River was really interested in him, Carol complained, they just wanted to protect themselves against his leaving and committing suicide. After a discussion of his case at the staff conference next day, Carol was sent back to his former building and Dr. Peters.

In the spring Dr. Peters received a letter from Miss Drake. Expressing her continued interest in Carol, though he had not officially been her "case," she now wanted Dr. Peters's permission to have Carol spend some time with her while she was visiting a nearby town. This was the first time she had been able to come to Vermont since getting her new job in western New York, though she had from time to time written Carol. On being told of her impending visit Carol became enthusiastic, asking Dr. Peters for a three-day pass. Feeling it would be preferable to have Carol spend his nights in the hospital, Dr. Peters gave him instead the first of a series of three one-day passes. That night Carol failed to return. The next morning he appeared back at the hospital, discouraged and unhappy. Upset and depressed by the personal interest Miss Drake was displaying, he had sat up all night in the local bus station. Finally, not knowing what to do, he had returned to the hospital. He did not take advantage of his other passes.

At the beginning of summer Dr. Peters received another letter from Miss Drake in which she explained more fully her interest in Carol. In it she told of how she had met Carol at Green River, of their many evenings together discussing religion, and finally of how he had confided to her the story of his life:

> ". . . including the idea that since he didn't know his father, he might be half Negro or Chinese or something and not good enough for people. Though he wasn't one of my cases I was very much drawn to him, particularly because all that year I had wished that I could have worked with an intelligent psychoneurotic."

She recounted their many visits to homes of her friends, her helping him pick out clothes, and how they had frequently talked of the strong relationship he had with Dr. Peters. Many times when she picked him up for the evening he was depressed but would become cheerful by the time he was ready to go back to the hospital. She also told of how she had on occasion given him money, about which he later expressed some misgivings. Occasionally when he didn't show up "for an appointment I realized I was forgetting he was sick." Ultimately her own family had begun to feel she was "meddling too much," but this had not dampened her interest. She now wanted Dr. Peters to know she had for sometime been sending Carol job suggestions, and would continue to look for "the proper employment for Carol."

For the next few months Carol went through a number of short-lived periods of depression. He was particularly upset at the beginning of weekends when he saw many patients going out on visit. His disappearances from the hospital also increased, particularly when plans for his ultimate discharge were discussed. On many of these "elopements" he went to a nearby town where he had homosexual experiences. Following such occurrences he expressed strong feelings of revulsion, guilt, and unworthiness. His periods of depression became more frequent. Even though he could have had a pass whenever he wanted one he preferred to leave without asking. On one such occasion he neglected to return from what was to have been an evening at the local theater. When he returned the following evening he again talked of being " disgusted with myself." Later he asked to be allowed to work on the outside with a view to ultimate discharge. A few weeks later, just as it seemed a job might be forthcoming, he again became despondent, disappearing one day but showing up again the following afternoon. At the beginning of September he again left the hospital because "everyone was going home for the Labor Day weekend." On his return the following day he was depressed as he told of visiting his mother, and of his finally realizing that her plans did not include him. Two weeks later, becoming "bored" at the beginning of a weekend, he again left for a day, and again returned depressed and disgusted with himself.

> "It seems like I'm not accomplishing anything here. I feel everyone knows the score about me and it bothers me. I don't fit in with the gang. I don't mingle with the other patients and sometimes I get to feeling awfully moody. That's why I left the hospital. I went into town and spent the night sitting in a park. I realized I did wrong but sometimes I get to feeling so that I can't help it."

Four days later Carol again left Green River, making his way to western New York State. After a few days of work as an itinerant laborer he found himself in the town where Miss Drake worked. When he called her to ask what he should do, she invited him to visit, in the meantime calling Green River to tell them of Carol's whereabouts. The hospital felt Carol could stay where he was if he could find a job. Two days later Miss Drake wrote to Dr. Peters, telling in detail what had transpired. When she first saw Carol he "looked badly, his face was broken out again and his suit was badly soiled. But his spirits were good." She had given him money, then found accommodations at a local clergyman's home, where Carol was to help as handyman. She and Carol went out job hunting the next day but without success. She even found him a date with a physically handicapped girl friend of hers. Feeling that Carol could make a good adjustment in a small, supportive environment, Miss Drake tried to get him a temporary job in the institution where she worked, hoping, ultimately, to help him to go to college. But her supervisor did not take so kindly to Carol, and suggested to him that he go back to Green River. Carol agreed with the logic of this, but told Miss Drake that much as he needed Dr. Peters, Dr. Peters could not see him often enough. Besides, he said, being alone in Green River was too difficult for him. At this point Miss Drake was not quite sure what to do. "I have asked all along for Divine guidance with Carol." She suggested he might take some courses at the theological school. In any event, Miss Drake wrote, it would be better for Carol to try something away from Green River than

> "work where he would be with people well below his intelligence level and with a group who might be less high morally. I thought he needed a mother—and I have tried to be that sort of person."

In her letter Miss Drake told where Carol might be reached. But on the day before her letter was received, Carol reappeared at Green River, content to remain "until I can get a job and the right place to live." He was not depressed, saying he had returned only because his funds and employment had run out.

For the rest of that year Carol seemed to make a better adjustment, overstaying just one pass. Then one day he became angry at another patient who had called him a "half-man, half-woman." Feeling he couldn't take any more such taunts he began to throw chairs at the man, but was soon restrained by the attendants.

At the turn of the year Carol again disappeared from the hospital. Late that night he and three soldiers were picked up by the police after they had been observed acting peculiarly in an alley. When returned to Green River the next day, Carol was depressed, crying: "Everything is hopeless." He denied knowing where he had been or what he had done the previous evening, saying that he had "blotted out" after some heavy drinking. He begged to be sent to the security building "so I won't do anything foolish." Within a week Carol was cheerful and his hospital privileges were restored. All then went smoothly for a while, and once again job planning was started. Within two months another outside job had been found for Carol. Just as he was about to be discharged he again became upset and disappeared from the hospital. After a heavy drinking bout in town he returned to the hospital in a belligerent mood. He openly expressed antagonism toward the hospital personnel, complained of the homosexual fantasies he still had, and demanded that he be treated. Despite his behavior the staff did not take away his privileges, since they felt confinement in the past had only aggravated his emotional state. On the following day Carol explained his behavior as being due to fear of going out. All his previous attempts at living away from the hospital had failed, he said, because he couldn't stand being alone. "You just can't have four walls to come back to at night."

Despite Carol's protestations and his repeated demands for a pension, the attitude of the hospital was gradually becoming firmer in the direction of getting Carol out to work. In September another job was found. Carol was to live with the family of an ex-patient, acting as a companion to the son. Knowing Carol had been friendly with him when he was at Green River, the parents felt Carol would be a good choice. Just to make sure, however, they invited Carol to spend a weekend with them. On Friday morning Carol left the hospital ostensibly to have his suit pressed for the occasion, but didn't come back until late that night. Shamefacedly he said he had been so afraid of being put to the test and found wanting, that he had run off to avoid it, spending the day in the public library. He now felt depressed and "just no good." Despite the ability of Dr. Peters and the social worker to buoy him up, once alone he couldn't maintain his courage. In contrast to his optimistic, confident attitude of the past few weeks as he had looked forward to this job, he now was fearful and unhappy. Even his acne had come back within the past couple of days.

Though he constantly expressed interest in getting a job, he regularly continued to become upset just as the social worker found one. But the hospital was not to give up so easily, some of the staff jokingly at times looking upon this as a struggle between them and Carol.

Two weeks later another job was found for him, the duties involving heavy physical labor in a manufacturing plant. After taking him to the job on the first day, the social worker secured for him a room at the "Y." From the start Carol worked hard at the job. His spirits were up and he became optimistic about the future. In his spare time he made frequent visits to the family for whom he was to have worked as companion to their son. Where before he had avoided visiting them he now felt no qualms. Almost immediately they became very much impressed with him, wanting him to come more and more frequently. All was well. But just as Carol was completing his second month on the job he and another employee without seniority were temporarily laid off because of material shortages. For two weeks Carol sought work elsewhere but without success. Gradually he again became depressed. His initiative diminished, but with each visit of the social worker Carol was moved to temporary activity. After another week of fruitless job hunting Carol returned to the hospital. He seemed no longer interested in working, giving the appearance of having "given up."

For the rest of that year and all of the following year Carol remained at Green River, despite many more attempts by the social worker to find him a job. He continued the same pattern as before, disappearing for from one to five days at a time rather than go through the routine of requesting a pass. Following each return his privileges were revoked. This would bring forth expressions of self-disgust and statements to the effect that Dr. Peters was losing interest in him. Because of the depression that followed each confinement, this type of punishment was eventually stopped. The hospital began to accept his frequent departures as a matter of course, ceasing to worry about him when he was not to be found. Sometimes he would get drunk on these disappearances, sometimes not. Occasionally he was returned by the police, but more often he returned by himself. His usual routine away from the hospital was to spend the day in the public library, the night sitting up in the railroad station. Occasionally, while under the influence of alcohol, he would indulge in a homosexual affair, following which he was disgusted with himself and depressed. As time went on he became increasingly resentful toward the hospital, threatening to make trouble and go off the grounds "no matter whether I have privileges or not."

Toward the end of that year Carol was asked by Dr. Peters to help out "like an aide." Immediately his attitude began to improve. He enjoyed working with sick patients, behaving as though he were "mothering" them. During this period Dr. Peters's lavish praise whenever he encountered Carol on the ward soon had marked positive effects. Before long Carol was trying to talk other patients into "working for Dr. Peters and getting something out of it." On the whole, he was now as happy as he had ever been.

At about this time Carol was transferred to the care of another physician, seeing Dr. Peters infrequently. Despite the change he continued to speak highly of Dr. Peters to the other patients, saying Dr. Peters was the "only one around here who knows anything." Whenever he heard anyone talk of Dr. Peters in a disparaging fashion, Carol became very angry. One side result of Carol's favorable remarks was the facilitating of rapport between Dr. Peters and new patients.

Through the winter Carol continued to perform some of the functions of an aide. He was such a help to the ward that he was given a gift paid for by the regular ward personnel. The pleasant working arrangement might have continued indefinitely had he not received a job offer from a friend out of the state. His disclosure of this offer was enthusiastically received by the physician, somewhat to Carol's chagrin. When told he would be discharged so that he might accept the job, Carol abruptly left the hospital in a huff, taking none of his belongings with him.

The job didn't turn out as Carol had anticipated, forcing him to look elsewhere for work. By means of many odd jobs, with a week or two layoff in between, he was able to support himself. But most of the jobs were menial, a source of irritation to Carol. He was finally able to secure a better-paying, more demanding job, but after a few weeks, during which time he became fearful and upset, he "blew his top" at the boss whom he had originally liked. "I put people I like on a pedestal, then I lash back at them once in a while and then bow again." When he lost this job he wrote to his mother, who invited him to stay with her. But at the end of two weeks Margaret's behavior forced him to leave. She had been upset and depressed, mentioning suicide so often that he himself began to feel depressed. He started to drink heavily, had a series of homosexual episodes, and became so disgusted with himself that he returned to Green River for readmission. He had been out of the hospital exactly six months.

On admission Carol said he felt "worthless as a human being," describing his problems as too big to be overcome. He felt neglected and in need of being cared for, "afraid something terrible in a homosexual way might happen if I didn't come back. I never want to leave the hospital again. I'm sorry I ever left." He constantly dwelt upon "my confirmed habit of homosexual relations," how he was a misfit, how he hated all women, and was terrified at the thought of sexual relations with them. If only he had had psychotherapy years ago, Carol felt, he might have overcome many of his problems, particularly those associated with his illegitimacy and feeling of not belonging anywhere. Despite his complaints, Carol was well dressed, neat, coherent, and in excellent contact. By the end of his first week back he seemed to have made a good adjustment. To the physician his mood and appearance now resembled boredom more than a severe depression.

Before many days had passed Carol returned to his habit of disappearing when the impulse came. Over the next few months there were many episodes of leaving the hospital because he "couldn't stand the monotony all of a sudden," then returning in a day or two. Sometimes he would ask the police to take him back. He drank from time to time, ending up occasionally by fighting with other patients in his ward. On one such occasion he attacked a patient who had tormented him about the homosexuality of which Carol had made no secret. Yet in his work assisting one of the women in the arts and crafts shop Carol functioned very well. In addition to helping her care for the more severely sick patients, Carol worked hard at improving the appearance of the classroom.

A few months later, after Carol had been back in Green River for almost a year, he was transferred to Marshview, a new hospital emphasizing rehabilitation. The staff at Green River felt that they had done all that could be done in the seven years he had been with them. Nor did they feel particularly optimistic about any possible success at Marshview. It was rather with a sigh of relief that they took Carol's name off the Green River rolls.

As soon as Carol arrived at Marshview he was put to work as a clerk in one of the administrative offices. Not only did he perform his job well but he began to get other patients to engage in recreational activities. He soon was given pass privileges, but within a few weeks was reported for drinking on hospital grounds. When confronted by the psychiatrist, he became quite agitated, making suicidal threats. For his protection he was put in the locked ward where he could be constantly observed. When visited by the psychiatrist the following morning, he claimed his threats had been "a hoax," a way of "striking back." Within two days he was back at work as though nothing had happened. From time to time Carol developed transient dislikes for individual patients, usually those with homosexual tendencies, but expressed no overt aggression toward them. His behavior was openly attention-seeking. He professed strong interests in various cultural activities but when questioned manifested only a superficial knowledge. The psychiatrist felt his mildly depressed mood to be more a manifestation of deep resentment and boredom than a true depression. In the interview Carol readily described himself as a "latent homosexual" who indulged in overt homosexual behavior when under the influence of alcohol.

Two months after Carol's admission to Marshview a series of supportive vocational counseling sessions was begun as part of a plan to work toward his ultimate release from the hospital. At the start of the first interview Carol was markedly hostile, partly because he was now being seen by a trainee rather than a psychiatrist. "I'm not going to be no guinea pig for some trainee. Who's this going to help, you or me?" Throughout the session he blithely tossed around psychoanalytic terms in describing his problems. As the interview went on he told of his many accomplishments since coming to Marshview, particularly in organizing recreational activities for the other patients. "Mind, not because of selfish purposes, but because I like to do things for others." He was proud of his knowledge of patients and of his ability to get regressed patients to do things where the staff had failed. But this was nothing new to him, he said. He had always been able to do things for others, but never for himself. He then began to talk of his past difficulties with authority, particularly in the Army where there were "big-cheese sergeants" and most officers were "thick-headed, stupid, unreasonable . . ." Here at Marshview, however, he found most of the staff sincere, though firm, with the exception of a woman physician. "I like her when she is alone with me, but I hate her guts when in a group, I don't know why. She plays two roles, sometimes nice, joking, and friendly, and other times a big cheese and two-faced."

Carol was late to the next two sessions, then missed the fourth completely. It seemed to the counselor that Carol came at first only because he was afraid of the disapproval of his work supervisor. He attempted to turn the tenor of the relationship from that of counseling to one of easy familiarity. Gradually he began to talk about his childhood, of his feelings of being "unwanted," "used," "pushed around," "spied on," and "lonely." Occasionally he spoke of his homosexual experiences, describing them as "one-night stands, then discard the partner." Repeatedly he talked of himself as "no good . . . I'll never amount to anything . . . my lot is to live from day to day." Along with his self-deprecation was his feeling of knowing more about patients than did the staff. "I can't make clinical diagnosis, but I know more than most professional people do here because I work with them."

Gradually, after three months, the sessions began to be turned to plans for work and for the future in general. With support and encouragement from the counselor he talked of his interest in hospital work, particularly in recreational activities. For the past two months, as part of the rehabilitation plan, Carol had been put on the "incentive plan." On this plan he worked a full day within the hospital, for which he was paid a nominal sum and lived in a separate building with other "working patients."

The white hospital coat he wore during work was a source of pride to him, a sign of his "professional status." Though he had no difficulty in putting in a full day's work now, he still was unable to cope with his feelings of loneliness when idle, particularly on weekends. He complained of having no real friends, no place to go, nothing to do. Most of his spare time he spent in hanging around the hospital, seldom going out on pass. At one point Carol struck up a friendship with an eleven-year-old boy whose mother he had met in a bar. Fearful for the boy's welfare and concerned with his being alone, Carol took him to the movies on those evenings when the mother was out drinking or entertaining men. As he explained it: "I'm trying to save the boy. His mother isn't a fit mother."

During the five months counseling went on, despite his good work, Carol got into a series of difficulties. Usually these consisted of arguments with patients, one of whom beat him up. On one occasion, after a visit to town, he was picked up by police on suspicion of rape, then later released. Though they had had no real suspicion of him specifically, they were rounding up all mental patients who might have been in the vicinity of the attack. This incident deeply disturbed Carol, giving support to his feelings of hopelessness.

When the counseling sessions began to deal with final discharge plans, Carol stopped coming to them. Instead, he began to ingratiate himself with many of the hospital personnel for whom he had been working. In addition to their usual warm, permissive attitude, they were particularly indulgent toward Carol because of his highly satisfactory work. Many of them hoped to keep Carol in Marshview, looking forward to using him as their assistant. Among them he enjoyed a special "non-patient" status. Concerned lest the combination of Carol's resistance to leaving and the encouragement he was getting in this from some of the personnel prove too much, the staff redoubled their job-seeking efforts. The following month Carol's supervisor discussed with him plans for taking a job outside the hospital. As they talked about this Carol became manifestly depressed. For the next two days he didn't report for work, but after some encouragement went back to his job. Two weeks later he was given some job "leads" to follow up, but instead of doing this, then returning, he stayed away overnight without having seen about any of the jobs.

The following month Carol became depressed again. When he had been absent from his hospital job for three days he was sent to the psychiatrist for evaluation. During this interview he spoke spontaneously, with no evidence of retardation. Though he claimed to be depressed, his appearance was not that of a depressed person. He blamed his unhappiness on the fact that some patients who were working under him had run away. He couldn't understand how patients with whom he had gotten along so well could do this to him. His feelings, he said, were hurt. He now wanted reassurance that he was not a "hopeless case." But when asked just what he would like to do Carol said: "I don't know. It's not up to me." He had now been at Marshview eight months.

Two weeks later Carol was discharged to a job as attendant in a hospital for crippled children, a job that had been located for him but for which he was made to apply by himself. From the start he was happy with his work. He wrote to Marshview, pleading for toys "to give to these poor kids. So please try and send something. They are not for me but for them." However, within two weeks Carol's feelings of inadequacy again began to plague him. In addition to finding it difficult to work under a female supervisor, he was being kidded by other employees who had found out about his mental-patient background. Unable to "take all this," Carol walked off his job, showing up at Marshview the following day. After talking things over with his former supervisor Carol began to feel better, allowing himself to be taken back to his job. A few days later he wrote to Marshview that all was well. Though he had been initially concerned about returning to work, all had turned out well.

Carol has now been out of Marshview almost a year. Since his initial period of difficulty he has done well on the job, receiving high commendation from his supervisors. He has become "pals" with a young boy, the son of a nurse there who Carol feels does not pay enough attention to her boy. There still are occasional periods when Carol gets depressed. On such occasions he may telephone Dr. Peters, saying: "You're the only one. I feel so low." Dr. Peters will listen, then tell him things aren't so bad as they seem. Whereupon Carol will thank him, saying he now feels much better.

Carol writes frequently to Marshview, expressing great interest in the patients and in the work of the hospital. On a few occasions he has returned there for a visit, spending the day with friends among patients and staff. To all he tells how well he is making out and shows them the nice clothes he has been able to buy. Yet he refers from time to time to the suddenness of his leaving Marshview, more or less joking about "when you threw me out."

Warlene

Sam Godsky

DEVELOPMENT OF PARANOID SCHIZOPHRENIA IN A MALE

When Sam's mother found she was pregnant she took to her bed. There she remained until Sam's birth. Since her two previous pregnancies had ended in miscarriages she was taking no chances with this one. A nervous, high-strung woman, Mrs. Godsky had always paid a great deal of attention to the state of her health. Now that she was again pregnant, she was even more concerned. At the end of nine months, after high forceps delivery, she presented her husband with a nine-pound boy. From the start she was oversolicitous in her treatment of Sam, resulting in a closer relationship than that usually found between mother and first-born son in the average Jewish home.

Sam walked at fifteen months, talked at two years. Toilet training was described by Mrs. Godsky as having been "easy." He had the usual childhood diseases without complications. As a young child he impressed his parents with the amount of energy he possessed. Though he had not had any nightmares, sleepwalking, or indulged in nail biting, at a very early age he became very much concerned about his health. He felt he had to have a bowel movement every day, working desperately to force one if none seemed impending. He quickly became alarmed over any cough, and if the weather seemed at all inclement, he would put on rubbers or a sweater without having to be told. Though well liked by the other children and able to get along with them, Sam was always shy and seclusive, preferring to play by himself. He rode his bicycle and played with his toys, but always apart from the other children on the street.

When Sam was four Mrs. Godsky had a second child, a girl. The two children were unable to get along together from the first. Whereas the mother praised Sam as a "very unselfish and obedient child," she complained of the many difficulties she had had with Esther even as a baby. Unlike Sam, Esther was considered by both her mother and brother to be "selfish and disagreeable." Esther, in turn, felt that Sam was pampered and spoiled by her mother, despite Mrs. Godsky's habit of doing everything she could for both children and not making them do anything for themselves.

Sam never did well in school, despite his mother's certainty that he was a bright boy. Disappointed in the first grade that he never got a "gold star" on any of his papers, Sam bought a box of stars, pasting them on all his work. In the third grade he was put into the "dumb class." After school each day, when the other children played games, Sam preferred to be off by himself. He repeated the fifth grade, but "slid by" all the others.

Even as a child Sam always wanted his own way, partly to prove that he was better than others. He had many temper tantrums to which his mother usually gave in. On occasions when she was firm with him he would disappear from the house, remaining away for hours. In his schoolwork Sam also expended much energy, but soon, when it became apparent to him that the others were doing much better, he devoted his attention to the subjects the other students didn't like. In junior high school his only good grades were in Latin, a subject unpopular with the other students. He himself explained his success in Latin as being due to "feeling and imagination rather than to fidelity of translation." As he grew older, with his efforts at achievement and dominance ending in failure, Sam more and more began to daydream about success. In his early teens he began to sleep excessively, finding it difficult to stay awake in school, and, in later years, on the job.

When Sam was fourteen his father was suddenly incapacitated by a brain tumor. He had always been a reticent person, keeping his problems to himself. For five years prior to his illness he had been unemployed, yet went out early each morning as if to work. To keep up the illusion he had cashed in much of his insurance. Now, however, there could be no more concealment of his lack of income. As he lay in bed, awaiting the inevitable end, he worried about what would become of his family. For two years he lay there, during the second year of which he was unable to speak. The sight of his dying father terrified Sam. Though the father had not been overly close to his son, Sam liked him. In describing him, at a much later date, Sam said he was "not a bad man—his brain caved in . . . He laid there like a corpse . . . He couldn't speak." Even when unable to speak, his father beckoned to him, but Sam just couldn't go near. While Esther in her childlike way tried to nurse her father, Sam hid out of sight. (Esther had always, said Mrs. Godsky, "stood up to problems like a little major.") Soon Sam himself began to have headaches, behaving as if he, too, had a brain tumor. Because four members of his father's family had died of cancer, Sam was sure he had, through his father, inherited a tumor tendency.

Sam was sixteen when his father died. Both the lingering illness and the death had grieved him deeply. In an effort to help out financially, Sam quit school, a change that was not wholly distasteful to him. At the same time a maternal aunt and her two children moved in with the Godskys to help Mrs. Godsky with the expenses. Through a relative who owned a nearby theater in the Bronx Sam was able to get work as an usher, working fourteen hours a day. From the start he disliked his job. He felt it unsuited to one who "was going to be an aeronautical engineer," a goal he had recently set for himself. He was particularly disturbed by "necking" in the theater, frequently "lecturing" couples who so indulged. Being himself "too serious-minded to be interested in girls," he felt it necessary to raise the moral tone of those who came to the movies.

About a year after he began working Sam became increasingly nervous, resulting in heart palpitation day and night. He felt this began shortly after he lost his temper at a noisy patron. His shouting at the man had been overheard by the manager, who threatened to fire him. But his being related to the owner saved his job for him. Sam worried about it for a few days, then seemed to have forgotten it. Some time later, during a long show, he became so nervous that he had to walk "around and around" until he felt better.

Gradually Sam's mood became melancholy and depressed. At home he spoke of being "fed up" and wanting to "end it all." He became generally uncommunicative, wanting only to be left alone, and reacting irritably when one of the family "interrupted my thoughts." Along with this Sam developed multiple physical complaints. He worried about his heart, becoming acutely conscious of its beating. He was afraid it would "wear itself out and collapse" from always beating so hard and so fast. Because of this Sam was afraid to exercise at all. He consulted a heart specialist but was told that he did not have heart trouble. Sam then decided he must have a "worry organ" in the cardiac region, like a "long, skinny nerve" which would swell up and inflame with "nerve impulses from worry" and then eject some fluid. He also developed headaches and constipation, from which he deduced that he had either cancer of the rectum, like his paternal uncle, or ulcerative colitis, like his paternal aunt. He regularly fished stools from the toilet bowl, dissecting them with a pencil in a search for blood. "Some days" he felt he had high-blood pressure, and on those occasions would not eat meat. He often felt "like urinating but can't." When nervous he frequently found it difficult to get enough air. Throughout all this Sam felt "always in the dumps."

At the suggestion of his mother Sam brought his complaints to the outpatient clinic of Bronx Hospital. There it was felt that his symptoms were nervous manifestations resulting mainly from the nature and long hours of his job and his irregular eating and bowel habits. He was given a more balanced diet and a lecture on the importance of regular food habits. Two weeks later, when he returned to the clinic, he said he "never felt better in my life." This he attributed to the diet. Also, as noted by the physician, "his bowels were splendid the first week, but not so good the second week."

Sam felt better for a while until the following summer when he visited an uncle who had been operated on for an intestinal tumor. When he heard how his uncle had suffered and of the "terrible things" that had been done to him, he became very much upset. Sam's symptoms returned, stronger than ever. In the meantime relations between Esther and her mother, which had never been too good, had now reached a point where something had to be done. On the advice of a friend Mrs. Godsky took her fourteen-year-old daughter to a children's clinic. A few months later, when Sam seemed to be more nervous than ever, Mrs. Godsky suggested to him that he seek help for himself from the same clinic where his sister was in treatment. He was now eighteen years of age.

At Children's Clinic

Sam was first seen by a female social worker. Though an hour and a half early for his appointment, he said he didn't mind waiting. When the social worker later came back to interview Sam he again assured her that he didn't mind waiting, that his job was "all waiting." With no mention of his sister, who was in treatment at the time, he immediately began to discuss his problems. He had been worrying a great deal about himself, was very health conscious, and became at times quite depressed. His mother didn't know he still had this difficulty, thinking he had gotten over it. He did get over it, but it always came back. He had been reading a lot about things, had been to see some doctors, was very conscious of his heart, and feared he might have heart trouble. When having one of his depressions usually bad thoughts began; then it seemed to go to his heart, and he'd get a constriction. This was followed by a feeling of something going out of his heart. There seemed to be an organ underneath his heart, although he was not clear in his description of it. When he could he "saved" himself. He found he went upstairs very slowly; whenever lifting something he was careful not to strain himself. Several times he mentioned bad thoughts. When asked about them he said things worried him and sometimes things on the job upset him. Following these feelings he would have depressions. "It's awful when it gets you like that." Several doctors had told him that lots of people think they have things wrong with them, but it didn't seem to help much to know about them.

Sam was very careful about his health, his posture, his stomach, and his elimination. In speaking of the members of his family who had died or been sick due to malignant growths he mentioned his uncle, who had been near death but had recovered. He seemed to associate his own illness with the visit to his uncle. Because of the intestinal difficulty it was soon necessary for his uncle to eliminate through his side. This had made a strong impression on Sam. He then mentioned his father's death but talked very little about it. His own difficulties had developed over the past year. He got better, but they always came back. The first thing he remembered about it was his attention to his health. First he took enemas, then he started to regulate himself. He now drank a cup of hot water each morning on arising, then later sat for about twenty minutes on the toilet at a regular hour. He was eating only what he felt was good for him. He was trying to change his whole manner of eating. He used to hurry through a meal, eating fast like his sister Esther, but he had stopped that. Now he took about an hour for his dinner, being very careful throughout the meal.

In fact, Sam was trying to change his whole personality. Though he hadn't assumed much responsibility when his father was alive he now wanted to find out what he was fitted for. He then spoke of his lack of friends and his demand for honesty in a friend when he found one. Occasionally during the interview Sam was near tears, at which times he complained of being sentimental about things. One of the things that bothered him was the fact that Esther often said terrible things to hurt his mother. He didn't like Esther at all, having no love for her himself nor knowing how anybody could. "Her behavior is so terrible."

Future appointments were made for Sam to see the therapist and the psychologist. When he heard the psychologist was a woman, he said he thought a woman would be better for him. He was a little afraid a man might think some of these things were not manly. He guessed he felt that way because he hadn't had a father, confiding always in his mother. When he got up to leave Sam again said how glad he was he had found this place, how much it meant to him to have someone to talk to about these things who would not tell him to forget them. He had found it hard to talk to his family.

The social worker described Sam as a nice-looking boy but with poor complexion and uncertain manner. At times during the interview he stuttered, appearing to have difficulty expressing himself, though most of the time he talked quite easily.

The First Interview

Sam was distressed during the first interview with Dr. Bettincourt. He cried as he told of his father's illness and death, and how he had become irritable and grouchy as he watched his father waste away. When he got a job after his father's death all his trouble became worse. For a short while after starting work as an usher in the theater he had felt superior to the other boys; he was better than they because he was more moral. But very soon he developed a terrible inferiority complex. The other ushers were interested in girls, even having intercourse with them. The head usher especially seemed very vulgar, as he talked so openly about intercourse with girls. He began to tease Sam, asking whether he had gonorrhea, in a tone that implied Sam was really afraid to go with girls. At one point Sam got into a fight with him but was beaten up. Nevertheless, at this time Sam had begun to get interested in girls. Soon he felt poisoned and began to masturbate. This caused him to worry all the more, making it necessary for him to use all his energy to put these ideas out of his head. He almost went out with a girl once but succeeded in beating down the temptation. Finally he conquered: he gave up girls completely, refusing to talk to them or even answer if they spoke to him. At night he had difficulty in sleeping. It was hard for him to keep his job because of his irritability.

As far back as he could remember he had been different, always by himself and without friends except for a boy cousin in the early days. His visit to his uncle in the hospital this past summer had upset him very much. He had become depressed, worrying all the time about his health. He soon became very much aware of his body and his organs, giving himself better care than any doctor could. He was careful to have a soft diet to insure a movement every day, although he frequently had to take mineral oil to help things along. He then talked of the organ under his heart that swelled up when he worried. It had nerves that were connected with the heart and the brain. "There are electric shocks in it and fluid comes out of it." The fluid went all over his stomach, causing different sensations over his body. Sometimes he feared his heart would stop. He thought the organ secreted adrenalin, about which he had read some articles. All people had that organ. Sometimes instead of swelling up it sank down. He felt terrible, he was so distressed. If he had the courage he would commit suicide. He had at times thought of taking poison. Because of his condition he had temporarily given up his job this week.

He then spoke of his being a scientific genius, not so much as fantasy but as an actual belief. He had understood that geniuses were always unbalanced and suffered a lot. When asked about his sister, Sam said she was terribly unmanageable, with no respect for anyone. When he again spoke of the organ under his heart he was asked to draw a picture of it and its relation to the heart and brain. After many erasures he finally made it rectangular, about four and a half inches long and an inch wide.

Sam was given an appointment for the next day but didn't appear. That day his mother telephoned the clinic. Excitedly she told how Sam had come home the night before, terribly upset, and threatening to do away with himself. Now he was in bed with a temperature of one hundred three, and, according to the family doctor, seemed to have the grippe. Dr. Bettincourt suggested she take Sam to the Psychiatric Institute if he became too disturbed, but if he calmed down, she was to let him come back to Children's Clinic. Mrs. Godsky then asked if she herself might come in to talk things over.

When Mrs. Godsky came in a few days later she described Sam as always having been a peculiar child, melancholy and dissatisfied. He had never seemed to get out of life what he should. Since the death of Mr. Godsky Sam had become worse. He resented being asked if he didn't feel well. For the past two weeks he had been pacing the floor all night, something he had previously done only occasionally. Last night he had threatened to leave home because he was no use to anyone and wanted to end it all. He now feared what had happened to his father would happen to him. He told his mother he hadn't missed his father so much at first but now felt he just couldn't take it. Not knowing what was wrong, she had tried to get him to talk about it. He told her he wasn't able to work, but she pointed out she needed to be taken care of. He cried, was hysterical for about an hour. He pulled his hair and seemed "terribly upset." Whenever he got that way, she said, he wouldn't talk or eat. He had had these depressed spells for some time, but since he hadn't talked about it lately she had thought he was better. Since he now had confidence in Dr. Bettincourt Mrs. Godsky was anxious to have him come back to the clinic. Mrs. Godsky then described the many times she had told Sam he couldn't bring back his father; now she worried that he would get sick and suffer as his father had. Because of this she was accepting his leaving his job. The children at the movies on Saturday afternoon had been too much for him. When he said he would like to go away on a boat she told Sam her family would stand by her; what she wanted was for him to get well.

In the meantime, Esther had been talking of Sam to her own therapist. She told how upset he was after seeing Dr. Bettincourt, complaining he didn't see why he had to go there so often. "Why can't I do something all at once and get it over with?" he would moan. Esther felt much of this was "put on" by Sam, that he wasn't really sick but was just acting up for the family's benefit. This had gotten on her nerves so much the other night that she had given him a good talking to, telling him to "buck up" and use some self-control. Sam then had broken down with a severe fit of crying and sobbing, saying he couldn't control himself, that he knew he couldn't. When Esther had realized that this was something different from what she had thought, she, too, had become upset, as had her mother. Then they had all cried. "Oh, it was awful!" Then Esther said: "You know I don't like my brother very well, I never did get along with him. We always fought, but I feel sorry for him, and I'm worried about what's the matter with him."

Esther then asked her therapist if she knew anything from Sam's doctor. The therapist said she did not, but she felt Sam was very nervous and upset and very frightened. Esther agreed, but then went on to say that there was nothing the matter with him. The family had had Sam seen by a "big specialist" at the Bronx Hospital who had gone over Sam from top to toe, and there had been nothing the matter with him. Sam just imagined he was sick. Why didn't he forget it? The therapist told her there were some people who imagined themselves sick and were really sicker than those with real ailments. Because they had no physical symptoms they got no sympathy or understanding. Instead, the therapist went on, everyone gave them lectures and talks that only increased their nervousness and apprehension. She then suggested to Esther that she leave Sam alone entirely, and not try to talk him out of his troubles. Esther said she would, and was very sorry she had upset him the other night.

The Second Interview

At the end of the week Sam dropped in for a short time. He was now over the grippe. He said he had felt terribly depressed at home, when he told his mother of his suicidal ideas, but he really wasn't serious about suicide. As he talked it was evident that Sam was still quite depressed. About the only thing he was able to talk of was his physical symptoms, particularly those of the stomach and the intestines. The only thing that gave him pleasure, he said, was having a good bowel movement.

The Third Interview

Sam was given a physical examination at this time. Afterward he talked quite freely. He was now very calm and without fears. He was able to smile and talk in an easy way. No attempt had yet been made by Dr. Bettincourt to give any particular direction to Sam's talk.

He told how his mother had babied him and how his father had been too moral and strict, with no interest in his son. He had always been mixed up about things. For example, he knew he was terribly mixed up about sex. He talked some more about the organ under his heart and again drew a picture of the heart with the organ underneath it. In a vague way he spoke of the organ's being able to go into the heart. On another piece of paper he drew a picture as he now thought the organ looked in its exact size.

The fourth interview

When Sam came in again a few days later he was smiling, seemingly relaxed and cheerful. The planned lack of direction by Dr. Bettincourt until Sam should relax now seemed to have been successful. Sam made no mention this time of any physical symptoms. He told of his recently having returned to his job, talking at length about the work and all the moving pictures he saw. He described his enjoyment in seeing action scenes over and over again, but had "absolutely no use" for love scenes. When Sam left at the end of the interview he was still smiling and relaxed. He and Dr. Bettincourt were fast becoming close friends.

The Fifth Interview

Sam was again smiling and happy when he came in this time. He felt "pretty good" and was still working. Over the weekend, however, he had felt depressed following a run-in with the assistant manager of the theater. That young man had been teasing Sam, calling him, among other names, a "jerk fiend," meaning a frequent masturbator. The two of them had had a heated argument during which Sam demanded he be addressed as "Mr. Godsky." Dr. Bettincourt pointed out to Sam that even worse than the lack of respect others had for him was the fact that he probably didn't have much respect for himself. Sam agreed, relating many incidents in which he had disappointed himself. He remembered that as a young boy he couldn't play baseball or any of the other sports like other boys who lived in the same block. Once when he was in the outfield an easy fly came in his direction. Having a feeling that he would be unable to catch it, he turned around, letting the ball hit him in his back. By doing this he was able at least to stop the ball. The other boys had no use for him, nor did they ever ask him to play with them. It made Sam feel very low.

For a long time Sam had had a casual acquaintance with some bad boys between the ages of eleven and fourteen. During this period he himself became a "very bad boy" just so he could feel superior and "big." He actually became a kind of leader in this gang of bad boys, of whom two at least later landed in the reformatory. Among other things, Sam and the others would "bum rides" on streetcars, smoke, make much noise, steal fruit from stands, steal articles from parked cars and tools that might be lying unattended. One night he and another boy went around breaking every window in all the schools in the neighborhood. Sam finally quit this gang without having been caught by the police. With them he had felt "big," he repeated. It was from them that he learned all about sex, having known nothing previously. Looking back, he felt that what they had told him was not always correct.

As Sam and Dr. Bettincourt talked about this area of sex, it became evident that Sam had known "some things" much before the boys had told him anything. More so even than in the discussion of other areas Sam's statements now were inconsistent, especially regarding time relationships. As the discussion went on, the time relationships became quite hazy as Sam got more and more mixed up. When asked whether he had really known nothing prior to his association with the bad boys, Sam said yes. But when asked specifically whether he had known about sex differences, it turned out that he had known about them before. When Sam was nine and his sister five, their mother used to bathe them together. The first time in the tub with his sister he had felt upset in some way as well as intensely curious. From the tenor of his discussion of the incident it was evident to Dr. Bettincourt that, without realizing it, Sam had been sexually excited at the time. The bathing together of the two children lasted for about a year or two. It was only through this that Sam had discovered that boys and girls were different. No, Sam later said, that wasn't the case either, because when he was five and maybe even earlier he had seen his mother naked. At any rate, he hadn't liked the idea of bathing with a girl, objecting to his mother frequently. Finally Mrs. Godsky had stopped the practice. No, this story couldn't have been true, either, because when Sam was eleven he had made some improper suggestions to his sister. At one point during their sharing the same room Sam had suggested to his sister that they indulge in some sexual behavior. Esther had then told her mother, who scolded Sam, telling him it was about the worst thing in the world he could do. For a long time then Sam had felt ashamed, afraid even to look at his sister or his mother, "like an outcast." He then told of several occasions when he had suggested to the gang of bad boys that they rape a girl, but none of these suggestions were carried out. Dr. Bettincourt pointed out to Sam that there was a difference in being afraid to do something wrong with his sister and being afraid to have anything to do with any girl. Sam then told how, when five or six, he and another boy had played dirty games with a little girl in the neighborhood. They had done all sorts of naughty things, at times sticking a clothespin "in her front and back."

Sam appeared relieved by the telling of these experiences. Dr. Bettincourt then told him that he didn't want Sam to think he was only interested in having Sam tell him all the naughty things he had done. Throughout the interview Dr. Bettincourt had the impression that Sam was deriving great satisfaction from being able to show that he had been bad and wild when younger.

The Sixth Interview

In general he was feeling much better now, Sam said. However, there were still times when he became depressed and worried about "the organ." He was now becoming religious. A young man he knew was going to teach him Hebrew for a very slight charge. In talking of his religious interests he told of having made his *bar mitzvah* at thirteen. On that day he was to have made a speech in the temple but being ill, he had been unable to go, postponing the ceremony one week. The following week the ceremony had not amounted to much and there had been no speech to make. He admitted having been quite terrified by thoughts of the ordeal of making a speech as well as by the general ceremonial aspect of the occasion. Like his father, Sam had not been particularly religious, but now when on Saturday mornings he went to the temple the men there complimented him very much because of the interest he was showing. This made Sam feel very proud.

Dr. Bettincourt noted that the interest in Hebrew began a short time after Sam had started to visit the clinic. He pointed out to Sam that he had had many conflicts that made him afraid to go out, and of which he himself was probably aware. He suggested to Sam that maybe he was aligning the therapist with one side of his personality, that of the bad boy, then counteracting this by developing the other side, that of the good boy, through his Hebrew lessons. Dr. Bettincourt then asked him how he felt about telling the things he had told in previous interviews. Sam said he felt a little ashamed. He was not pressed to make any more revelations, but was told that he had been afraid and mixed up about things, and that Dr. Bettincourt would be patient and would help Sam see just what his conflicts were.

The Seventh Interview

Sam came in eagerly, showing Dr. Bettincourt the new overcoat he had bought. All week he had been happy and proud of himself because he had started in on his Hebrew lessons. It was clear that to Sam this signified being a good boy and conforming. He spoke of his interest in Hebrew as being an interest in the finer things in life. It was the kind of interest that would make people proud of him and compliment him on being so good. He had tried to put out of his life the other side that was opposite to what he considered the finer things. He thought he was now losing all interest in girls. However, this past Saturday, while in the temple, he had suddenly developed a terrible pain in his rectum.

At this point in the record Dr. Bettincourt commented on the obvious meaning of this symptom: One part of Sam's personality had been dominant all week, being expressed in Sam's pleasure in being good and interested in the finer things of life. This part of Sam's personality had said: "This is the nicest thing in life: to be interested in religion." But on Saturday the other part of his personality had manifested itself by saying: "This is a pain in the . . ."

To Sam, however, Dr. Bettincourt simply pointed out that there was a conflict and that Sam realized it. But Dr. Bettincourt emphasized that Sam need not feel that he had to overcome it immediately. Nor did he need to feel inferior about it, despite the prodding by the boys at the theater for Sam to go out with girls, just the thought of which had frightened Sam. Dr. Bettincourt then told Sam it would be better for him not to force issues but to be patient until, together, they could find out just what it was about the topic that so frightened Sam.

Sam then described how necessary it had always been for him to conciliate people so that they would like him. As he talked he gave Dr. Bettincourt the impression that he really wished people not to hurt him. He had always wanted to be approved of, so much so that he became fearful and timid. For example, Sam said, if in a restaurant he picked up a bottle of plain milk by mistake, he would be afraid to put it back to pick up a bottle of chocolate milk, though he would be entitled to do so.

With a great deal of hesitancy Sam later said that he would like to go to the Bronx Hospital clinic for physical examinations. For some weeks now he had not talked of "the organ" or the sensations to it from the nerves. Dr. Bettincourt told him it was all right to tell of his wish but that he had recently been examined at various clinics. Also, if Sam just went from clinic to clinic he would in short order exhaust all the possibilities. However, if he wished reassurance he might go for examinations at intervals but not too frequently.

At one point in the interview, in talking about possible areas of interest, Sam expressed a liking for sports. Dr. Bettincourt did not press this because of Sam's current disinclination to associate with people. However, Sam had been getting a little friendly with some of the other ushers, going out with them on his day off. He was praised for this by Dr. Bettincourt, and encouraged to continue doing so.

The Eighth Interview

Sam now seemed more confident and assertive in his manner. He was thankful and appreciative toward the clinic, saying he was now feeling very happy. Nothing bothered him any more. He was also making good progress with his Hebrew lessons, an achievement that had prompted his grandmother to reward him with a dollar.

Dr. Bettincourt then talked to him about "being a good boy," pointing out that Sam had made too sharp a distinction between being a good boy and being a bad boy. Little children, he went on, often get the idea that they will be liked only if they are good in the sense of not doing things. People are really liked for their own personal likeable qualities, not simply because of their ability to be compliant and obedient.

Later Sam told of his intention to have a hobby, specifically, learning about radio sets. With a cousin he was now going to the "Y" to build himself up physically. Last week he had had a cold but didn't let it bother him one bit. He mentioned how confident in himself he now felt. He no longer thought of his old symptoms, such as the organ under his heart. Recently, on seeing a young fellow usher feeling his pulse, he laughed heartily and told him not to be a hypochondriac. On another occasion a boy with whom he was walking had expressed a fear of going insane. Sam had immediately told the boy of his being treated "some place," and that it would be a good idea for the boy also to get some advice.

Girls were now definitely out of the picture, as far as Sam was concerned. He planned to keep himself chaste until he married. He had recently read the pamphlet on sex that his sister had been given by her therapist. The pamphlet said that people who had intercourse before marriage felt guilty about it and so didn't get any fun out of it. Sam said this wasn't true. He knew from lots of people who had premarital relations that they didn't feel guilty about it.

Sam enumerated three factors that he considered to be responsible for his trouble. One: He had had carnal desires that produced a conflict. Two: About two or three years ago he and a boy cousin almost four years his junior were inseparable companions. Despite the age difference they both had had the same outlook, being interested in sports but not in girls. Sam had known some boys who even at twelve liked to go out with girls! But he was not like that, having no such interest even at sixteen. About three years ago the cousin had moved away, and it was as if something had been taken away from Sam. Three: Finally, and most important of all, he had always been rather sheltered, always being played up as a good boy. Then, suddenly, he had plunged into a world he didn't know anything about. Without his cousin he had no friends. All at the same time he had been (1) faced with illness and deaths in the family, (2) thrown into conflicts about sex, (3) disturbed because of feeling inferior to the other boys, (4) faced with financial worries. He had felt completely lost. Dr. Bettincourt agreed with Sam that it was really as though he had suddenly been thrown into a jungle.

The Ninth Interview

When Sam came in he told of having had a fairly good week, and that Dr. Bettincourt must surely have noticed how calm he was. He had spent most of his time studying his Hebrew lessons. Dr. Bettincourt told him that this was all right but that it was also a defense and that Sam really knew this; the more he studied Hebrew the less chance there was for him to go out with girls. This past week Sam had been a little worried by one particular girl who came to the theater frequently. He apparently was struggling quite vigorously against the temptation to look at her or talk to her. Some time ago he had had sex fantasies about her. On one occasion he had even put his arm around her. He knew some of the other boys had taken her out, and he had heard stories of her sex activities. Once he had gone out with another girl who had frequented the theater a good deal and who had been taken out by most of the other ushers. Anticipating some sexual activity, Sam had a condom in his pocket when he took her out. However, the date had been very disappointing, both Sam and the girl being restrained and cool toward each other. Yet once, while at work, Sam had seen one of the other ushers fool around with this same girl, doing "everything except actually have intercourse with her." Sam had become quite excited as he watched them.

When asked about his sexual activities at present, Sam said there were none. He hadn't masturbated from the time he first began coming to the clinic. He said before he had been ashamed to talk of this, denying at first any other motive for his reticence, such as being afraid to masturbate and then telling Dr. Bettincourt about it. As the discussion of masturbation continued, Sam began to express many fears long associated with it in his mind. He thought it would rob him of pleasure later on in intercourse with a wife, that his procreative organs would be injured, that his penis would in some way be harmed, perhaps ruptured. He considered masturbation "dirty," having found it defined in the dictionary as a "self-pollution." Over and above all this perhaps masturbation was one of the ways in which one lost his chastity. Dr. Bettincourt corrected many of these ideas. He then asked Sam about nocturnal emissions. Sam told him that the first one had occurred at the age of thirteen, when he was living with an aunt at the beach. One day he had accidentally seen her maid naked. That night Sam had had a "wet dream," an experience that had horrified and frightened him. He had felt as though he had committed some terrible crime. Even now, just having an erection evoked in him much distress.

Sam was then asked to tell of the sleeping arrangements at home. Until the death of his father Sam and his sister had slept in the same room. Since then, however, Sam had been sharing his mother's room, but not her bed. He knew his sister's therapist had spoken to her about the sleeping arrangements at home, since his mother had been quite upset when Esther told her. Dr. Bettincourt told Sam he agreed with Esther's therapist that it would be better for Sam not to sleep in the same room with his mother. At first, Sam said, he used to notice his mother when she undressed, then he would have fantasies of other girls. However, now there was not any particular distress on his part connected with the sleeping arrangements. Nevertheless, he would take the clinic's advice about this matter.

The Tenth Interview

Sam called to cancel his next appointment. One month later he again appeared at the clinic. Three weeks ago, he reported, he had had "a little attack." After expectorating he had looked at his throat in the mirror, afraid there was something wrong. On telling this he quickly went on to talk of how his father's brain tumor had caused some throat paralysis. Sam's attack had quickly worn off, however, and for the past three weeks he had been "in utopia." He felt absolutely cured, so much so that he was a little resentful about continuing at the clinic on the basis of receiving treatment. However, he welcomed very much Dr. Bettincourt's suggestion that he could come just as a friend to tell how he was getting along, independently of whether or not he needed treatment for his symptoms.

Sam then told of having spoken to a girl recently, and how he now had a date to visit her in a few days. He felt very confident that it had all been foolish, his having ideas that he wasn't a ladies' man or that he could never have anything to do with girls and would always have to be lonely. He now had some catalogues describing evening courses he might take. He wanted to educate himself, perhaps with courses in philosophy, psychology, and engineering. He was also continuing his study of Hebrew.

Sam spent a good part of the interview criticizing his sister's doctor, to whom he always referred as "Miss." He and his mother had talked it over a great deal, and both now felt that Esther had only gotten worse since coming to the clinic. They felt her doctor had put wrong ideas into her head, meaning about sex. Her doctor had no right to say that the mother was old-fashioned, or imply that there was anything in the home atmosphere responsible for Esther's trouble. The home atmosphere was perfect, his sister was a rat, and it was all her fault, Sam shouted.

Despite the advice of the clinic, sleeping arrangements at home had not been altered, nor did it seem that they would be. Since the topic was so disturbing to Mrs. Godsky, and because her daughter now seemed to be even more disrespectful than before, she had just about decided not to let Esther visit the clinic any more. Sam was told it was necessary to be patient and sympathetic with Esther, and that Dr. Bettincourt would talk to her therapist about her.

The Eleventh through Seventeenth Interview

For the next two months Sam continued to visit the clinic regularly. He talked of how much braver he was in his contacts with girls, going so far one day in the theater as to take the liberty of touching a girl's buttocks. Most of his attention, however, was concentrated on studying Hebrew. However, he was now a little concerned about his sister who, he said, went out too much and stayed out too late.

He told of being depressed one day, but not knowing why. Dr. Bettincourt told him it was important that they discuss it so that they could try to discover the reasons for Sam's feelings. Gradually Sam remembered that on that particular day he had seen a very pretty girl. What had depressed him was the realization that he had great desires for girls but felt so inferior to the other boys that it had seemed hopeless to him about ever going out with a girl. He was becoming a little irritated with his being such a good boy. Everybody was saying this about him, even the kids in the street. He was getting sick of it. He was thinking of taking up dancing lessons, he said.

In still later sessions he appeared alert, lively, talkative, full of all sorts of ambitious plans for the future, such as going to college. Dr. Bettincourt suggested that this might be too difficult at present, but it was fine that he could assert himself and tell his therapist about it. The important thing, he continued, was that Sam's idea was essentially correct and in the right direction. Sam no longer seemed concerned over his health, rarely mentioning it. He was frank in admitting his uneasy feelings regarding girls, being encouraged by his doctor to try to overcome them gradually. Sam referred again, later on, to his younger cousin, saying that they had been so inseparable that he had had no chance to make other friends. He considered this important in causing him to be shy and unable to get along not only with other boys, but particularly with girls.

Additional Interviews

One month later Sam came to the clinic after having called for an appointment. He wanted a little help. He had been studying very hard a college textbook on how to study and work efficiently. One of the chapters had called for the students to carry out an experiment in which they had to account for every minute of every day for a whole week to determine how much time they had been wasting. Sam thought there was something ridiculous about the whole theory, feeling quite relieved when Dr. Bettincourt agreed with him.

Dr. Bettincourt then explained to Sam the struggle between, on the one hand, his attempts to liberate himself, or feel freer in his impulses and, on the other hand, his keeping tabs on every minute of his day as a very nice way of protecting himself by making sure no unwholesome impulses could come to the surface to upset him. Sam was very much impressed by this explanation. He had already mentioned his inability to skip anything in the book, feeling a compulsion to carry out every order and experiment. At the same time he had talked about how everything in the book was overdone, that by expanding what should have been a good ten-page pamphlet into a four-hundred-page book, the text on efficiency had itself become an example of waste and inefficiency.

Sam then told of having spent fifteen dollars on a course of dancing lessons, in which he now felt he had been gypped. He had felt quite uncomfortable at first in dancing with the girls, but this later wore off. Throughout all this recounting Dr. Bettincourt was strongly encouraging. At the end Sam said he would go back for more lessons. He also reported at this time that his health was still absolutely perfect, that he had a lot of confidence in himself and, except with girls, was not upset in his relationships with people.

Four months later, in midsummer, Sam paid a surprise visit to Children's Clinic to tell Dr. Bettincourt how things were going. Tanned and looking well, he described himself as a new man with a great deal of confidence in himself. He was a cured case, he said. His health was perfect. He bragged a good deal, as he told how much he now liked his work at the theater. It was a great place to meet people, something he was now enjoying despite his formerly having been so miserable in doing so. He wasn't afraid of girls any more. He now walked home with lots of them, went to their houses, had even had one sexual experience. Though he did not mention it to Sam, Dr. Bettincourt wondered whether Sam's return was primarily to tell him of this experience.

The girls with whom he walked home, Sam said, were nice girls, but the girl of whom he now spoke was a "douche bag." He and another boy had taken a walk with her. In order to make a big impression on the other boy, to show him what he could do and what a big shot he was, Sam had asked the girl to masturbate them both at the same time. This she had done. For about a week after this Sam had been disgusted. But as Sam told of this it was evident that he had also gotten much satisfaction out of the incident, not only as a sexual experience but because he had been able to impress the other boy.

Recently Sam had been investigating night schools. He wanted to take up auto mechanics, since an uncle had promised to get him a good civil-service job if he could obtain some training. Despite his now talking of being an auto mechanic, Sam had not completely given up his grandiose ideas. Hesitantly he talked of how it was only human to have daydreams about being a genius. From auto mechanic there was but a step to becoming an engineer, and then there were many further things ahead!

Sam spoke only briefly of his sister, saying she was still a little spoiled. Recently she had dropped some things on the floor, then refused to pick them up. It was only after he "really beat her" that she had picked them up.

For a while after his series of visits to Children's Clinic Sam's mood underwent an upswing. At the same time many of his physical symptoms disappeared. He became "happy most of the time," active and sociable, taking part in family conversations, and occasionally going out with the boys. In his own words, he became "bold and brazen" with some of the girls who came to the theater, "insulting them" in an obscene and loud fashion. When alone he daydreamed much "about sex," though he "never had time" for dates. The rest of the time he daydreamed about "airplanes and zeppelins" and "inventions" as he had done for years.

A few months later Sam enrolled in the Municipal Trade School, hoping to fulfill his dreams of becoming an aeronautical engineer. Despite his good intentions he failed to do well there, being "tired and sleepy all the time." Nevertheless, he persisted ("I drove myself"), recounting later how he would not let himself "sleep or rest." Throughout all this he continued to work nights in the theater.

In the summer, after school had let out, Sam was very active. According to Mrs. Godsky he was "always on the go," spending his days playing golf by himself, his nights working at the theater. In September, one evening about a week before classes were to begin, he became anxious, pacing the floor at home. He told his aunt he was "blue," "down in the dumps," and afraid his old "nervous trouble" was coming back. The following night he called his aunt into his room to tell her he felt sick, tired, and exhausted. It seemed to him that he was "hanging on the edge of a precipice." He appeared very discouraged and anxious. Suddenly he broke into uncontrollable laughter, saying he could not stop. This was followed by a crying spell, which in turn gave way to a discussion of the theme: "I am a superman but there's a cloud over my brain that won't let me concentrate." After this episode he slept most of the time, day and night, being chronically exhausted before and after sleeping. There were occasional spells of uncontrollable laughter. Usually on these occasions he took a walk so as not to alarm the family. For the first time in his life he began to talk of sexual matters to his aunt and mother, though not in an obscene fashion. He complained that there should be places where men could go to release their sexual energy. He was much disturbed by his inability to achieve a "limited type of concentration," a peculiar power he felt was possessed by some persons whereby they could accomplish great things.

Sam's aunt suggested he return to Children's Clinic, but he said this time he wanted to go to a "big psychiatrist." About a week later, after he had lost all interest in his usual activities and seemed to be preoccupied with his fantasies, Mrs. Godsky took him to a private psychiatrist. However, she refused to accept the suggestion that Sam be hospitalized and given electro-shock treatments. At the recommendation of the next physician she visited, Mrs. Godsky took Sam to the psychiatric clinic of the Bronx Hospital.

During the interview at the clinic Sam appeared sleepy but was able to carry on a conversation. He complained of being unable to do anything but sit for hours "half sleeping" and preoccupied with daydreaming about zeppelins and airplanes. At the same time he had noticed increased thirst and urination. During the interview he was not depressed, nor did he seem to have any hallucinatory experiences. Because of his sleepiness, the question of midbrain pathology was raised. When Sam returned to the clinic five days later he showed a striking improvement. His sleepiness was gone, and along with this there was an increase of interests. However, a week later he was brought back by his mother, again preoccupied and in a state of sleepiness. He told the physician: "I sleep all the time. I'm always tired. I can't think." He complained of frontal headaches "all the time." His eyes were dull and heavy. At this time he was admitted to the hospital for study.

Despite the suggestion of neurological disturbance raised by the sleepiness, all chemical, physical, and neurological examinations were negative. Skull plates, done to rule out the possibility of brain tumor, were also negative. During the E.E.G. recording Sam kept moving, smiling, frowning, and grimacing all through the overbreathing. During the rest of the record artifact head movements and eye movements were introduced. In between these artifacts there was normal ten per second alpha activity undisturbed by overbreathing. The examination was considered normal though unsatisfactory.

Sam's behavior in the psychometric examination was described as "verbally energetic and aggressive, alternating at times with very easy giving up." He frequently discoursed on how easy the problems would be for him if he were in his normal condition, that there was "nothing to" mathematics anyway. With each response he asked: "Is that right?" in a challenging tone. On the Wechsler-Bellevue Intelligence Scales he did well in the verbal areas, achieving the lower limits of college level. On the performance subtests, however, Sam had great difficulty. On block designs he began very well but broke down completely in the last two problems, surrendering after a relatively brief attempt.

On the ward Sam made a poor adjustment, taking an immediate dislike to the nurses and some of the patients. Though occasionally anxious and depressed, most of the time he was bright and cheerful. During the interviews his stream of talk was rapid, continuous, and often excited, consisting of big words, abstract phrases, obscenity, and scientific terminology. His memory was intact, his mental grasp normal. At times he described himself as a genius, a superman, capable of great inventions. He again expressed his belief in his "worry organ." Occasionally he talked of his dreams of killing people in violent ways.

On Sam's first visits to the occupational-therapy shop he was very talkative, claiming to know a great deal about woodworking. When questioned specifically, however, he admitted not knowing many things. He frequently complained of being tired, but stuck to the work. He was pleased when helping to make decorations for the hospital party, saying: "I feel so much better when I am doing voluntary work." A few days later, while in the shop, he talked a great deal about himself and his ideas, of his search for Truth, the proper use of time, and "perfect concentration." Though he helped others with their work he wouldn't begin a project of his own. Many times he would play ball with the other patients but was always very careful not to "overtire" himself.

A month after his admission Sam was discharged from the psychiatric ward of Bronx Hospital. Diagnosis at that time was deferred.

After a few weeks at home Sam was inducted into the Army. Before very long it became evident that Sam Godsky was not going to be a success as a soldier. From the start he had difficulty in keeping up with the others. He had "no ambition to march." His tendency to sleep all the time reasserted itself. Whenever there was a job to be done Sam was fast asleep somewhere. One typical incident occurred each time his company moved out on maneuvers. Fast asleep at the time, Sam would be left behind. After a few months of this Sam was sent to the station hospital for evaluation. There he stayed for three months, at the end of which time he was diagnosed "psychoneurotic" and discharged. In all he had spent eight months in the Army.

For a while after Sam's return he seemed quite happy. On one occasion he dropped in on Dr. Bettincourt to tell him of his Army experiences and of how well he now felt. Then his mood began to change. He wanted to be left alone, not talking to anyone. From time to time he got a job in a defense plant, but quickly lost it when found asleep when he should have been working. His mother tried to get him to see a psychiatrist but Sam felt he could work things out by himself. Occasionally he returned to the outpatient clinic at Bronx Hospital, complaining of his usual somatic symptoms. A year later, at the age of twenty-three, he again went there after having lost another job because of his sleepiness. While working at the Army base he had fallen asleep a few times. Interpreting this as laziness, his foreman had fired him. Now Sam was asking the hospital for help in getting his job back. The hospital could not offer him much help in this direction but they were able at this time to rule out narcolepsy as a possible cause of his sleepiness.

For the next six months Sam appeared to be getting along without much difficulty. Unable to get a job, he seemed to accept his enforced idleness without much apparent difficulty. However, just when the financial situation at home was getting desperate, a letter came to him from a successful uncle in Chicago in which he offered to teach Sam the upholstering business. On his mother's urging Sam left for Chicago and his new career. For the next two months he lived at his uncle's house but in all that time not once felt well enough to go to work. Meanwhile, he called several Chicago hospitals, and, after identifying himself as Dr . . . or just as "a big brain doctor," would tell them he was sending in a patient for a brain-wave test. Shortly thereafter Sam would himself appear at the hospital, ready to be examined. During this same period Sam began to telephone married women in the neighborhood asking to see them. After two months of this kind of behavior on Sam's part the uncle felt something had to be done. But when he told Sam he would take him to see a doctor Sam left the house. For a few days he worked as a janitor, but was fired because of inefficiency. For the next three weeks he was broke and hungry, getting an occasional meal by washing dishes in cheap restaurants. Finally, unable to take it any longer, he wired his mother collect for enough money to get back to New York. Two days later he arrived back in the Bronx, surly and disagreeable. From the time of his return he talked incessantly. He announced to his family that there was a cure for cancer and a new gun that would quickly end the war. He claimed everyone in Chicago was suffering from a goiter, that he had had one but had cured it himself by taking "pills." He also was sure he had colitis and an ulcer. His appetite was poor, and though he slept well, he did not sleep so much as he used to. He became quite irritable, threatening his mother. At one point, in a fit of temper, he put his fist through a door.

After a few days of this behavior Sam complied with his mother's urging to pay a visit to the psychiatric clinic. When seen there he was in a state of what seemed to be manic excitement. There was a press of speech, with a rapid flow of associations. Throughout the interview he was quite aggressive. He manifested much concern about his heart, his brain, and his stomach. Alternating with this was his belief that he had discovered the secret of the atom. Deciding that Sam was now "violent and in need of immediate hospitalization," the psychiatrist had him sent to State Hospital for observation. On arrival there Sam was co-operative and completely oriented. He blithely explained away the statements he had made at the psychiatric clinic, saying he was just interested in electricity but had not made any discoveries.

Physical and neurological examinations were entirely negative. Physically he was "stocky," well developed, and well nourished. On the ward Sam was quiet and in good contact, mixing well with the other patients. Overtalkative, though relative and coherent, he gave the impression of being more of a talker than a doer. There was no flight of ideas, no blocking, no rhyming, or preoccupation. His psychomotor activity was normal. Emotional tone was flattened but appropriate and mild when questioned about his personal affairs. He talked freely about his theory of the integration of matter by waves and about the German character as being "so destructive." His philosophy of life was that you get out of it what you put in and most of the time less. He was sorry about having created such a disturbance at the clinic where he had "told everyone off." "They must have thought I was crazy." Though in the past he had worried much about his health, certain in his own mind that he had syphilis, gonorrhea, and/or a brain tumor, Sam said he now wasn't going to worry about anything.

When asked about his marital status Sam said he was "single, thank God!" and that he didn't believe in marriage. He admitted having been approached at times by men but had had no relations with them, nor did he feel attracted to this behavior. Contrary to his earlier religious interests he now didn't believe in religion or God, nor was he at all worried about his lack of faith. Where he used to spend much time in the synagogue, for some time now he hadn't gone at all. His major problem at this time, he felt, was his need for a rest. He felt tired all the time, although otherwise he felt "pretty good." There was definitely nothing wrong with his mind, he asserted. He said he had made plenty of mistakes in his work, usually realizing it after he had committed them. When discharged, he would like to "do my work and mind my business." Five days after his admission Sam was diagnosed as not insane, and released to his mother.

Again Sam tried to hold down a job, but was unsuccessful. Though the war situation made it easy for him to find a job, his feelings of fatigue and inferiority, combined with his belief that others were taking advantage of him or wanted to do him bodily harm, soon led to behavior that resulted in his being fired. About a year after his brief stay in State Hospital he finally found a good job in defense construction work. Though his earlier symptoms persisted he managed to keep from being fired. Two months later he was involved in an accident at work, in which his right eardrum was punctured. All of his previous attitudes and symptoms immediately became markedly more severe. Soon he became suspicious of the physician treating his ear, refusing to let him examine. Then he became suspicious of his mother, fearing that she might be trying to poison him. He felt he had "polio," but "cured" himself by taking twelve sulfa tablets. On the following day he saw a caption in the newspaper, "Boy cured polio with sulfa." Immediately he was sure someone was trying to steal his glory. A few days later he saw another headline, this one beginning: "President says . . ." Certain that his words and thoughts had been used by the President, he suddenly realized that the whole world was listening to him, Sam Godsky! But because he was important and different, people were trying to harm him.

Within two weeks he was sure the telephone operator was spying on him. He immediately told his mother. When she was not properly sympathetic, which only increased his suspicion that she was trying to poison him, he beat her. A few days later Sam visited the courthouse to sit in on a trial, something he had done from time to time while unemployed. On this occasion a man, a complete stranger to Sam was on trial for rape. Suddenly Sam cried out, disrupting the proceedings. The defendant was being railroaded, he shouted. If they could put an innocent man like this one in jail they might next put Sam Godsky in! He was then forcibly ejected from the court.

At home during the next couple of days he began to worry about what might be done to him for his behavior in court. At the same time he accused his mother of having had sexual relations with many men, calling her "foul" and "degraded." At the end of the second day he began to "see" plain-clothes men, with guns pointed, searching for him. When the police came to pick up a stolen car near his home he was sure they were using that only as a ruse to surround his house and trap him. Seeking to avoid capture and bodily harm, Sam abruptly left home. He went to a small town in Connecticut where he quickly came to the attention of the police. At the request of his mother, who had been notified, he was brought back. En route he broke away from the guards, attempting to commit suicide by jumping off the train into the river. He was still sure it all had to do with the scene he had created in court. At one point he was sure that he recognized the menacing figure of the judge among his captors in Connecticut. He begged the police to shoot him.

When Sam was brought back to New York, he was immediately taken to Psychiatric Institute. In the admission office he was quite disturbed, attempting, unsuccessfully, to escape. On the ward from the first he was difficult to handle. At one time he attempted to attack one of the nurses, at another he was accused by one of the patients of making advances to him. During the interviews he frequently talked of the evil in the world, of how the weak were ground into dust and spit on. He ardently wished for communism. Damning his government, he wished aloud that he lived in Europe. He mentioned that he had had sexual relations with women, but looked on it as a fulfillment "of higher emotions."

Mrs. Godsky was able to add a few new details for the record. She told how he had been so close to her in growing up, a dependency she had encouraged. When she later tried to change this Sam had insisted things be kept the same. On one occasion he had flown into a rage when she asked him to drain the tub after using it himself. One of the factors keeping them so close, she said, was that he had always been "a good boy and never went around with girls." Ever since adolescence he had been greatly disturbed by immorality in others. Within the past few months, Mrs. Godsky said, he had many times accused his sister, Esther, of sexual promiscuity, often threatening to beat her because of it.

Several times during the interview on his first day at the institute Sam knelt before the examiner, agitatedly begging for mercy. He promised to do anything if only he could be spared, then burst out crying. When the ward door was open he again tried to escape. On the second day he made good an attempt to escape, but returned quietly, an hour and a half later, in the company of a policeman. He was irritable back on the ward, brooding when alone. If approached by a staff member, however, he immediately became suspicious, escaping to the other side of the room.

When interviewed again, ten days later, Sam's face was tense and drawn. He was restless, casting frequent quick glances over his shoulder. At times, raising his voice, he loudly declared that no one was going to do him bodily harm, meanwhile looking nervously about him. As he talked he seemed preoccupied with inner thoughts. He mentioned a plot against him, directed by an important man whose name he refused to reveal. His thinking was muddled and disordered. In his speech he shifted rapidly from his being head of the communistic world to his discovery of the cure for cancer, and then to his own somatic complaints. When asked a direct question he became evasive. There was a curious mixture of weird statements of bodily changes and discussion of the problems of evil and of the government.

Sam's mood was generally depressed, whether he was restless, agitated, or fearful. When asked how he felt he always responded with: "How can I feel well with polio and the poisons eating me away?" If at such times his polio was discounted he immediately began to bemoan the evil in the world. His main preoccupations, however, to which he invariably returned were his worries about the threat of physical harm to him from others and his own physical diseases. He complained of polio, of brain tumor, and myriad other conditions. He was particularly concerned because of "hydrogen osmosis in my gut," as a result of which a tumor formed on his left side, pulling his gut out of line so his "sh— comes out sideways."

Along with some superficial knowledge he evidenced much interest in medicine. Declaring himself to be pre-eminent in the field, he announced that he would cure all diseases in the world. There was no possible element of failure in his life. He was the key figure in the world to whom all would ultimately have to listen. He believed himself possessed of the ability to govern the world. He would first establish a communistic state, then by his own good example eliminate all evil. He possessed great scientific knowledge, controlling a secret of power greater than the atom bomb. In addition to his forthcoming announcement of a cure for cancer he also was at work perfecting a mechanical heart through which he could assure everlasting life. The world was already listening to him, the President of the United States constantly quoting him.

On the ward Sam still saw police pointing their guns at him. Though realizing that he was in a mental hospital and that his fellow patients were mentally ill, he was sure he was being persecuted by being confined. However, his good example would be a "guiding light" to the other patients. His complacency about being the most important man in the world did not seem to be affected by his awareness that he was in a mental hospital.

Four days later and two weeks after his admission a bilateral frontal lobotomy was performed on Sam Godsky. Following the operation Sam was returned to the ward in good condition. At first he was very restless, tossing about and trying to tear off the dressing. An hour later he was responding, mumbling: "They're trying to kill me." About four or five hours later he was quiet and co-operative. The following day he slept most of the time. When awake he was friendly and co-operative, despite the headache of which he complained. Two days later he was quiet and friendly. Though his mental content was the same as before the lobotomy he was not at all upset by it. "If they want to do it, I am going to fight them. After all, everybody has the right to live the way they want." During the next month Sam became more cheerful and co-operative, volunteering to help with the ward work. In contrast to his prior state he was now under-talkative, showing less spontaneity and willingness to carry on a conversation with members of the staff. After a period of shying away from the other patients because "they're not really patients" but spies sent to check up on him, Sam began to take part in games with some of them. He was now somewhat negligent about his appearance. To some of the staff his polite, friendly attitude seemed only a front. He avoided answering specific questions, responding only with a smile. Exactly two months after his admission to Psychiatric Institute Sam was transferred to State Hospital for prolonged care. He was twenty-five years of age at this time.

At State Hospital Sam was talkative, coherent, and relevant. There was some emotional flattening and depression. He felt he was going to be tortured. There were police watching the grounds, he was sure, waiting for him to make a break. However, he denied his previous delusions, admitting he might have had them but they were nonsensical and silly. No longer did he believe he would rule the world or be able to prolong life. "I also thought I was a great man, I guess. I thought so up until a short time ago. If you let your imagination run away, that is what happens." He also denied having said he was being quoted by the President or that he defecated from the side of his body. "I did say that the police of the Psychiatric Institute had jumped on me. I don't believe that now. That's a lot of foolishness. That's another thing I believed up until a few days ago."

When asked about the earlier episode during which he had fled to Connecticut, Sam was quite frank and now better able to tell of it. He explained that he had felt the police were after him because of speaking out in court. When he had approached a policeman in the town where he had stopped, to ask if they were still looking for him, to his surprise he was arrested. He was taken to the local police station where he was locked up. This frightened him very much. The police then got in touch with Mrs. Godsky back in New York, who told them she would send Sam to Mountainview, a small private hospital. When Sam was told this he immediately became suspicious, knowing his mother couldn't afford this "because they charge at least thirty-five dollars a week. I figured she wanted me back so the police would inflict bodily harm on me." On the way back to New York he jumped off the train.

> "I was chased by policemen who had been wired ahead of me. I entered into the river near by and started to swim away from them. They followed me in a rowboat and I tried to drown. I went down twice and they pulled me up. I was afraid of being beaten up and I was also afraid of the judge and the court. I was locked up in a police station there and the judge, the same man, was brought over. I heard him say, 'He won't want to live when I get through with him!' Now I realize that he wanted me to go home and not to run away.
>
> "I'm quieter now. I'm not really suspicious, like I used to be. I used to think that everyone was against me."

While talking Sam had been raising his voice slightly. He still believed the world should be communistic, but he emphasized that he would have nothing to do with it; it was purely a political matter. His knowledge of current events, geography, and calculation was found to be good when tested at this time. When seen a week later Sam was still well-balanced, co-operative, and quiet, still oriented to time and place. His depression was still with him, as evidenced by the tears in his eyes during the interview. He still was preoccupied with his paranoid delusions, continuing to believe the police were still after him because of insulting the judge, and that he had been framed by the police into the hospital. "A lot of people didn't like me and they made remarks about me." Recently he had begun to feel that the attendants and some of the patients had taken a dislike to him and were for this reason mistreating him.

For the next three weeks there was no change in Sam. There was a definite flattening in his emotional reactions. Though he repeatedly assured the physician that he felt depressed he now did not seem to be so. Though he still believed "the cops are after me," he denied hearing any whisperings about this. When seen at the staff conference two weeks later he expressed definite active paranoid trends; e.g., police and plain-clothesmen were following him everywhere, and the judge was going to burn Sam's eyes out. In telling of his experiences he enjoyed describing "the merry chase I gave the cops." As he spoke, his affect toward these experiences seemed inappropriate and non-critical.

Gradually Sam became neater and more co-operative, even to helping out on the ward from time to time. Though his paranoid ideas were still present they were much less vivid. At the same time he began to sleep less during the day. Two months later he was allowed home for the Jewish holidays, being returned by his mother three days later without incident. Because of his good behavior on this visit he was allowed home every weekend. Beginning with his first weekend visit Sam's ideas seemed to become more rational. He was neater, cleaner, and more prone to enter into activities about him. He became more respectful as he listened to the psychiatrist explain why it was so important to work about the ward. When asked about the ideas he had held in the past Sam described them as "water over the dam. When you are sick and nervous those things seem so real and you actually believe them. . . . Now I feel better and see them as fragments [sic] of my imagination." After Sam had been making weekend visits for two months, Mrs. Godsky asked to have Sam home for an extended visit. The request was granted. When asked, on leaving, what his plans were, Sam said he would "take it easy for a while on a light job and then get into salesmanship if I can." He was to visit the hospital for regular checkups every month or two.

Sam came in by himself for his first checkup two months later. He was living at home with his mother and sister. He was not working, spending most of his time at ball games or the movies. He still intended to go to work but didn't yet feel strong enough to do so. He wanted to be sure he had gotten enough rest before taking a job. He complained of severe gripping precordial pain. The pain was worse on arising in the morning, but seemed not to be so bad when he was occupied, as at a ball game. Throughout the interview he had been well composed though moderately tense. After some reassurance he was told to return in a month. When he came back on that occasion he described conditions as no different. He was still unemployed, but otherwise there were no real problems. At one point in the interview, however, he described his tendency to talk a great deal. "I am talking too much. I drive my folks crazy with my talk. I have to admit I am overbearing." No delusions or hallucinations were elicited.

One month later Sam got a job clerking and delivering orders from a local delicatessen. On the next three monthly visits he still had this job. But though he had solved the employment problem he was not having much success with his social life. Finding it difficult to make friends, he went out alone each evening. Occasionally he felt people were talking about him, but these feelings soon decreased in frequency. Sam seemed to be making a good adjustment.

However, at the end of the seventh month on parole Sam reported that he was becoming frightened about his masturbation. He was still working, but was getting a little worried about things in general. One month later Sam was brought in by Mrs. Godsky. A short time before, feeling the President was after him, he had telegraphed him about the A-bomb. He was soon visited by two men from the F.B.I. who relieved his feeling when they told him not to worry about it. Now he was concerned about the mayor of New York City. Sam was now beginning to act like his old self, said Mrs. Godsky. He was exhausted all the time. Still afraid of policemen, he continually checked the windows each night to make sure they were locked. When Sam was asked about this he said he realized that his fears were imaginary but that there was no way he could control them. A week later Sam was returned to the hospital.

Over the next month Sam was in insulin subshock therapy, receiving twenty-one treatments. During this time he was quite introspective with some insight. However, he was never without some somatic complaint. Despite a chronically sneering attitude he was clean, oriented, and willing to work. His delusions continued unabated. Four months later, when Mrs. Godsky again asked for Sam to be allowed to visit her, her request was turned down. Sam still believed all of his statements were being recorded by radio, and that the President was still after him. He became more upset as time went on, describing himself as a coward with "no guts." At times he referred to himself as "a woman." He began to hear voices, was unable to sleep. Everybody, he felt, was talking about the bad sexual things he had done, and even the voices called him names.

Six months after his readmission Sam underwent insulin-shock therapy, but without apparent change in his mental condition. He said he no longer wanted to go home, that it had done no good the last time when he had lied his way out of the hospital. A few weeks later, after last being seen on the ward talking to his mother, Sam escaped from the hospital. The following day he was returned by the police. Three weeks later, at the request of Mrs. Godsky, Sam was discharged to a small private mental hospital. After a month the visiting psychiatrist told Mrs. Godsky to take her son home. By not co-operating, he told her, Sam was wasting the psychiatrist's time and his mother's money.

Back home again, Sam got along well at first. On advice of the State Hospital clinic he was not to look for work. His usual routine was to go to the movies, return directly home, and get to bed at a regular hour. However, at times Sam went out at night, wandering around the streets until three or four o'clock in the morning. On several such walks he was picked up by the police and taken home. During all this time he never did any harm or did he manifest any anti-social activity. About a month after his return home he again began to have difficulty sleeping. He became more quiet and seclusive, staying out late every night. One morning his mother asked him where he had been the night before. Sam became very angry, shouting that there were spirits and ghosts in the house and she herself was a wicked witch. He said he wanted to get rid of her, that she was a hypocrite only pretending to be good to him. Whereupon he attacked her with a golf club, hitting her across the back. Fleeing from the house, Mrs. Godsky called the police to take Sam back to State Hospital.

Back on the ward Sam was slow and deliberate in his movements. At times he behaved in a bizarre manner, standing in a corner like a soldier at attention. His speech was irrelevant, incoherent, tangential, and circumstantial. Despite his behavior and speech disturbance his mood remained neutral, with flat and inappropriate affect. He was both hallucinated and deluded. His mother lied, he said, when she claimed he had hit her on the head with a golf stick. Not so! He had hit her in the spine! Beyond this he wouldn't talk about the incident or about his mother. He then told of seeing many black bears coming out of his mother's room. Throughout the house there had been ghosts and spirits, the presence of which had bothered him. He hadn't been able to sleep because of the dark, the "pitch dark." He had always been afraid of the dark. At night he had heard screams as heads were being cut off. Even his mother began to look like a ghost to him. He had felt that his only escape lay in jumping out of the window or dynamiting the house.

Sam told how he'd always been fired from his jobs. Despite hard work he had accomplished nothing except to make trouble. However, money wasn't everything, he said. All a man wanted was the love of a good woman, and you couldn't buy that. He then complained of his position in society as a Jew, that Jews were halfway between Negroes and whites. From this he went on to talk of gassing people and how he could smell them, and of how the Negroes were the master race. Then Sam went back to the topic of his masturbation, saying that when he did it blood came out of his penis. His penis was now no more than a peep-hole, in fact his whole body had dwindled away to nothing. There were all sorts of holes, Sam said, the mouth and the rectum. Babies were born through the mouth.

Sam wouldn't co-operate in any of the psychological tests, immediately starting in on his delusional material. He was oriented for place and person but not for time. He had no insight. All physical and laboratory tests were negative.

Sam's condition remained essentially unchanged for the next few years. As reflected in the yearly reports, Sam continued to maintain his delusions, although his affect did not fit their disturbing content. Over the next two years he gradually became more co-operative, occasionally working about the ward. His clothes always seemed soiled, fitting in with his generally disheveled appearance. His mood remained slightly agitated, modified from time to time by inappropriate smiles. When interviewed he would sit quietly in the chair, talking fast and continuously of the "fifth dimension out of the world" floating in space. Or sometimes he talked of death—"At least they should have a plain white pine box and sheets with your head showing—if they do die. Do they allow this in the state? Of course you can have your own box if a person deceases . . . Have you got the paper? I had treatment at Psychiatric Institute. Lost my head, that's all." He continued his religious interests, making a strong effort to observe the various Jewish holidays.

As time went on Sam became cleaner in appearance and more co-operative, although he was still disheveled. He ate three meals a day without exception. He was irritable and still deluded. Smiling inappropriately as he talked, he gave no evidence of any real insight—"I think I am suffering from insecurity. I'm not sure what it means to anybody. People get puffed up with importance then make a mistake and feel sorry. On the outside I said some things. I feel badly hurt. I hate to be hurt or fall down. I'm still afraid, afraid of doing it again." Sitting quietly in his seat, his hat in his hand, Sam continued: "I feel like a damn fool. Most people I always meddle in other people's affairs. I am always wrong. Can't tell, I could be still highly sensitive. I'm a patient here. I don't want to make a complaint. I was brought up this way."

By the end of another year Sam had become quite co-operative. He was now thirty-two. He talked of how much better he now felt, and that he didn't have so many fits of fear. However, he was still afraid of being attacked, usually by two or three persons at the same time. Sometimes he heard "a little tiny voice coming from the middle of the room," a voice that came from a dwarf. His memory for recent events was good, but he had much difficulty in temporally locating remote events. He now frequently asked the doctor to let him go home and go to work.

At the present time Sam is still in State Hospital, a young man of thirty-five years. Two years ago he had a convulsive seizure during which he struck his head against the sidewalk, fracturing his skull. Since that time he has been put on dilantin therapy "for life." On the ward he is active, infrequently helping out with the work. Though usually quiet and co-operative, he sometimes talks loudly of wanting to go to Italy and of how he has been mistreated. On the whole, he seems fairly intact. He dresses neatly although in rather dirty clothes. His emotional state is flat and even. Occasionally there is an empty smile on his face.

When asked why he is in the hospital Sam gets involved in such a long, detailed, rambling story that he mixes up time, sequence, and locale without being aware of the contradictions. With great composure he discusses his hallucinations, suicidal thoughts, and previous hospitalizations, saying he used to be "a hypochondriac." Though wrong in answering questions about what month it is, he knows the details of world series games, recent election results, etc. He admits having been ill in the past, when he was scared and irrational.

Sam is apathetic about his present situation, showing little initiative for leaving the hospital and establishing a life of his own. He no longer talks of getting a job. Despite the still negative physical and neurological examinations, Sam psychologically is not considered ready for another visit home. Nor is it considered likely by the staff that he ever will be ready. Mrs. Godsky sees him regularly, bringing clothes as well as parcels of food delicacies Sam as a child had always liked. His sister neither visits nor writes. As far as Esther is now concerned, she has never had a brother.

Cluny Standish

MANIC–DEPRESSIVE PSYCHOSIS IN A WOMAN

PAUL AND MELISSA STANDISH were both strong willed and independent. Melissa had been a secretary in Paul's department store when she married him, capable and efficient. She was thirty at the time, he fifty. From the start married life was marked by incompatibility, though each was too genteel to give vent to violence. Partly perhaps the friction was due to Melissa's failure to give Paul a son, partly perhaps it was Melissa's coldness, particularly in their sexual relations. Not once did Melissa have an orgasm in the many years of their marriage. On occasion Paul would leave Melissa for another woman, and sometimes he would be involved with another woman without bothering to move out his belongings. Whatever the case, Paul always provided well for his wife, giving her whatever she might ask for in the way of material things.

Paul was a self-made man, a former haberdasher who over the years had worked his way up to where he now owned a large downtown department store. He was a quiet, generous, though domineering person who enjoyed solitude. It was only in his work that he mixed with others. At night he preferred to be at home by himself, reading or listening to the radio. He was a fastidious dresser who liked expensive though conservative clothes. He rarely became angry, although for the greater part of his life he was subject to asthmatic attacks. Paul had been an only child, inheriting the family pride in an ancestry that went back to the first settlers in New Hampshire. His father had been a domineering person with a strong, violent temper that used to frighten Paul as a child. His mother had been a gentle person who for years had suffered from frequent attacks of asthma.

Melissa, like Paul, had come from old Yankee stock. Her father had been a passive, gentle man who rarely raised his voice at home. Her mother had been the tyrant of the household, domineering with a steady, implicit authority. Her word had been law in the home, and Melissa's father had quickly learned not to question it. Melissa grew up into a poised, very much self-controlled woman who "felt inwardly," as she later described it. Unable to express warmth, she had many acquaintances but few close friends. She was dramatic in her actions, and somewhat overbearing.

After nine years of childlessness Melissa finally gave Paul a daughter. At first Paul didn't care for Cluny, seemingly disinterested because he hadn't gotten a son. Gradually he began to worship his little girl, giving her anything she wanted. At the same time Cluny began to love her father very much. Despite this feeling for each other, the two could never establish an easy, give-and-take relationship. Between Melissa and Cluny a different relationship developed. Melissa was quite close to her daughter, idolizing her yet at the same time exerting steady pressure to make sure Cluny would someday amount to something. She kept Cluny with her much of the time, taking her along whenever she made her social calls.

Cluny was a model child in Melissa's estimation. She was bright in school and got along well with the other children. As a child Cluny never quarreled, either with her mother or with the children with whom she played. Should a disagreement arise in the course of a game, Cluny would quickly be in tears. At twelve Cluny had her first menstrual period. She had been prepared for it by Melissa, who had been very careful to instruct Cluny in what she felt to be the proper attitude toward sex. Years later Cluny explained that her mother's talks had made her develop ideals in regard to sex, and to look forward to the day when a man would approach her almost spiritually. "I expect," said Cluny, "to find a little god in a man."

When Cluny was sixteen she graduated from high school with honors, entering a well-known college for women the following September. In college she achieved excellent grades, was very popular with the other girls and their dates. But Cluny herself did not go out with any male friends. Instead, she busied herself with her studies and with class activities. When with a mixed group she never actively took part in "petting parties," although she confided to her mother that she had submitted twice "out of curiosity." In all her relations she was a very proper person.

Cluny's father died at the beginning of her junior year at college. To her friends she seemed not to be particularly upset by the loss but immediately threw herself into more and more college activities. For the next year she was very active and restless, the leader in whatever group she joined. Despite her great popularity at college and her many friends, Cluny continued to dress in the old-fashioned clothes that her mother chose for her, resisting the attempts of the other girls to "bring her up to date."

Cluny graduated from college at the time of the great depression. She could neither find a job nor could she and her mother get along without some sort of financial aid. Paul's death and the economic depression had left the family almost penniless. To add to the difficulties, Melissa had developed a heart condition that made it all the more necessary for Cluny to live near home, where she could watch out for her mother. After a long period of job hunting, Cluny was able to find work as a social secretary for a very wealthy family where she stayed for the next two years.

During this period Cluny continued her policy of not having anything to do with men because she had not found any who, she felt, were mentally compatible. She hoped to marry sometime and to have children, but her policy of no dates made it difficult to get started. On one occasion, shortly after graduation, she was driven home from a party by a young man who lived near by. At the door he gave her a perfunctory good-night kiss, the first she had ever received from a man. She ran into the house and, in line with her long-standing custom of telling Melissa everything, told of the kiss. Though it had been "only a peck," she was so disillusioned and disappointed that she wept until four o'clock in the morning. She had long before formed ideals as to how a kiss between a man and a woman should be given and received, and the experience that night had not measured up to it. For the next three years she repeatedly told her mother that she would never again let a man kiss her until "the right man" came into her life. On her job as social secretary she never had any male visitors, spending her evenings reading in the library.

On the job Cluny continued her pattern of hard work. Though she always presented a cheerful, smiling exterior, just as at college, when alone she worried and grieved. Many nights she cried herself to sleep because she was doing what she considered menial work rather than the writing she had always wanted to do. She had always been a worrier, though none of her friends had realized it. At night, even in college, she frequently had difficulty in falling asleep because of her habit of thinking over what she was going to say in each situation the next day. But the next day, when others were around, she gave the impression of great self-confidence and efficiency.

At the end of the second year Cluny lost her job because of a curtailment of staff. She began to worry about her mother's physical condition and about the family finances. She became increasingly irritated at Melissa's constant complaints of how little money they had, yet curtailed many of her social activities because she felt guilty about spending the money. Though Melissa's complaints were not new, spoiling Cluny's enjoyment even at college, they were now bolstered by Cluny's loss of the job.

For the next year Cluny stayed at home, unsuccessful in her many attempts to find a job. To keep herself busy she worked about the house, and even did unpaid volunteer work at a settlement house. She had to be constantly on the alert to economize, even to the point of having to worry about her carfare when going to the settlement house. Her clothes, which had never been very stylish, now had to be mended frequently. During the latter part of that year she was somewhat depressed on hearing of the marriages of several of her college classmates, and she didn't even have a boy friend! There was also a series of mishaps that excited Cluny for a time. Within a period of three months she was in two minor auto accidents, and an older woman, a widow who had confided in Cluny, suddenly got married and left town.

One day Cluny answered a help-wanted ad for women trainees for personnel work. She attended a number of lectures, becoming increasingly enthusiastic about the work. Within a few days she began to have difficulty in sleeping because of the many things about the job that kept running through her mind. Otherwise she appeared to be well and happy. The somewhat depressed state of the past six months seemed suddenly to have disappeared.

Two weeks after answering the ad Cluny suddenly had her first major breakdown. At eleven o'clock at night she ran into her mother's room crying in a loud voice that she was dying. In a few minutes she seemed to be calm again, seemingly responding to Melissa's reassurance. Then she told her mother of having just had a vision from God who had told her she would marry a boy she had known in childhood and that he would die in a year, leaving her pregnant with a son. Before that was to happen, the vision had said, the wife of her training supervisor would sue Cluny for alienation of her husband's affections. Cluny told her mother she didn't even know whether or not this man was married. The vision had also said, continued Cluny, that she would go to Chicago with this man.

Cluny didn't sleep the rest of that night. Next day she complained of being completely worn out, and was able to sleep for an hour in the afternoon. Later that afternoon she visited a girl friend and told her of the vision. The following day she went to the settlement house, but left early because of feeling sick to her stomach. On the way home she stopped at the osteopath's for a treatment (which in the past had relaxed her) and a sleeping pill. Back at the house she seemed her old self for a while, then began to insist to Melissa that the vision was true. She became excited, and apparently aware that something was wrong she insisted on calling the Psychiatric Hospital to prove she was in a peculiar frame of mind. She called the hospital but became furious because the doctor wouldn't listen to her on the telephone.

Hastily she dressed and with Melissa went to the hospital. She was restless, talkative, and excited, and when she repeated to the doctor the story of her vision, she was admitted as a patient.

Physical examination of Cluny was negative except for a tendency to obesity, about which she had in the past been very sensitive. There was also noted at the time a tendency to masculine distribution of hair at the pubis.

During her first week in the hospital Cluny was restless and in a continuous state of excitement. She spoke continuously but in an incoherent and irrational manner. Frequently she sought the examiner's hand. She acted confused, and with her eyes half closed, moaned and groaned in a loud tone as if she were delirious. She was distracted by outside noises, speaking of them as she heard them. On the first day she frequently got out of bed to speak to the nurses, telling them she understood her condition because she had studied psychology. Next morning she insisted no photographers be allowed in to take her picture, that her mother was locked up in the toilet, and that one of the patients was a spy. At one point she threw herself caressingly upon another woman patient, insisting she was "Fred" who had come back to see her. She banged herself about the wall, and seemed to be aware only at intervals. At times she called for whisky, then asked, "Why do I do this?" She was overactive, exposed herself, and pulled the bedclothes from the bed. She was incontinent for a few days, speaking of it with remorse, but would then rub her feet through the urine or sit in it. Attempts at getting a coherent story from her were futile.

Cluny's speech was of a stuttering type, very artificially made out, though she was quite able to speak the words correctly when urged. Here is an example: "Just, just, just, br–, br–, br–, br–, bring them here, Voi–, voi–, voi–, voi–, v-o-i-c-e. Voice. I hear the dishes rattling." When asked the date, she was able, after much urging, to give the correct month and year, but gave the date as of the day prior to her admission. She correctly named the hospital and herself. At times she responded to specific questions, at times she didn't. The content of her speech centered about "Michael," but there was little actual material expressed. She spoke of the voice of a man, but it was difficult to determine whether this was a true hallucination.

Cluny's push of talk and actions didn't let up that first week. She was observed at times to be masturbating. At first paraldehyde quieted her, but soon it took several drams just to give her one hour's sleep. When seven and a half grains of nembutal were injected prior to a spinal puncture, she slept only an hour and a half. Her excitement seemed steadily to increase. Along with this her temperature went up to 104.6° F. Medical examination revealed no apparent physical basis for her elevated temperature. Tubs and wet packs seemed to have no calming effect. Her excitement became intense as she talked and threw herself about. After ten days sodium amytal in frequent doses began to quiet her until finally she slept for six hours. Along with this sleep her temperature dropped five degrees overnight. However, despite the heavy dosage of sodium amytal, Cluny continued to have the push of talk and activity. But it seemed as if she were too tired to move much. Her eyelids would half close, then open as though she were driven by a great drive that was only restrained and not abolished. She seemed anxious, and moaned a lot.

During this period some of her statements were, "I can't be a Catholic—I can't. I'm dying. I'm dead. I feel I'm dying." She spelled out many words, particularly "Graham," a name she repeatedly mentioned. "Don't let them pull my mother. It's not too late. My mind is unclear for the last few days. You can help me get well." She considered many of her visitors to be reporters, repeatedly saying, "I do not want any publicity. My mind is all right, at least it was all right one month ago." She frequently asked to be allowed to go home.

On the evening of the twelfth day, just before she came out of the warm tub where she had been spending ten hours a day, Cluny's entire reaction seemed to change. She appeared relaxed and at ease, smiling easily and talking naturally. She was oriented to place, but didn't know the exact date. She walked to the bathroom with a nurse, was co-operative, and spoke rationally on a very superficial level, asking how long she had been in the hospital. She did not answer any questions of a probing nature. This lucid period lasted two hours, then she again became restless, talking about "Freddie." She got out of bed, had to be held down, and soon was put in restraint. Later, somehow getting out of restraint, she put her head in the elevator shaft. Sodium amytal was started again but she didn't sleep. The next day she was in the tub all day, and was fairly quiet. Though still agitated, there was not the push of speech seen on previous days.

Her mood now changed to a somewhat depressed one. She was oriented but her recent memory was impaired. She had several delusions and admitted to auditory hallucinations. She said she now felt "punk." She felt Fred Graham was there and that people on the ward were telling her "Graham" was dead, that the examiner was dead, that she might have a baby by the examiner. "Rather depressing. It's a state you don't want to get into unless you're married." She claimed to have heard bells tolling and that the nurse had told her of the examiner's death. She accused the hospital of trying to make a Catholic of her. At such times she would kneel on the floor in an attitude of prayer, uttering such vague and uncomprehensible statements as: "He bled for me" and "I can't share my religion." She would lie on the floor, stick her head into the elevator shaft to listen, and claimed her mother was not really her mother. She felt she had conceived while in the hospital. She heard shots being fired at her continuously. She asked for another vaginal examination, and after it was completed talked of having masturbated since the age of fourteen with accompanying feelings of guilt. "I'm very passionate and masturbated a lot, and they think I have to masturbate every night here but I don't have to do it very often.

Cluny's mental condition continued to improve, with ever-increasing periods of lucidity. During her confused periods she was delusioned, was resistive, and listened to hallucinatory voices. During her clear periods she talked rationally on almost any topic except the delusions to which she clung. By talking to herself she was gradually able to reassure herself enough to make her delusions disappear. ("You silly nut, they can't kill you in this hospital.") In the meantime a strong transference had developed toward the examiner that disturbed Cluny very much, but it was gradually broken down by indifference on his part.

Mrs. Standish had visited Cluny each day. After two months she began to take Cluny home for a day, then overnight. On her first night home Cluny was very fearful of the dark, and imagined many fearful shapes. This, she told herself, was only imaginary, and after a distinct effort to control this fear she soon went to sleep. After that she had no more such fears.

Three months after her admission Cluny was discharged to her mother. She had been steadily improving, and once home began to go out socially more and more. She soon got a job, and for the next two and a half years made a good adjustment.

When Cluny was twenty-eight she decided to go to a class reunion during commencement week at her alma mater. As she made her plans to go she became somewhat depressed. With a woebegone air she told her mother she didn't have any suitable new clothes, and that she felt bad because she would have to compare her own record over the past few years with that of others in her class who had made successes, been married, and had children. And here she was with no accomplishments except for a period in a mental hospital. However, her mother got her some clothes, told her to be proud of her intelligent efforts in recovering from the illness, and to go and have a good time. Two days later Cluny left, cheerful and content. On the day she was to return she called her mother to say she was having such a good time that she wanted permission to stay two days more. Three days later she called to say that she wanted to stay on for a gathering at a friend's home.

When Cluny entered the house on the evening of her return she was so active, cheerful, and spry after the long trip that her mother became worried. Though Melissa was tired, Cluny insisted on telling her the story of her week away from home in a rapid-fire, fragmentary manner. An hour and a half later Cluny was still talking, not having yet covered the topic. To Melissa the conversation seemed normal except that it was very rapid. Cluny jumped from subject to subject without any connection that her mother could follow, but attributing it to Cluny's enthusiasm, Melissa did not worry. At half-past eleven that night Melissa let the little dog out. A few minutes later a policeman knocked on the door and said the dog had been run over by a car and was dying. Cluny immediately became very much upset, waving her arms and saying, "Oh, God, we can't have the little dog die." Despite her mother's objections Cluny drove the dog into town to a veterinary hospital where she was told the dog was beyond aid. A few minutes later they killed the dog. Cluny returned home a few hours later, very nervous and excited, talking about the dog's death, the dog's life, the dog's character and, confused with this, about her week at the college. Finally her mother was able to persuade her to go to bed and talk the next day. When she awoke, Cluny was still overtalkative, excited and rambling, combining the dog's death and the story of her week away in a seemingly disconnected fashion. But her mother felt that a quiet day at home would take care of the excitement, that Cluny was just fatigued from a difficulty in sleeping while away that week. Cluny went to visit some friends, and while there was very overtalkative, excitable, inefficient in her work, overactive, and frequently praying. On the second day of Cluny's visit her friend called Cluny's family physician without consulting Melissa. On his recommendation Cluny was sent to a private mental hospital, again without consulting Melissa. The following day, as soon as she was told, Melissa went to the hospital. She didn't like the way Cluny was being treated and had her transferred to the hospital where she had previously been.

On her admission this time Cluny was again overactive and talkative, demanding to see the doctor she had had before. She gesticulated, grimaced somewhat, and was very restless. That afternoon she was so overactive and overtalkative that she was put into an isolated room. She was brought somewhat against her will into the examination room with a blanket wrapped tightly about her. When she walked in she had her left hand extended in a manner suggestive of Napoleon. She immediately addressed the examiner by the name of the physician she had previously had. When told he was not the same physician, Cluny said, "That's all right. I know that the doctors do change." She then walked to the window and looking out said, "Today is going on." When asked by the nurse to remove the blanket, Cluny refused. "I've never done that." "That is beyond me." She walked up and down the room, clutching the blanket tightly to her. During the examination she was restless and unco-operative. Frequently during the physical she would sigh and moan, and close her eyes, the lids fluttering in a hysterical, dramatic manner. Many times she moved her arms about, grasping the examiner's hands and holding on to his coat in a manner suggesting erotic impulses. During the examination of her blood pressure she lay back limp, closed her eyes, fluttered her eyelids, and moaned, "I am going, I am going." She then sat up suddenly and said, "Must I go through all this again? It is so terrible! Oh, God! It is too terrible." After the physical examination she was very restless, fidgeting with her clothes. At times during the interview she broke away from the subject under discussion and posing her head in a supplicating manner toward an apparent deity prayed, with arms outstretched, in a loud, rather dramatic voice.

In her room Cluny's behavior was of two sorts. Sometimes she would wander around, patting the wall with her hands, exposing herself, talking and praying loudly; at other times she would lie on her bed, covered up with a blanket and apparently asleep. Occasionally she threw food on the floor, and smeared feces, urine, and food over the walls, bed, and floor. During the day she was kept in tubs where she talked and prayed at a very fast rate most of the time. At night considerable sedation was required to make her sleep.

Cluny's mood was labile, shifting from one extreme to the other. When asked how she felt, she might say, "I feel perfectly fine—never better in my life—I am well in every way." At other times she would say she was dying and that all was ended. Occasionally she broke out into laughter and at other times into tears.

In her stream of talk there was a definite, connected type of flight of ideas with no abnormal use of words or sentence structure. Usually monosyllables or two or three words hooked together flowed out rather than complicated and complete sentences. There was no singing or rhyming. She answered most questions inaccurately but with some degree of meaning. For example, on one occasion Cluny said she was in a dog hospital; at another time, that this was a maternity hospital. Her flight of ideas was illustrated by the following response to a question about her health:

> "It is just about to begin—thank you Mary—Mary Astor—Queen Mary—I like Queen Mary—hell and Maria!—General Grant—There are several in the family—they don't know who I am yet. Keep your shirt on—I will be speaking through you."

On another occasion the following came forth:

"Michael, oh Michael! Father, dear! My husband, Graham —God is love! My life is finished! Oh, oh—where are you? Where are you going? I can't stand this—all is ended—all, all, all—all is ended!"

Within four days, after sedation and repeated warm tubs, Cluny began to calm down. At the end of ten days she was quiet and reacting appropriately. At the end of the third week Cluny was taken home by her mother, despite the advice of the hospital to let her stay there a little longer.

Cluny stayed out of the hospital for the next five years, living at home with her mother. She was working in the office of a private school for girls and soon began to acquire a group of friends. She was going out on dates from time to time, and all seemed well. When Cluny was thirty-three she again became ill. Her mother seemed to feel it was related to their being asked to vacate the apartment they had had for so many years. Cluny was very upset at being uprooted, just as she had always in the past been upset by any change of location or job. She spent a week looking for an apartment, but with each day of failure she became more discouraged. She began to have difficulty in falling asleep but didn't tell her mother. At last she found a suitable apartment, and one of which her mother approved, but Cluny couldn't seem to get over the chronic fatigue she now had. She became more tense, smoking much more than she had.

On the day after she and her mother moved to the new apartment Cluny called a male friend to meet her to hear "the most wonderful news." At dinner with him she impulsively yanked the tablecloth off the table, saying it was soiled, and demanding another. She told her companion not to talk, that she had things to tell him. She then told him of the difficulties in getting the apartment. With another couple they then went to the theater. During the evening she seemed hardly able to walk, saying she was exhausted. Later she cried as she told him of her past and of her having been in a mental hospital and that her mother had told her she must never marry because of her mental illness. At another point in the conversation she said she was going to let her mother have her independence, then threatened to kill her mother. (Later she reversed this, telling Melissa this friend had advised her to do away with her mother.) She went on to tell him how during her last two years at college she had vowed she was going to be popular and could prove her success by the yearbook. She said in her new home she was going to have a room away from her mother. All of the preceding came forth very fast and in excited fashion.

The following day Cluny had an osteopathic treatment and massage to relax her. But her excitement continued. The next day her girl friend tried all day to calm Cluny, who was rational but overtalkative. That night she went to bed early but got up after midnight, sneaking past her mother who had fallen asleep on guard outside Cluny's room. A few hours later she arrived at the dwelling of the man she had had dinner with two days before. Entering by the back stairs, she stole into his apartment. When asked why she was there, Cluny complained she was cold, went into the bathroom, and shut herself in. She then took a prolonged bath, talking and singing loudly throughout. After this she dressed in a pair of her friend's pajamas and walked out into the living room. Her conversation was profane and so loud it could be heard all through the building. She demanded the radio be turned on, saying she felt like listening to music. Throughout she persisted in referring to her friend as her husband. She then criticized the arrangement of the furniture and demanded changes in it. An ambulance was called. When it arrived, Cluny shouted, "Put me in a straight jacket. No, you can't take me out of my house." She ran about in the apartment, then quieted down and walked out to the ambulance.

On arrival at the hospital Cluny had insight into her condition. She told of having gone to a physician the day before, ostensibly for a physical complaint, but that her reason had been her feeling that she was beginning to have a recurrence of her old disorder. She was fairly co-operative, although rather active. After a few hours she became markedly overactive and overtalkative, remaining in this state for the next few weeks. She stayed in her room, becoming so active that the bed had to be removed. She draped herself in a blanket after removing her clothing, then rolled about on the mattress on the floor. Frequently she threw off the blanket, rolling about nude and at times banging her head and body against the wall. Frequently she would stand in the nude, her back to the door. Occasionally she was on all fours on the floor, remaining in this position while the physician visited. She was combative and resistive, refusing to take medication by mouth so that it was necessary to inject it. During her continuous warm tubs she was considerably quieter, and at times talked only in a low voice. More commonly she splashed about in the tub, talking constantly and rather loudly, but seeming to enjoy the tub. Her appetite was poor, but she ate adequately.

Cluny's speech consisted primarily of short phrases with much repetition. She used profanity frequently in a repetitive fashion with little variety. She was markedly distractible, and at times rhymed and punned. The following is a verbatim excerpt from her speech as she lay in the tub one day, with a medical student in the room:

> "No, I haven't—my God, what next?—God damn these men, they can't even if you want them to. That boy, God damn it, he's a mouse. How many words in a minute can you say? I can beat it. Virgins—utterly impossible. Now we'll see whose mind is running the New Hampshire Retreat. We'll date it October 15.—Yes, paralyze her—that's right, dear—did you really?—this is psychiatry—who cares? [Kicking.] This is co-operation. One of the greatest triumvirates since Julius Caesar—no Caesar was a dictator—Didn't you know?—the bitches had penises called clitorises—My God, you're putting words into my mouth. We're not looking at each other—I'm cold—The Chinese do have a fire burning constantly underneath their tubs. Where did I read that?—Whose show is this?—See, I'm all words. Oh boy, I never wanted to direct a show as much as I do now—Don't let them scare you. God damn you. You just keep your mind and I'll keep mine—We do choose whom we want—Everybody, stop calling me Miss Standish. I won't answer to it—that's for me to know and for you to find out—the greatest egoists on earth, all men—Get yourself a harem—See you how? Latin. It helps. God damn boy. [Laughs.] I don't need to, not now, or tomorrow, or next week—I'm scared of mice, so are most women—He made a motion that to me alone has sufficient significance to make

me blush. [To student.] Thank God you're leaving. [Student goes out.] God damn Dante, Dan. My God, we will come out of this together even if we have to get in this tub together. [Patient has been shouting; gradually becomes quieter.] Battle Creek, Michigan. Did I send my mother there with my own hand? I hope so. Mother, I see what you have said. My God, you are good. It was on the seacoast. Don't kill me now—Where the wind threw up the surf against, what do you think of that, the wind threw up the surf in a tidal wave. Two Greek servants conditioned me for life to be afraid of water—This is Cluny Standish speaking. Don't forget that—I think I'll go out of here as free as air. Kill me, dead, whoever wants to—That was Michael. I hope. —you have to be careful what you say here—So long as I've omitted the M he doesn't have to commit.—It's not cold enough. [Splashing, noisier.] Who am I saving now? Water panacea. Oh, my God. I want to see you more than ever. Now we're getting the source of it—Stay out, Doctor—, you're not God. [No one had entered.] All is sex. I'll remember that. This is October 17. Three days. I'm Christ. I came to earth—It's a good place for you to be. I wouldn't care to be there —Who the hell told me that? My mother, what? I always knew that. But I didn't think she'd have to die for me to be entirely free. Oh, my God, Jesus Christ, who did that? [Pause.] This is getting a little bit too deep for me, God damn right. [Pause.] Yes, I think so. I'll take care of his own dirt, I hope—That's the arm, Sam."

During her hospitalization this time Cluny had no hallucinations or systematized delusions. The tubs were quite effective in quieting her, and at the end of a month she was transferred to a convalescent ward. There she showed a mild hypomania, enjoyed socializing with the other patients, and was willing to discuss some of her problems with the physician. Three weeks later she was discharged. At the time she was quiet, emotionally level, and in good contact. She expressed the wish to get employment away from home, but had very little hope she would be able to do so.

Over the next ten years Cluny went to the hospital four more times, staying about four months each time. There was an average interval of about two years between hospitalizations during which she made a good adjustment working as a clerk in various schools for girls. During the fourth of these periods in the hospital Melissa died, making major readjustments necessary when Cluny was released. In less than a year Cluny was rehospitalized, this time at one of the state hospitals.

Cluny has now been at the State Hospital for the past four years. Now forty-five, she seems likely to remain a patient for some time. Whenever she is moved to one of the convalescent buildings, she becomes briefly depressed, then very excited. On such occasions she is transferred back to her old ward, put into the tubs, and in a few days she is again quiet.

In group-therapy sessions Cluny stands out, using her superior intelligence and wit to understand the therapist long before the other patients can grasp what is being said. For a while the group was led by a woman physchologist. Cluny felt a great kinship toward her, as though the two of them could discuss matters which the other patients couldn't comprehend. Whenever this therapist was late, or had to miss a meeting, Cluny was sure she had died, and even her reappearance the next day was sometimes not enough to reassure Cluny.

Cluny's only interest now seems to be the annual meetings of her college class. Though she can't go to them, she eagerly awaits news of what transpires, hoping perhaps next year to join them. She will tell the psychologist where she will buy her dress, what she will wear, what she will eat, and in many other details savors the possibility. Perhaps, says Cluny, she can make the twenty-fifth reunion—or will it be the thirtieth?

A NOTE ON THE TYPE

The text of this book is set in Caledonia, a Linotype face that belongs to the family of printing types called "modern face" by printers—a term used to mark the change in style of type-letters that occurred about 1800. Caledonia borders on the general design of Scotch Modern, but is more freely drawn than that letter.

The book was composed, printed, and bound by The Plimpton Press, Norwood, Massachusetts. Paper manufactured by S. D. Warren Company, Boston, Massachusetts. Designed by Harry Ford.